to. sussie Benson

from, Devan
Chapman

Linda Benson

06-07-2015

with Love ♡

DISCOVERING OUR

CHRISTIAN FAITH

AN INTRODUCTION TO THEOLOGY

DISCOVERING OUR
CHRISTIAN FAITH

AN INTRODUCTION TO THEOLOGY

SAMUEL M. POWELL

BEACON HILL PRESS
OF KANSAS CITY

Copyright 2008
By Samuel M. Powell and Beacon Hill Press of Kansas City

Printed in the
United States of America

ISBN-13: 978-0-8341-2354-0

Cover Design: Brandon Hill
Interior Design: Sharon Page

All Scripture quotations are from the *New Revised Standard Version* (NRSV) of the Bible, copyright 1989 by the Division of Christian Education of the National Council of the Churches of Christ in the USA. Used by permission. All rights reserved.

All hymns quoted are from Franz Hildebrandt and Oliver A. Beckerlegge, eds., *A Collection of Hymns for the Use of the People Called Methodists*, vol. 7, *The Works of John Wesley* (Oxford: Clarendon Press, 1983).

Library of Congress Cataloging-in-Publication Data

Powell, Samuel M.
  Discovering our Christian faith : an introduction to theology / Samuel M. Powell.
    p. cm.
  Includes bibliographical references and index.
  ISBN 978-0-8341-2354-0 (hardcover)
  1. Christianity. 2. Theology, Doctrinal. I. Title.

  BR121.3.P69 2008
  230'.7—dc22

                     2007048185

10 9 8 7 6 5 4 3 2 1

CONTENTS

ACKNOWLEDGMENTS

I would like to thank those who rendered help in writing this book: Beacon Hill Press of Kansas City, which has undertaken the cost and labor of publishing a series of textbooks in theology and related fields; Alex Varughese, who, as editor, provided valuable comments and encouragement; Point Loma Nazarene University, which has over the years provided a stimulating and nurturing environment for intellectual work and which reduced my teaching schedule so that I could expedite the writing of this book; my colleagues at Point Loma Nazarene University, especially Brad E. Kelle, Michael Lodahl, and Thomas E. Phillips, as well as Craig Keen (Azusa Pacific University), who tirelessly read the manuscript and offered invaluable advice and insight; and above all my wife, Terrie, whose unfailing support and patience have seen me through many days of study, writing, and editing.

FOREWORD

Discovering Our Christian Faith is designed to be used as a textbook for general education courses that aim to introduce college-university students to the essentials of Christian faith. The usefulness of this volume, however, is not limited to students in general education courses in institutions of higher education. It is also intended to be a valuable resource for anyone who seeks a general understanding of the classical doctrines of the Christian faith.

The writer and the publisher of this book stand within the Wesleyan tradition of Protestant Christianity. Therefore, the reader will find in this volume the author's articulation of the normative Christian faith as understood and interpreted by the Protestant-Wesleyan tradition. The connection of this volume to the Wesleyan tradition is clear at the beginning of each chapter where the author introduces its content with an appropriate and theologically profound Wesley hymn. These hymns set the agenda of each chapter.

Since the book is an introduction to Christian faith, this volume does not enter into a conversation with other theologians in the Wesleyan tradition. As in any Christian tradition, the Wesleyan tradition also has its share of divergent theological voices that, while remaining true to the core convictions of Wesleyan theology, may utilize different language and ideas to express their understanding of Christian faith. This volume presents only one of those voices and does not assume to be the only voice of Wesleyan tradition.

This volume presents various topics of the Christian faith following the order of the biblical narrative, and it is richly supplemented with references to biblical texts. Readers are frequently presented with biblical texts that inform and shape our understanding of the Christian faith. This volume also takes seriously into account the classical doctrines of the Christian faith and interfaces them with the doctrine of the Trinity and shows the latter as central to the overall arrangement of Christian theology.

As a textbook, this volume seeks to serve both students and faculty by giving attention to pedagogical concerns. Each chapter has a set of student learning objectives, list of key words, sidebars that give expanded treatments on special topics, summary statements, and questions for reflection.

The author of this volume is a well-established theologian and writer in the Wesleyan tradition. The imaginative and skillful ways in which the author presents the doctrines of the Christian faith are meant not only to inform but also to invite the readers to engage and to participate in theological thinking and dialogue in their own imaginative ways. The fundamental aim of this volume will have been attained if the readers are challenged and helped to live out in their daily life the faith that is confessed in its pages.

—Alex Varughese
Managing Editor
Centennial Initiative
Beacon Hill Press of Kansas City

PREFACE

Theology is the knowledge of God.

However, there is much more to be said about this knowledge, for it is unlike other sorts of knowledge. Theology is not, for instance, a type of scientific or historical knowledge. It is not a matter of calculating probabilities or projecting forecasts or predicting results. It is instead "the teaching that is in accordance with godliness" (1 Tim. 6:3). Unlike other sorts of knowledge, theology is not a purely theoretical or cognitive discipline. On the contrary, it is that teaching whose truth is measured by the yardstick of godliness. And, unlike other sorts of knowledge that aim at information or understanding, the principal aim of theology "is love that comes from a pure heart, a good conscience, and sincere faith" (1:5). Theology, in other words, has an ethical or practical dimension. It is not simply a body of knowledge but is instead intimately connected to a way of existing and conducting ourselves in the world. That is why we find it to be contradictory when people profess to know God and live in an ungodly way. In the language of John's Gospel, they do not "do what is true" (3:21). Christian theology, then, is both belief and practice in their inseparable unity. *Faith* is the word we use to denote this unity of belief and practice.

Of course, a textbook will necessarily focus on the belief-dimension of faith, since it is this aspect of the Christian faith that is most easily conveyed with words. We learn the practice of the faith through the godly examples of saintly people and in the context of Christian fellowship and worship. Nonetheless, the ethical and practical dimension of faith must be constantly in mind in the study of theology, for otherwise we will think of theology as an objective, factual study like other modes of investigation, and we will forget that the purpose of theology is not simply to provide information but is instead to be an instrument in the transformation of our minds as we seek to have the same mind that was in Jesus Christ.

Besides its ethical dimension, theology has a normative content that can be specified in terms of beliefs. The Church finds this content in the

11

Bible and gives it a succinct form in creeds. Of course, it is important to note that people and churches interpret the Bible in various ways and that there are numerous creeds in the Christian Church, none of which completely agrees with others. Consequently, it is necessary and helpful to distinguish the normative Christian faith from the ways in which that faith has been understood across the centuries. The faith is one; understandings are many. The faith is normative and authoritative; the understandings are not. Every branch of the Christian tradition, while affirming the Christian faith, understands that faith in distinctive ways based on its historical development. As a result, any textbook of theology will stand within and represent the scriptural interpretation and creedal formation of a particular branch of Christianity. This textbook stands within the stream of the Christian Church that sees in the life and thought of John Wesley and those that influenced him a sound and powerful understanding of the Christian faith. The convictions of this tradition have inevitably and intentionally shaped the way in which this textbook interprets the Bible and presents the Christian faith. As the reader will notice, interspersed in this textbook's exposition of the Christian faith are references to "the creeds in our tradition." These creeds are the doctrinal statements of churches that draw upon John Wesley and those who influenced him. These creeds include the Articles of Religion of the Methodist Church, the Wesleyan Church, and the Free Methodist Church, and the Articles of Faith of the Church of the Nazarene. However, the fact that this textbook speaks from a particular branch of Christianity does not mean that other branches are wrong or that they lack "the teaching that is in accordance with godliness." It simply means that they understand some matters differently from the understanding set forth in this textbook and that they differ from the branch that supports this textbook about which doctrines should receive special emphasis.

Every textbook seeks to accomplish some things and not others. The purpose of this textbook is to set forth the central doctrines of the Christian faith as they are expounded in the biblical narrative and understood in the Wesleyan tradition. Its purpose, in other words, is to introduce readers to the Christian faith more than it is to introduce them to the study of Christian theology. This purpose dictates that many important things are not included. For instance, there is no significant discussion of the history of Christian thought, even though that is a worthy topic and one that is indispensable for serious students of Christian theology. Similarly, this textbook contains no substantive comparison of the Wesleyan tradition with other traditions within Christianity and no engagement with philosophy or other disciplines. These are issues that deserve serious study; however, they properly belong in more advanced textbooks. At the same time, this textbook is not a biblical theology. It does not, for example, attempt to do full justice to the variety of witnesses within the Bible, and it does not engage the results and methods of biblical criticism. Instead, it seeks to follow the main thread of Christian doctrine as it unfolds within the biblical narrative. Finally, this textbook contains no extensive discussion of the many points of theological method that are routinely covered in advanced introductions to theology.

In accordance with the purpose of this textbook, the topics of the Christian faith are presented according to the order of the biblical narrative. Consequently, some doctrines, such as creation and sin, are discussed in early chapters in a preliminary way and are not fully developed until later chapters. Indeed, it is a deep-seated conviction of Christians that no doctrine can be fully understood without a grasp of eschatology—the doctrine of last things—for the end determines the meaning of everything. As a result, readers must allow the biblical narrative, and not our natural desire for completeness and coherence, to lead the discussion. This means that the reader cannot expect any single chapter, especially early chapters, to provide a full exposition of any given doctrine.

Theology is the knowledge of God. To engage the subject matter of theology is to open ourselves to hearing God's word to us and to do so with understanding. It is the act of engaging both our faithfulness to God and our intellectual powers in the attempt to discern the divine movement into the world that begins with the Father, passes through the Son, and reaches its end in the Spirit. It is an act of worship by which we offer to God our thoughts and our words, in the hope that the God who makes all things new will take those thoughts and words and make them instruments of grace and insight. It is, accordingly, one part of our calling as Christian disciples to devote every aspect of our existence to God. In theology we thus come face-to-face with the beginning and end of our being. Let us therefore enter into it with the spirit of prayer, for in it we encounter God.

PREFACE FOR INSTRUCTORS

Those who instruct beginners in the Christian faith make use of tools like this textbook. It hardly needs to be said that the usefulness of the tool is proportionate to the knowledge and skill of the instructor. It therefore behooves all of us who are instructors to attend to our task with the greatest reverence and dedication. But the reverence that our task demands is balanced by the free attitude that users of this textbook should adopt toward it. This textbook, in other words, is only a tool and as such exists for the tasks of teaching and learning. Users, therefore, should feel free to use it as we should use all tools—carefully, but keeping in mind that it is only a tool placed in the service of a greater goal, the instruction of students in the Christian faith. For that reason, instructors should expect and encourage students to question and probe this book's affirmations and exposition. For although I have striven to be faithful to the Church's tradition, this book remains only one way of presenting the Christian faith; it is not the only authentic way of presenting that faith. Disagreement with this or that aspect of the book is, consequently, an encouraging sign that students are actively engaged with its subject. The purpose of this textbook is, accordingly, to bring students into dialogue with the Christian faith. Instructors will use it most effectively if they employ it as a means of engaging students in that dialogue.

With this purpose in mind, I have written this book with careful consideration of its intended readers. These readers are students of the Christian faith who have little or no acquaintance with theology. Accordingly, this textbook is an introduction to the Christian faith; it is not an introduction to the discipline of theology. It is, therefore, a catechetical document, for through it I am trying to convey to its readers the substance and structure of the Christian faith. However, as it is not an introduction to the discipline of theology, it does not contain many things customarily associated with such introductions. Readers will immediately notice, for example, the absence of footnotes. This is due to the fact that I am not attempting to acquaint students with contemporary theological literature or to trace out the history of doctrinal discussions. Also absent is theology's engagement with other disciplines such as philosophy. Although Christian theology has a rich heritage of dialogue with philosophy, the purpose of this book demanded that I focus on the substance of the Christian faith and not expound the historical development of that faith. For the same reason, theologians will quickly notice that this book has no sustained discussion of points of controversy between branches of the Christian tradition. This book provides students with a rudimentary instruction in these controversies; however, the focus remains on the historical faith that Christians have affirmed throughout the centuries. Keeping in mind the intended readers, I have written this book in such a way that the Christian faith is presented on the basis of the main parts of the biblical narrative.

Although my goal has been to present students with the substance and structure of the Christian faith, every such presentation inevitably proceeds from some definite understanding of that faith. The understanding from which this presentation proceeds is given by the Wesleyan tradition—that branch of the Christian tradition that encompasses John Wesley, all those who influenced him, and those who have been significantly influenced by him. For that reason, I have placed, in appropriate places, references to the statements of faith of several Churches in the Wesleyan tradition: the Articles of Religion of the United Methodist Church, of the Free Methodist Church, of The Wesleyan Church, and the Articles of Faith of the Church of the Nazarene. In this book I have drawn from the consensus that these statements of faith represent and I refer to them collectively as "the creeds in our tradition."

Instructing beginners in the Christian faith is a high calling. It deserves our best efforts and our finest tools. My prayer is that this book will be a tool suitable to the task and that it will prove to be helpful to those called to this task.

DISCOVERING OUR
CHRISTIAN FAITH
AN INTRODUCTION TO THEOLOGY

THE BEGINNING AND END OF GOD'S CREATION

ONE

THE CREATIVE POWER OF GOD

OBJECTIVES

Your study of this chapter should help you to:

1. Understand the Bible's teaching about God the Creator.

2. Appreciate the importance of books such as the Psalms and Isaiah for helping us understand the Bible's teaching about the Creator.

3. See the importance of thinking about creation and the Creator from the perspective of God's purposes.

4. Understand the meaning of theological terms used in connection with the doctrine of the Creator.

5. Understand the connection between the doctrine of the Creator and the practice of the Christian life.

KEY WORDS TO UNDERSTAND

Creation from nothing	Omnipotence
Eschatology	Omnipresence
Eternity	Omniscience
Holiness	Providence
Immutability	Theodicy
Infinity	Transcendence
Monotheism	

QUESTIONS TO CONSIDER AS YOU READ

1. What does the Bible say about God when it portrays God as the Creator?

2. How is Christian faith in the Creator different from scientific ways of thinking about the origin of the universe?

3. What does the doctrine of the Creator say about our practice of the Christian life?

Father of all, whose powerful voice
  Called forth this universal frame;
Whose mercies over all rejoice,
  Through endless ages still the same;
Thou by thy word upholdest all;
  Thy bounteous love to all is showed;
Thou hearest thy every creature's call,
  And fillest every mouth with good.

In heaven thou reign'st enthroned in light,
  Nature's expanse beneath thee spread;
Earth, air, and sea, before thy sight,
  And hell's deep gloom, are open laid.
Wisdom, and might, and love are thine;
  Prostrate before thy face we fall,
Confess thine attributes divine,
  And hail the sovereign Lord of all.

Thee, sovereign Lord, let all confess
  That moves in earth, or air, or sky,
Revere thy power, thy goodness bless,
  Tremble before thy piercing eye;
All ye who owe to him your birth,
  In praise your every hour employ;
Jehovah reigns! Be glad, O earth,
  And shout, ye morning stars, for joy.

This Wesleyan hymn expresses the Christian faith in the Creator, who "called forth this universal frame" and whose "word upholdest all." It affirms that the Creator is exalted and transcendent ("In heaven thou reign'st") and calls on creatures to worship the Creator. But the transcendent Creator is also the one "whose mercies over all rejoice" and whose "bounteous love to all is showed." In short, this hymn invites us to consider the Creator who is holy and exalted but who also comes to us in love and grace.

▶ INTRODUCTION

The opening words of the Bible are simple and majestic. They speak of God, in the beginning, creating the heavens and the earth. These words have the power to grip our minds and hearts with wonder and awe. They speak of a divine reality incomprehensibly greater than our world and our conceptions. They point us to the mystery of the universe's existence and to the inconceivable divine reality that lies outside our world of space and time. In short, they point us toward the Christian doctrine of creation and of the Creator.

But we will miss important aspects of the Bible's teaching about creation if we focus too narrowly on the opening chapters of Genesis and find the doctrine of creation only there; we should not identify the act of creation with a single, originating event in the past. We see other aspects of creation when we study other biblical books, especially the Psalms and Isaiah.

▶ THE CONTEXT OF THE BIBLE'S TEACHING ABOUT CREATION

In the context of exile in Babylon, biblical writers affirmed the power and supremacy of the God who was about to liberate Israel from exile and re-create it. They proclaimed that the God who was about to redeem Israel was the God who had created the world. In this proclamation, they portrayed redemption as a new act of God's creation.

One way to get beyond a narrow conception of creation is to study chapters 40—55 of Isaiah. The context of these chapters was Israel's exile in Babylon, in the 6th century B.C. As a result of the war with Babylon, Jerusalem was destroyed, the national life of Israel was brought to a close,

GOD, MAKER AND PRESERVER OF ALL THINGS

The creeds in our tradition affirm the doctrine of creation by calling God the "Maker" or "Creator" and "Preserver of all things both visible and invisible."

and several thousand Israelites endured a forced evacuation to Babylon. There they lived a difficult life throughout the greater part of the 500s B.C. In this situation a prophet arose with the hopeful message to the exiled people that Israel's God, the Creator of all, was about to redeem Israel by an act of re-creation. God's creation, in other words, flows seamlessly into re-creation and redemption.

Consider, for example, Isa. 42:5-9. Here the God who does "new things" is the God who in the beginning "created the heavens and stretched them out, who spread out the earth and what comes from it, who gives breath to the people upon it and spirit to those who walk in it" (v. 5). Creation, therefore, is not a once and for all event, lying solely in the past. On the contrary, it is the continuing act of God's creative power. In the context of Isa. 40—55, this divine movement of creation-redemption meant the end of exile in Babylon and the restoration of Jerusalem.

The lesson to draw from Isa. 40—55 is that, in order to think rightly about creation, we must see it not only as an original event but also as the paradigm of all divine activity and as continuous with redemption and new creation. Original creation, considered abstractly, is meaningless apart from its relation to the sum total of God's creative acts, acts that all have an end in God's purposes.

▶ The Eschatological End of Creation

The Bible's teaching about creation goes beyond Israel's destiny. It embraces as well the destiny of the entire created world, so that God's creative power and presence extend from the beginning of the world to its end. This means that God's creation has a goal—an end. This end is fellowship between Creator and the created world.

Thinking about redemption and new creation introduces another aspect of the Bible's teaching about creation. This aspect is suggested by Rev. 1:8, "I am the Alpha and the Omega," that is, the first and the last, the beginning and the end. This important verse reminds us that God is not only the beginning of all things but is also the end of all things. But the word *end* may confuse us because in English this term means cessation or termination. For example, the end of someone's life means the conclusion of that person's life. When we say that God is the end of all things, we are not speaking about the termination of the world. We are instead speaking about the goal of creation.

The theological term that denotes the end of creation is *eschatology*. Discussions of eschatology customarily focus on Christ's return, the final judgment, and other events mentioned in books such as Revelation. These are important matters that bear on human sin; however, apart from sin, creation would still have an end—an eschatological fulfillment. Eschatology, then, is above all a doctrine about God's desire for the created world, a desire that remains unchanged in spite of sin. Christian thinking about creation, therefore, moves in an ellipse whose foci are (1) God's originating creative act and (2) the end of creation. The ellipse itself is the universe's history, a history that revolves around God's creative activity.

What is the eschatological end toward which God's creative activity points? Genesis 3 helps us here. It pictures God walking in the garden and calling out to Adam and Eve (vv. 8-9). This brief episode is important for it indicates God's desire for fellowship. God does not remain in heaven, distant from us. On the contrary, God comes into the world for the purpose of fellowship. That is what makes verse 8 so poignant: "The man and his wife hid themselves from the presence of the Lord God." Whereas God came into the world seeking fellowship, humankind withdrew from God's presence.

God's quest for fellowship is a pervasive theme in the Bible and the Book of Revelation concludes with this theme. In portraying humankind's destiny, it does not think of us as journeying to heaven to be with God. It instead portrays God as coming from heaven to dwell with us: "I heard a loud voice from the throne saying, 'See, the home of God is among mortals" (21:3). In the end, God overcomes alienation, the history of which goes back to the events narrated in Genesis 3, establishes unhindered fellowship with us, and thus restores the world to its status as God's creation. We can understand the doctrine of creation only in the context of eschatology and God's quest for fellowship.

At this point it is important to ask whether God's creative power, in all of its manifestations, is aimed only or principally at communion with humankind. The answer is no. God comes into the world seeking fellowship with the entire world. But in order to think about the significance of the nonhuman world, we need to attend once again to biblical passages besides Genesis. Most instructive in this regard is the Psalms' affirmation that God provides for animals as well as for humans as in Ps. 147: God "covers the heavens with clouds, prepares rain for the earth, makes grass grow on the hills. He gives to the animals their food, and to the young ravens when they cry" (vv. 8-9). Other examples include Pss. 36:5-6 and 145:15-16.

In response, nonhuman beings offer praise to God. Psalm 19, for instance, affirms that "The heavens are telling the glory of God; and the firmament proclaims his handiwork" (v. 1) and Ps. 148 exhorts every creature to praise God (v. 10). It may be difficult for us to think of the nonhuman portion of creation praising God, perhaps because we think of praise as something verbal arising from thinking. But Pss. 19 and 148 show us that praise is not always verbal. On the contrary, these psalms envision each kind of being in the cosmos as playing a role in a great symphony of silent praise. But in what does their praise consist? It consists in the act of declaring God's glory, which each thing does by acting according to its created nature. The sun, moon and every created thing declare God's glory by their nature and existence. Just by being what they are, they show forth the glory of God and thus praise God.

Consequently, the beginning and end of God's creative activity extend beyond the human world. Of course, being human, we can speak much more fully about our destiny and end than we can speak about the destiny and end of the nonhuman world. It is impossible for us to imagine what it is like for other beings in the universe to enjoy communion with God and what it is like for God to enjoy communion with them. We are likewise puzzled at some of the harsh facts of the world such as the death and suffering associated with predation. It is difficult to reconcile these facts with our image of a loving God and of God's providential care for the world. Nonetheless, our lack of imaginative power and our intellectual perplexities should not prevent our affirming the significance of the nonhuman world to God and of God to the nonhuman world. Doing so is required not only by the Bible's express teaching but also by the need to remind ourselves that we are not the only creatures of importance in God's universe.

We have noted that the Bible defines God in terms of creative power, so that the doctrine of creation spans the totality of God's activity. It is now time to inquire more carefully into what the Bible says about God's creative power.

▶ THE CREATIVE POWER OF GOD: FAITHFULNESS

The act of creation not only is the world's beginning but also is God's act of sustaining the world and its rhythms. God's faithfulness to the created world assumes concrete form as God's blessing. Because of this blessing the world is characterized by natural and predictable processes.

One of the dominant themes of Isa. 40—55 is the Creator's promise to be with Israel in spite of all of Israel's troubles and sins. For the prophet, God's creative power was much more than the cause of Israel's beginning. It was also God's faithful promise to be with Israel and to bless and provide for Israel: "He will feed his flock like a shepherd; he will gather the lambs in his arms, and carry them in his bosom, and gently lead the mother sheep" (40:11).

Other biblical writers expressed this belief in God's faithfulness in their conviction that God's creative power faithfully sustains the universe in its continued existence. A classical expression of God's faithfulness toward the universe is found in Gen. 8:22: "As long as the earth endures, seedtime and harvest, cold and heat, summer and winter, day and night, shall not cease." This confidence in God's sustenance is stated picturesquely in those passages, such as Ps. 104:5, that portray God as constructing the world so well that its continued existence and well-being are secure: "You set the earth on its foundations, so that it shall never be shaken."

The characteristic of God that inspires this confidence is faithfulness. God's faithfulness is the promise of God's continued creative power and, therefore, the promise of God's perpetual will to achieve fellowship. It is God's promise to conquer everything that hinders this fellowship. The term *immutability* designates God's unwavering faithfulness and the steadfast character of God's intent. It points to the meaning of *hesed,* a Hebrew word that denotes God's pledge to remain true to a covenant. So, when Genesis portrays God's relation to the world as a covenant, it is stating that the promises that God makes are backed up by God's *hesed—*

God's utterly dependable faithfulness and promise to remain creatively present with us.

Psalm 136 is an especially powerful testimony to God's covenantal faithfulness toward the world. "O give thanks to the LORD, for he is good, . . . Who by understanding made the heavens, . . . who spread out the earth on the waters, . . . who made the great lights, for his steadfast love endures forever (vv. 1, 5-7). Psalm 33:5 similarly affirms that the earth is full of God's *hesed*, finding God's faithfulness in every part of the created world. These psalms express the conviction that the world and its continued existence rest on God's faithfulness and covenant with the world.

The New Testament affirms God's faithfulness by associating God's creative power with Jesus Christ. Colossians states that "In [Jesus Christ] all things hold together" (1:17) and Hebrews asserts that Christ "sustains all things by his powerful word" (1:3). Describing God's sustaining faithfulness in terms of Jesus Christ signifies the eschatological character of that faithfulness. It reminds us that God's creative activity is oriented toward an end, which is fully understood only from the revelation of Jesus Christ. Jesus Christ is accordingly the meaning and fulfillment of God's creative activity. The God who is faithful toward the created world is the God who in Jesus Christ comes to the world in redemption.

However, to speak of God's sustaining the universe does not convey the full extent of God's faithfulness. The Bible also presents God as faithfully blessing the world. Psalm 65:9-11 is instructive in this regard: "You visit the earth and water it, you greatly enrich it; the river of God is full of water; You provide the people with grain . . . You water its furrows abundantly, settling its ridges, softening it with showers, and blessing its growth. You crown the year with your bounty."

For the biblical writers, the regular, predictable processes of nature were in fact God's blessings upon the world and resulted from God's covenantal faithfulness. The theological term for God's faithfulness in the processes of nature is **providence.** As God's creative activity has a universal scope, so God's providence and blessing are given to the entire world. This means that it is not only the people of God who receive God's blessing. As Matthew's Gospel states it, God "makes his sun rise on the evil and on the good, and sends rain on the righteous and on the unrighteous" (5:45). The point is that God's blessing on the world is seen in the regular rhythms of the natural order, which benefit everything in the created world. The world thus sustains life of all sorts through the kinds of processes that the natural sciences study. Without nullifying the validity of scientific inquiry, Christians believe that these processes reflect God's universal faithfulness and blessing.

At the same time, recognizing that God's blessing takes the form of natural processes enables us to understand that these processes are subject to variation. In some years we receive more rain, in other years less rain. In some years there is so much rain that crops are destroyed. In other years there is so little rain that crops wither. We understand that the rhythms of nature do not guarantee that things will always work out for our immediate benefit. It is no sign of God's displeasure when we suffer at the hands of nature just as it is no sign of God's favor when the unrighteous benefit from nature. As a result, the praise that we give to the Creator for blessings is based not so much on the fact that we have benefited as on our recognition that the world as a whole and all of its processes are generally life-sustaining, even if sometimes they are not directly good for us.

▶ The Creative Power of God: Wisdom

The creative power and presence of God, which is God's faithful blessing, is also God's wisdom.

The predictable processes of the natural world lead us to consider God's wisdom. God's wisdom is God's creative power establishing the conditions for fellowship with humankind by fashioning an ordered world that makes creatures' well-being possible. To call the created world ordered is to say with Proverbs that "the LORD by wisdom founded the earth; by understanding he established the heavens" (3:19).

Sometimes God's wisdom is seen in the sheer variety of beings within God's world: "O LORD, how manifold are your works! In wisdom you have made them all; the earth is full of your creatures" (Ps. 104:24). At other times (as in Prov. 8:22-31) God's wisdom is seen in the stability of the world. And sometimes it is manifested in the incomprehensible realities of the world, as when God asks Job, "Who has the wisdom to number the clouds?" (Job 38:37). In every case, the Bible testifies to the conviction that the world is rooted in God's wisdom and that this wisdom is an expression of God's creative power.

But to fully understand this conviction about God's wisdom we must see it in relation to the biblical idea of God's word, which is a way of speaking about God's acting with creative power. To say that God is wise is to say that God creates and acts wisely. This emphasis on action underlies the Bible's concept of God's word:

> As the rain and the snow come down from heaven, and do not return there until they have watered the earth, making it bring forth and sprout, . . . so shall my word be that goes out from my mouth; it shall not return to me empty, but it shall accomplish that which I purpose, and succeed in the thing for which I sent it *(Isa. 55:10-11)*.

This passage vividly portrays God's word as an effective and creative power that proceeds from God and performs his purpose. This helps us understand the first chapter of Genesis, in which God creates merely by speaking. God speaks and things come into being in such a way that God's wisdom is manifested. God's word is God's wisdom in action.

The connection between God's word and wisdom is reinforced by the New Testament's insistence that Jesus Christ is both the wisdom of God (1 Cor. 1:24) and the word of God (John 1:1). As the divine wisdom and word, Jesus Christ is the world's Creator (Col. 1:16). Jesus Christ is, therefore, the wise, creative and active word of God—the movement of God into the world that creates fellowship.

God's wisdom is transcendent. Humans are able, with great effort, to attain to a measure of knowledge and, with experience, can accumulate some wisdom. But God possesses wisdom that is unsurpassable. Sometimes the Bible represents God's knowledge as amazing in extent, as when Isaiah affirms God's knowledge of each star: "Lift up your eyes and see: Who created these? He who brings out their host and numbers them, calling them all by name" (40:26). However, the Bible more customarily portrays God as creating and therefore knowing things that are incomprehensible to us: "Can you find out the deep things of God? Can you find out the limit of the Almighty? It is higher than heaven—what can you do? Deeper than Sheol—what can you know? Its measure is longer than the earth, and broader than the sea" (Job 11:7-9). Consequently, to say that God is wise is not merely to acknowledge that God knows so much more than we know. It is not even to affirm that God knows things that are in principle impossible for human beings to know. It is not that God knows things as we know them, except that God knows everything whereas we know only a few things. Such an understanding would violate the Bible's sense of God's incomparable nature. It is better to think of God's knowledge as coinciding with God's creative activity—with God's word. To say that God has created the world is to say that God knows the world. This means that God's knowledge is of a different order from human knowledge. For us it is one thing to know, another to act. For God, however, knowledge is identical with creative action. God's knowledge is God's action; God's action is God's knowledge. And since the scope of God's creative activity is universal, the scope of God's knowing wisdom is likewise universal.

The theological term that designates the universality of God's wisdom is *omniscience.* The identification of God's knowledge with God's creative activity means that God's knowledge is not composed of isolated facts (as our knowledge tends to be) but is instead God's wisdom, that is God's act of creating an ethical order that sustains human well-being. As a result, we are compelled to acknowledge a paradox. On one hand, we can share in God's wisdom and knowledge (Prov. 2:6-7). Indeed, our well-being depends on doing so. On the other hand, God's wisdom and knowledge infinitely exceed ours. This helps us grasp the difference between our transitory, fragmented wisdom and God, who is wisdom itself. This is the truth to which the idea of omniscience points.

▶ THE CREATIVE POWER OF GOD: RIGHTEOUSNESS

God's wisdom passes over into the created world in the form of an ethical order that establishes the conditions for human well-being. This ethical order indicates the righteousness of the Creator God.

Besides emphasizing God's faithfulness and wisdom, Isaiah 40—55 stresses the Creator's righteousness. For the prophet, God's righteousness was evident principally in God's judgment on Israel (42:8-25) and also in the coming destruction of Babylon (47:1-15). But righteousness is also

God's desire for the entire created world: "Shower, O heavens, from above, and let the skies rain down righteousness; let the earth open, that salvation may spring up, and let it cause righteousness to sprout up also; I the LORD have created it" (45:8).

This verse speaks of the connection between God's creative power and righteousness. This connection tells us that the universe exhibits a righteous moral order just as it exhibits a wise natural order. Just as there are reliable, predictable processes in the physical world, so there are reliable, predictable processes in the ethical world. And just as God's faithfulness, expressed in wisdom, sustains the natural order of the world, so that same faithfulness, expressed in righteousness, sustains the moral order.

God's righteousness is God's power that creates justice in human affairs, thus establishing the conditions for fellowship with humankind and for human life well-lived. It is God's act of destroying everything that hinders this fellowship and the good life.

The world's moral order is grounded in God's own righteousness, for "the word of the LORD is upright, and all his work is done in faithfulness. He loves righteousness and justice" (Ps. 33:4-5). Although God's ways are at times incomprehensible, biblical writers never depart from the fundamental conviction that, ultimately, God is righteous. In turn, just as the wise Creator wants human beings to be wise, so the righteous God demands righteousness from us. Hence the sadness of the early chapters of Genesis, in which God is persistently disappointed by human actions of unrighteousness. Adam and Eve prove to be disobedient. Cain spills his brother's blood. People strive for divinity by building a tower into the heavens. And, in general, "The LORD saw that the wickedness of humankind was great in the earth, and that every inclination of the thoughts of their hearts was only evil continually" (Gen. 6:5). The early chapters of Genesis as well as the rest of the Bible show that God responds to unrighteousness as a judge (see for example Gen 6:7; Ps. 14:2). Thus, according to Paul: "[God] will repay according to each one's deeds: to those who by patiently doing good seek for glory and honor and immortality, he will give eternal life; while for those who are self-seeking and who obey not the truth but wickedness, there will be wrath and fury" (Rom. 2:6-8).

However, the Bible does not regard the Creator's demand for righteousness as burdensome, for righteousness is simply a matter of doing good, as Paul indicates in Rom. 2:6. Righteousness is doing what is right, just as God does what is right.

In summary, God's faithfulness is the promise of God's continued creative power among us and the promise of his perpetual will to establish fellowship with us. It is God's promise to conquer everything that hinders this fellowship. God's wisdom is God's creative power fashioning an ordered world in which we may live. God's righteousness is God's creative power that brings about a moral world ruled by justice so that human beings can have fellowship with God, with each other and with the rest of the created world. Faithfulness, wisdom and righteousness are ways in which God expresses his love as he relates to the world.

▶ THE CREATIVE POWER OF GOD: INFINITY AND TRANSCENDENCE

God the Creator is the powerful Lord of all things, who is not limited by worldly realities such as time, space, and power. God is not a part of the created world but instead is the creative presence that sustains that world.

God's faithfulness, wisdom, and righteousness differ from human faithfulness, wisdom, and righteousness. Theology uses terms such as omniscience and immutability to indicate this difference. These and similar terms express the conviction that God is not constrained by the limitations that characterize humans and that, in important respects, God is not like beings in the created world.

It is important to emphasize God's difference from created beings for without this difference God would not be the creative power that redeems and re-creates. This is the point made in Isa. 46:1-7, which makes fun of the Babylonian gods by noting that they are unable to save anyone and have to be carried about by animals. Although people cry out to them, they cannot answer, for they are really only a part of the created world: "They hire a goldsmith, who makes it into a god; then they fall down and worship!" (46:6).

Israel's God, however, is different. Israel's God is not a being that belongs to the created world. This God is radically different from the created world and everything in it. In Isaiah's words, this God is incomparable: "To whom will you liken me and make me equal, and compare me, as though we were alike?" (46:5).

Two theological terms that express God's incomparability are *transcendence* and *infinity.* God's transcendence means God is neither a part of nor dependent on the created world. God's infinity means God is not limited by anything and, more important, that God's creative power knows no boundaries and that God's will to create fellowship with humankind is unconquerable. The infinity of God and the transcendence of God mean that God alone is the Creator. Since only Israel's God is the power of creative activity, only Israel's God is truly divine, for nothing can be considered divine unless it has the power to create. Other gods are really no gods at all (see Jer. 16:20); they lack creative power and they can do nothing. Israel's God is the living God, the God who is creative power. The belief that Israel's God alone is the living God of creative activity is the basis of *monotheism,* the belief that the word *God* points to a single and unified reality.

THE ONENESS OF GOD

> The creedal statements in our tradition assert the oneness of God by affirming belief in "one living and true God" who "only is God."

The one God—the infinite God—is not limited by the realities that limit creatures. One of these realities is time. The existence of every created thing is inscribed within the structure of time. Everything has a beginning and an end. But with God it is different. In the picturesque words of Ps. 90, "Before the mountains were brought forth, or ever you had formed the earth and the world, from everlasting to everlasting you are God" (v. 2). Here the psalmist considers first the oldest things thinkable—the mountains and the earth—and finally confesses that, as unimaginably old as these are, God is before them. Job goes further, in perplexity observing that "Surely God is great, and we do not know him; the number of his years is unsearchable" (36:26).

The psalmist's confession, "from everlasting to everlasting you are God," makes clear that God's life is not limited by time, and hence it cannot be measured by time. As Creator, he is not confined to or controlled by time. Instead, time is subject to God, and thus he is the Lord of time. The theological term *eternity* points to this idea of God as the Lord of time. Psalm 90 goes on to say, "For a thousand years in your sight are like yesterday when it is past" (v. 4).

This verse does not imply that time is meaningless to God, but it does affirm that, with respect to time, God is free in a way in which we are not, for God is the Lord of time. Because God is the Lord of time, he can truly be the Creator, the one "who gives life to the dead and calls into existence the things that do not exist" (Rom. 4:17). As the Lord of time, God does not suffer the limitations inherent in beings that are bounded by time. The psalmist laments about the brevity of human life, extending to seventy or eighty years, filled with toil and trouble (see Ps. 90:10).

Human life is thus a vain attempt to stave off the inevitable vicissitudes of time. Because God is the Lord of time, the psalmist finds him as our refuge, "our dwelling place in all generations" (Ps. 90:1). This means that his creative activity can bring about the renewal of our life, which is otherwise transient and filled with trouble. The biblical conviction that God is eternal—God is the Lord of time—thus also means that the creative power of God and God's will to create fellowship with us transcend the boundaries of time.

The same is true concerning space. Creatures are bound by space, even if that space is very large. Every entity occupies some space. But God is not bound by space; Isaiah speaks about God's immensity in this way: "It is he who sits above the circle of the earth, and its inhabitants are like grasshoppers; who stretched out the heavens like a curtain; and spreads them like a tent to live in" (40:22). This verse metaphorically affirms God's incomparability with respect to space. Nothing in the created world, regardless of its immensity, can be compared to God's greatness. But this does not mean that God possesses a larger size than any other created thing or that God is located in some region of space. If this were the case, then God would be bound by space and would be limited in the same way in which every created thing is limited. On the contrary, as the psalmist indicates, God is the Creator of space and is free from spatial limitations: "If I ascend to heaven, you are there; if I make my bed in Sheol, you are there. If I take the wings of the morning and settle at the farthest limits of the sea, even there your hand shall lead me" (139:8-10).

In contrast to the pagan gods, who were thought to inhabit a specific territory, Israel's God knows no spatial limits and consequently is the Lord of space. This is the truth expressed in the theological term *omnipresence.* By this term we mean that the creative activity of God that sustains our being and our well-being is not limited to this or that place. The psalmist believed that God would be found even in *Sheol,* the place of the dead. Elijah encountered God in the silence of the desert (1 Kings 19:4-13). John heard the voice of God on the island of Patmos (Rev. 1:9-11). The creative power of God and God's will to create fellowship with us cannot be conquered by the limitations of space, for God is the Lord of space.

God is unlimited with respect to time and space. God is also *omnipotent,* that is, unlimited with respect to creative power. We are familiar with the exercise of power by human beings and political institutions. But in

GOD'S INFINITE POWER AND HUMAN FREEDOM

The idea of God's infinite power has been a point of contention and the subject of long discussion in Christian history. The main point of debate is whether God's infinite power excludes human freedom. In medieval theology, theologians generally held that God acts in and through all human deeds but without compromising human freedom. In the 20th century some theologians have proposed that we think of God's power as inherently limited, so that there are some things (for example, preventing the evil acts of human beings) that God cannot do. Others suggest that God's power is not inherently limited but that God voluntarily limits the exercise of divine power in order to preserve human freedom. Other theologians have found these proposals flawed and instead have argued for a version of the medieval view.

every case there are limitations to that power and its exercise is not always creative. However, God's power is unlimited: "Whatever the LORD pleases he does, in heaven and on earth, in the seas and all deeps" (Ps. 135:6).

The infinitude of God's power with respect to creation is expressed in the theological concept of **creation from nothing** (often referred to as *creatio ex nihilo*). This is the idea that nothing constrains God's creative power, especially with respect to the originating act of creating the world. This concept denies that the universe is eternal and that the originating act of creation is merely a transformation from a previously existing state of the universe. To affirm the idea of creation from nothing is to assert that only God is the Lord of time and space and that the created world exists only through God's creative power.

THE ETERNAL GOD

The creeds in our tradition affirm God's Lordship over time by confessing that God is "everlasting" and "eternal." They assert God's Lordship over the limitations of space when they affirm that God is "without body or parts." They proclaim God's limitlessness by affirming that God is "of infinite power, wisdom, and goodness" and is the "Sovereign of the universe."

The concept of infinite power and the idea of creation from nothing are puzzling. But we should not become obsessed with the logical and theological puzzles arising from these concepts. Instead, we should see that because God's power is unlimited God is an inexhaustible source of life and blessing for us, who suffer from the limitations and distortions of power: "The LORD is the everlasting God, the Creator of the ends of the earth. He does not faint or grow weary; his understanding is unsearchable. He gives power to the faint, and strengthens the powerless" (Isa. 40:28-29).

The power of which this passage speaks is the creative power of God's presence among us. In exile in Babylon and with hope nearly exhausted, Israelites heard the declaration that their God was not only powerful but also the everlasting source of strength. To say that God is the

Lord of power is, therefore, to affirm that God's creative power, which establishes fellowship with us, never comes to an end and that this power creates the hope that sustains life and provides us with a future.

To speak of the Creator as the infinite creative presence who acts powerfully raises a difficult issue, expressed in those passages of the Bible that represent God as the power that determines everything. For example, consider Ps. 104: "[living creatures] all look to you to give them their food in due season; when you give to them, they gather it up; when you open your hand, they are filled with good things. When you hide your face, they are dismayed; when you take away their breath, they die and return to the dust" (vv. 27-29). This passage gives clear expression to the conviction that the life and death of every living being depend directly on the creative activity of God. But it is not only life and death that the Bible attributes to God's will. Events of all sorts are attributed to God: "I form light and create darkness, I make weal and create woe; I the LORD do all these things" (Isa. 45:7). "Does a disaster befall a city, unless the LORD has done it?" (Amos 3:6). Some biblical passages, then, portray God as determining the course of all events, both the great and the small.

Of course, the Bible does not provide a philosophical theory of God's power and as a result does not deal theoretically with the problem of reconciling God's power and humankind's sense of freedom and our notions about the contingency of historical events. The Bible also does not devote much space to the difficult problem of explaining how God can be good yet be responsible for woes and disasters. Philosophers have devoted much thought to this issue, which is called the problem of *theodicy.* None of the various attempts at forming a theodicy has been fully satisfactory.

The Bible's ultimate response to this issue is that of Job. Throughout his discourses, Job has enunciated a persistent complaint against God and God's use of power: "He crushes me with a tempest, and multiplies my wounds without cause" (9:17).

Job regards God as the force behind his problems and argues that he is suffering unjustly. As a result, he repeatedly demands an audience with God: "I would speak to the Almighty, and I desire to argue my case with God" (13:3). At last Job receives his audience with God. He finally has his chance to present his case and to press God for justice. But when he encounters God, his quest for justice evaporates as the tables are turned, with God posing questions to Job: "Where were you when I laid the foundation of the earth? Tell me, if you have understanding. Who determined its measurements—surely you know!" (38:4-5).

Job does not receive an answer to his query about God's justice and God's role in his suffering. In the presence of God, Job is reduced to silence as he realizes that God's mystery cannot be contained by his concept of justice: "I know that you can do all things, and that no purpose of yours can be thwarted. . . . Therefore I have uttered what I did not understand, things too wonderful for me, which I did not know" (42:2-3). This is obviously not a philosophical solution to the problems associated with God's power and our need of an adequate theodicy. But it is one of the Bible's responses to these issues. It is a response that calls upon us to acknowledge that God's reality cannot be measured by us and that it is we who must answer to God and not God to us. It is a response that leads us to see that we do not fully determine the course of our lives. We do not act in complete freedom. There are realities that lie outside our control that shape the contours of our existence and establish constraints upon our actions in ways we do not understand.

How are we to deal with the intellectual perplexities that the Bible's convictions generate? We certainly should not affirm that God is the only causal force and that humans are mere instruments of God's power. Although the Bible occasionally portrays things in this way, as when Paul discusses Pharaoh (Rom. 9:17-18), it more routinely recognizes that God's determination of life does not annul the causal efficacy of human behavior. Proverbs expresses this paradox when it notes that "The human mind plans the way, but the LORD directs the steps" (16:9).

The paradoxical relation between divine action and human action—the fact that both are somehow operative in the same events—means that we cannot formulate a philosophically precise account of this relation. Nonetheless, we can make several affirmations as matters of Christian faith. First, because we cannot comprehend God, there will always be something enigmatic about divine action. Theology's task is not to resolve perplexities but instead to point to them and honor them. Second, God's will is accomplished through human action in ways that we do not understand. For example, Isaiah proclaimed that God had raised up the Persian king, Cyrus, specifically in order to liberate Israel from exile in Babylon. Isaiah perceived matters from God's perspective. Cyrus was certainly not aware of being an instrument of Israel's God. From Cyrus's human perspective there were factors such as Cyrus's desire for conquest at work. The Bible, then, invites us to perceive that there are various ways of viewing the same event. To be a person of faith is to acknowledge that in every instance of creatures' acting there is also a dimension of divine action, even if we cannot provide a satisfactory explanation of the matter. Third, the Bible's conviction that God determines all things points us to an affirmation of great importance, namely that human life depends radically on God and that our well-being is a matter of acknowledging that dependence and living in response to that dependence. In other words, regardless of how we think about God's power philosophically, its religious significance is clear. Human life is lived in the presence of God and cannot exist outside that presence. But it can be lived well only when God's power works within us and leads us into fellowship with God.

The God who is love—who is faithful, wise, and righteous—is also infinite and transcendent. The Bible's word for designating God's infinity and transcendence is *holiness*. To say that God is holy is to affirm that God is radically unlike us and unlike anything in the created world. It is to affirm that God differs from the world and everything in the world.

The Christian faith affirms that God is both love and holy. God is the transcendent power that infinitely exceeds us and whose faithfulness, wisdom, and righteousness cannot be compared to ours. But this transcendent, infinite power creates and comes into the world for the purpose of creating fellowship with creatures. This fellowship-creating power is God's love. In order to think truly about God, we must think about God's love and holiness together. We must see that God's holiness is not lessened by his coming into the world and creating fellowship with creatures. And we must see that God's love is the expression of his holy transcendence and infinity. In love God identifies with the world. In holiness God remains transcendently different from the world. Christian theology is the work of holding together this identity and difference.

CREATION AND THE TRIUNE GOD

The Early Church stated the doctrine of creation in the creed of Constantinople (381). This creed's doctrine of creation was fashioned in response to a religious movement, Gnosticism, some types of which held that the Creator of the world was not the Father of Jesus Christ but instead a different god. Although its statement is brief, it declares the main points of the Church's convictions: "We believe in one God the Father all-powerful, maker of heaven and of earth, and of all things both seen and unseen. And in one Lord Jesus Christ . . . through whom all things came to be. . . . And in the Spirit, the holy, the lordly and life-giving one." This creed affirms (1) that there is one God; (2) that this God is all-powerful and therefore has no rivals; (3) that God has made everything, so that every being (except for God) is a part of the created world; (4) that Jesus Christ is the Word through whom the Father created the universe; (5) and that the Holy Spirit is the source of creatures' life. We will consider the trinitarian dimension of this doctrine in subsequent chapters.

▶ A POSTSCRIPT: THE TRIUNE CREATOR

In this chapter we have asked about the Creator's identity. We have seen that the Bible sets forth this identity in terms of creative power. Yet there is more to be said about the Creator who comes into the world to create fellowship, for Creator is the triune God—the Father, the Son and the Holy Spirit. The triune being of the Creator will be discussed in detail in later chapters. But it is profitable to remind ourselves of this truth at the beginning.

The Bible testifies to the trinitarian Creator in its affirmation that the Father God creates the world through the Son (Heb. 1:3) and when it sees the basis of creatures' life in the divine Spirit (Ps. 104:30). To speak of the Creator, then, is to speak of the Father, from whom all things proceed, and the Son, through whom all things come to be, and the Spirit, in whom all things subsist. To speak of creation is to speak not only of the beginning but also of the revelation of the Father through the Son and in the Spirit. It is, finally, to speak of the world's redemption accomplished by the triune Creator.

▶ THE ETHICAL DIMENSION OF FAITH

Faith in the Creator is more than a cognitive belief that the universe was caused by a transcendent power. It is also a commitment to conduct our lives in a way that imitates the Creator's faithfulness, wisdom, and righteousness.

The Christian doctrine of the Creator is not a scientific or even quasi-scientific theory about the origin of the universe. It is instead a statement of our faith in the Creator. Accordingly, the appropriate response to this doctrine is not merely belief, as though, having believed the truth of this doctrine, we were through with it. On the contrary, our response must involve the totality of our being.

In particular, it is not enough that we acknowledge the Creator's faithfulness, wisdom, righteousness, and justice. The Christian faith demands that we not only believe but also reflect God's nature. This means that we should respond to God's faithfulness with our active faithfulness, that we should receive and embody God's wisdom as best we can, and that we should practice righteousness and pursue justice as does God. By practicing faithfulness, wisdom, and righteousness, even in our finite and fallible way, we truly believe in the Creator. We also thereby cooperate with God's eschatological goal of fellowship with humankind. This is because fellowship with God is a matter of living faithfully in the world that God is creating and of conforming our lives to God's life.

SUMMARY STATEMENTS

1. In the context of exile in Babylon, biblical writers affirmed the power and supremacy of the God who was about to liberate Israel from exile and re-create it. They proclaimed that the God who was about to redeem Israel was the God who had created the world. In this proclamation, they portrayed redemption as a new act of God's creation.

2. The Bible's teaching about creation embraces the destiny of the entire created world, so that God's creative power and presence extend from the beginning of the world to its end. This means that God's creation has a goal, which is fellowship between Creator and the created world.

3. The act of creation not only is the world's beginning but also is God's act of sustaining the world and its rhythms. God's faithfulness to the created world assumes concrete form as God's blessing. Because of this blessing the world is characterized by natural and predictable processes.

4. The creative presence of God, which is God's faithful blessing, is also God's wisdom.

5. God's wisdom passes over into the created world in the form of an ethical order that establishes the conditions for human well-being. As the source of this ethical order, the Creator God is the righteous God.

6. To say that God is the Creator is to say as well that God is the powerful Lord of all things, who is not limited by worldly realities such as time, space, and power. God is not a part of the created world but instead is the creative presence that sustains that world.

7. Faith in the Creator is more than a cognitive belief that the universe was caused by a transcendent power. It is also a commitment to conduct our lives in a way that imitates the Creator's faithfulness, wisdom, and righteousness.

QUESTIONS FOR REFLECTION

1. In what ways do biblical books such as Proverbs, the Psalms, and Isaiah supplement the teaching about creation that we find in Genesis 1?

2. How is our thinking about creation and the Creator affected by considering them from the perspective of eschatology?

3. What, if anything, do scientific theories about the universe have to contribute to our understanding of the Creator?

TWO

THE WORLD THAT GOD CREATES

OBJECTIVES

Your study of this chapter should help you to:

1. Become acquainted with the main features of the doctrine of creation.

2. Appreciate the Bible's use of metaphor in describing creation.

3. Reflect on God's relation to the created world.

4. Understand the meaning of theological terms used in connection with the doctrine of creation.

5. Grasp the distinction between the doctrines of faith and the understanding of faith.

6. Understand the connection between the doctrine of creation and the practice of the Christian life.

KEY WORDS TO UNDERSTAND

Conservation	Faith seeking understanding
Contingency	Natural evil
Cosmology	Natural theology
Dominion	

QUESTIONS TO CONSIDER AS YOU READ

1. What does the Bible say about the world that God creates?

2. What does scientific inquiry have to contribute to our understanding of the doctrine of creation?

3. How does the belief that God creates the world affect the way we practice the Christian life?

Praise ye the Lord! 'tis good to raise
Our hearts and voices in his praise;
His nature and his works invite
To make this duty our delight.

He formed the stars, those heavenly flames;
He counts their numbers, calls their names;
His wisdom's vast, and knows no bound,
A deep where all our thoughts are drowned!

Sing to the Lord; exalt him high,
Who spreads his clouds around the sky;
There he prepares the fruitful rain,
Nor lets the drops descend in vain.

He makes the grass the hills adorn,
And clothes the smiling fields with corn;
The beasts with food his hands supply,
And the young ravens when they cry.

What is the creature's skill or force,
The sprightly man, or warlike horse,
The piercing wit, the active limb?
All are too mean delights for him.

But saints are lovely in his sight,
He views his children with delight!
He sees their hope, he knows their fear,
And looks, and loves his image there.

This hymn, adapted from a work by Isaac Watts and first published by John and Charles Wesley in 1737, calls on us to praise God, the Creator. We are to praise God in response to God's creative power manifested in the created world ("He makes the grass the hills adorn, And clothes the smiling fields with corn") and also because praise is to be both our duty and delight. Accordingly, this hymn is a fine example of Christian reflection on the Creator and on the world that God creates, for it helps see how our faith is related to the practice of praise.

▶ THE WORLD'S DEPENDENCE ON GOD

One of the principal aspects of the doctrine of creation is that the existence of the world and everything in it is utterly dependent upon God's creative power.

One theme that emerges from the Old Testament's *cosmology* (i.e., its view of the universe) is the world's dependence on God. This dependence is total with respect to the world's being, for the world would not exist at all and would not continue to exist if it were not for God. The world's dependence on God is clearly affirmed in the first chapter of Genesis by the majestic refrain "And God said. . . . And it was so." These words assert that the existence of the world rests strictly on God's command.

The theological concept of *creation from nothing* (see chapter 1) expresses several aspects of this radical dependence of the world on God. For one, it signifies that there is no reason for the world's existence except the command of God. The world's existence, in other words, is characterized by radical *contingency.* If it were not for God, there would be no world.

Creation from nothing signifies also that the universe cannot be eternal as God is eternal. As discussed in chapter one, God is the Lord of time. God is free from the constraints of time. That is what eternity means. But the world is, by definition, the domain characterized by time, whether in the form of physical time or time as psychologically experienced by human beings. The world is not, therefore, free from the constraints of time as is God and consequently is not eternal.

Creation from nothing implies, finally, that the world's continued existence is as contingent as its origin. We take it for granted that the universe continues to exist from one moment to another but, philosophically considered, the universe's continued existence is as mysterious as the beginning of its existence. The Bible expresses this point in the story of the flood (Gen. 6—9) when God allows the world to return to a formless, watery, chaotic state and thus (theologically stated) nearly to return to the nothingness from which it emerged. The theological term that designates the creative power of God that sustains the world in its being from moment to moment is *conservation.* But we should not think of conservation as an activity different from God's other creative activities.

To speak of conservation is simply to affirm that God's creative power is ongoing and that God sustains the created world.

The world's radical dependence on God means also that, apart from God, the world and beings in the world are incomplete. The world emerges from nothingness and, apart from the conserving, sustaining power of God, returns to nothingness. The world cannot sustain its own existence and therefore needs God. This conviction points us toward the world's eschatological destiny, which is to be united with God in fellowship. But until the eschatological consummation, the world abides in incompleteness.

It is important to note that neither the doctrine of creation nor the idea of creation from nothing implies anything about the age of the universe or about the way in which God creates. As is well known, scientists today give estimates of the universe's age that range from 10 to 20 billion years. Whether these estimates are correct or not is a matter for the scientific community to decide; however, most Christians have wisely refrained from taking a stand on this issue, recognizing that the truth of the doctrine of creation in no way depends on the results of scientific inquiry, although we can have confidence that there can be no ultimate disagreement between the Christian faith and confirmed scientific discoveries. On the basis of this conviction, and clinging to the fundamental

CREATION FROM NOTHING

Early Christian theologians developed the idea of creation from nothing in their attempt to refute the view, asserted by ancient philosophical schools, that the universe of matter is without beginning and without end. For these schools, the extent of God's creative activity was accordingly limited and the nature of the universe was thought to place definite constraints on what God could do. Early Christian writers, convinced of the infinitude of God's power, were led to accept the idea that the world was not created out of any pre-existing, everlasting reality. They concluded that the world depends wholly and only on God.

convictions of the Christian faith, Christian disciples are free to think about the created world, its age and its origins in whichever ways seem to be most intellectually responsible.

▶ THE STABILITY OF GOD'S CREATED WORLD

To say that God is the world's Creator is to say that God is the creative power that conquers chaos and sustains hope.

Both the biblical picture of chaos (the "formless void" of Gen. 1:2) and the idea of creation from nothing point to the precarious nature of the world—the fact that, apart from the ongoing creative power of God, the world would relapse into a state of chaos or nothingness. As the Bible often attests, humankind's experience of chaos or nothingness produces despair. Despair is the loss of hope that occurs when our world is shattered and all seems to be lost and chaos overtakes us.

Despite despair, the world reflects God's wisdom and faithfulness. Because of God's wisdom and faithfulness, the world is well made and so stable that it continues to exist and to resist the encroachment of chaos. A fine statement of this conviction is Psalm 104:5-6, 8-9: "You set the earth on its foundations, so that it shall never be shaken. You cover it with the deep as with a garment; the waters stood above the mountains. . . . They rose up to the mountains, ran down to the valleys to the place that you appointed for them. You set a boundary that they may not pass, so that they might not again cover the earth." Here the psalmist imaginatively portrayed God as placing the earth onto pillars sunk deep into the primordial waters so securely that it cannot be shaken loose from its place. The psalmist also depicted God as establishing a definite place for the sea and forbidding it to cover the earth as it did at the beginning. However, we miss the message of this passage if we try to understand it in an overly concrete way. We don't have to believe that the world literally rests on foundations sunk into the primordial sea.

But if Psalm 104:5-9 is not to be interpreted literally, how are we to understand it? The critical point to grasp is this: the Bible's affirmation of the world's stability is not a statement about geology but is instead a statement about the creative power of God and the way in which it faithfully establishes a world that sustains life. Amid the difficulties and struggles of life, God faithfully maintains the world that God creates: "When the earth totters . . . it is I who keep its pillars steady" (Ps. 75:3). Here is a frank recognition that the world (i.e., our existence—our family and community and our larger environment) does in fact totter at times. Sometimes our world seems destroyed. Nonetheless, the shaking of life's foundations is overcome by God's creative power, which keeps the pillars of life steady. The world's stability, accordingly, has an eschatological dimension. When our world is shaken or destroyed God comes to us as the power of the new creation and fashions new heavens and a new earth. In this way, humankind's eschatological destiny—fellowship with God—is continually renewed despite the depredations of chaos. God's creative activity, therefore, is the infinite power that conquers chaos and nothingness and sustains the hope that overcomes despair.

▸ THE GOODNESS OF GOD'S CREATED WORLD

The world that God creates is a world characterized by order. In this order, all beings, including human beings, have distinctive places of habitation and modes of activity. The world's order constitutes its goodness.

In chapter one, we noted that God blesses the world. God's blessing follows from God's faithfulness and also from the fact that God conquers chaos in order to establish a world in which we can live. This world is good because it is the object of God's blessing and because everything in the universe has an appropriate place and role. This is the point of Ps. 104, which marvels at the way in which all things in the created world fit together: "You cause the grass to grow for the cattle, and plants for people to use" (v. 14). The goodness of creation, which rests on God's blessing, means that there is an order whereby each thing fits together with others to form a universal system.

It is important to observe that the world's goodness is compatible with the reality of pain and death. The roaring of the young lions means that their prey will die. In this universe, death accompanies organic life. Nonetheless, the presence of death in the world does not negate the goodness of God's creation. The world's goodness lies in its order, not in the way that individuals benefit from that order. Rain is good but it may destroy a house that is built in a low-lying area. Geological faults that create stunning coastlines also produce earthquakes that kill people. The parasite that causes sickness is a part of the good creation but is harmful to its hosts.

NATURAL DISASTERS AND GOD

Christian theologians have traditionally followed the lead of the Old Testament in seeing God as the ultimate cause of all that happens in the universe. However, the Wesleyan tradition and most contemporary theologians have come to see that much happens in the world for which God is not directly responsible. Natural disasters, for instance, are caused by physical systems, not by God.

These and related issues are traditionally discussed under the heading of *natural evil*. This term designates those natural processes that result in pain and destruction. The experience of such evil has often led people to question the existence of God or at least the goodness of God's creation. But, as we have seen and as the Bible makes clear, the goodness of the world means that beings in the world fit together into a system. It does not mean that natural processes always produce the results that we wish. To put it differently, the world has not been created for the exclusive benefit of humankind. We are a part of a universal system of laws and processes. We benefit from them but we can suffer from them as well. Although benefiting from them is a sign of God's general blessing upon the world, suffering from them is not a sign of God's anger.

Even with the reality of death and other forms of natural evil, the world that God makes is good, for it is a system in which the various parts fit harmoniously together. As such, it manifests God's wisdom. Psalm 104, having surveyed God's world and the way in which each thing fits into its place and role, exclaims, "O LORD, how manifold are your works! In wisdom you have made them all" (v. 24). This verse expresses the Bible's sense of wonder that the universe works in regular and life-sustaining ways. For biblical writers, these aspects of the world are grounded in God's wisdom. Of course, the Bible's writers knew very well that much happens in the world—especially the human world—that does not reflect God's wisdom. Error, evil and, pain abound. But this observation does not nullify the fact that the universe's processes operate in dependable ways.

In the New Testament, the conviction that the created world is good and reflects God's wisdom is joined to teaching about Jesus Christ, who, Paul affirms, is God's wisdom (1 Cor. 1:24) and the Creator (Col. 1:16). The scriptures thus remind us that when we speak about creation we have to keep eschatology in mind. By grounding creation in Jesus Christ, these verses help us see that the created world has a destiny that is disclosed to us by the life and death of Jesus Christ.

▶ THE WORLD'S REFLECTION OF GOD'S GLORY

The world as a whole and each thing in the world is an image of God's power and perfection. As such, the existence of each thing expresses God's praise.

Because the universe is grounded in and reflects God's faithfulness and wisdom, it speaks of God and God's greatness—God's glory. We can see this point if we attend to Ps. 148:1-10:

> Praise the LORD! . . . Praise him, sun and moon; praise him, all you shining stars! Praise him, you highest heavens, and you waters above the heavens! Let them praise the name of the LORD, for he commanded and they were created. . . . Praise the LORD from the earth, you sea monsters and all deeps, fire and hail, snow and frost, stormy wind fulfilling his command. Mountains and all hills, fruit trees and all cedars! Wild animals and all cattle, creeping things and flying birds! *(vv. 1, 3-5, 7-10).*

According to this psalm everything in the entire created world offers praise to God. It may seem odd to us that the nonhuman things are called upon to praise the Creator but the psalm's message becomes clear if we meditate on verses 7-8. They speak of sea monsters, the deep, fire, hail, snow, and frost fulfilling God's command. How do they fulfill God's command? They do so simply by playing their role in the created world, thus fitting into the scheme of natural processes that God has created. Fire, hail, snow, and frost, as well as sun, moon, and the other things of the world, obey God's command simply by being what they are and taking part in natural processes. In this way they praise God as they fashion the world into a symphony of praise. As in any symphonic orchestra, some parts (such as the stars) are loud and obvious; others (such a bacteria and animals at the bottom of the ocean) are quiet and unobtrusive. But each sort of being in the universe, by participating in physical and other natural processes, contributes its part to the cosmic symphony of praise. We will return to this subject in chapter three, for human beings have a very important role to play in this symphony (through the gift of speech) but are notoriously reluctant to play their part. Every other being offers praise spontaneously by playing its created role. Humans, however, do not offer praise spontaneously but must decide to do so.

NATURAL THEOLOGY

The conviction that the created world bears witness to God's greatness and glory is the basis of *natural theology.* Natural theology is knowledge about God that is given to us by consideration of the created world. For example, the fact that the physical laws and realities that govern the world's processes seem to be particularly suited to allow for life can lead to the conclusion that an intelligent being created the world. Theologians do not agree on the validity of natural theology. Some believe that it provides an important confirmation of religious faith. Others believe that the evidence available from studying the world is too ambivalent to yield firm conclusions about God. Still others believe that natural theology is an illegitimate attempt to substitute human reason for God's revelation.

The orchestral character of the universe and the fact that each sort of thing in the universe offers praise to God by its existence and its function suggests to us the importance of ecological responsibility. Human beings tend to think of the universe as the stage upon which we offer a solo performance. Thinking thus, we feel free to manipulate the universal stage to suit our needs. It does not bother us if our actions destroy parts of the universe because we feel that it exists for our sake. But things look very different if we see ourselves as having just one part to play in the great cosmic symphony of praise. Even if it is an important part, it is still just one part. Human beings are neither the conductor nor soloists. Consequently, it is important to preserve other sorts of beings so that they can perform their parts. Above all, we should not see the universe as merely the background upon which we perform our part but should instead see ourselves as involved in a cooperative endeavor whereby we take our place with the rest of creation in the symphony of praise.

MYSTICAL THEOLOGY

In the middle ages, Christian theologians devoted considerable effort to articulating the ways in which created realities reflect the nature of God. This endeavor was an important part of that age's mystical theology. According to this approach, things in the created world are like mirrors, each reflecting God's perfection in its own way. Meditation on these created things allows us to ascend by degrees to the knowledge of God.

▶ GOD'S CREATION AND THE RETURN OF CHAOS

Chaos and nothingness continue in the world that God created. Accordingly, the doctrine of creation anticipates the doctrine of God's new creation.

The Bible sometimes pictures the act of creation as God's conquering the power of chaos (e.g., Job 26:12-13; Ps. 74:13-14). Some biblical passages affirm that the chaos has been overcome but not utterly destroyed. As a result, a relapse into chaos is possible at any time—such a relapse being prevented only by the creative power of God (Pss. 46:2-3; 75:3). In other words, the world's coherence and stability depend entirely

on the conserving power of God, for the power of chaos lurks at the periphery of our world. Accordingly, when Jeremiah wished to portray the
devastating results of God's judgment on Israel, he portrayed these results
as the return of chaos: "I looked on the earth, and lo, it was waste and
void; and to the heavens, and they had no light. I looked on the mountains, and lo, they were quaking, and all the hills moved to and fro. . . . I
looked, and lo, the fruitful land was a desert, and all its cities were laid in
ruins before the LORD, before his fierce anger" (4:23-24, 26).

For the biblical writers, disasters of all sorts—national and individual—were experienced as the return of chaos, in which the world or some
part of their world returned to the condition of nothingness that threatens the world apart. So, it was very important for the biblical writers to
depict God as holding back the forces of chaos and destruction not only
at the world's beginning but also in the midst of Israel's history: "Yet God
my King is of old, working salvation in the earth. You divided the sea by
your might; you broke the heads of the dragons in the waters. You
crushed the heads of Leviathan; you gave him as food for the creatures of
the wilderness" (Ps. 74:12-14). However, biblical writers acknowledged
that chaos can break out and damage God's creation. In the midst of history God's creative power is not all-conquering, for the power of chaos
and nothingness still threatens. Human existence in the midst of history,
then, is poised between the creative power of God and the destructive
power of chaos and nothingness. The eschatological new creation signifies the event in which God's creative power will prevail over chaos and
bring it to an end (Isa. 27:1). To believe in God the Creator, therefore, is
to trust in the divine creative power that conquers chaos and nothingness
and sustains hope.

▶ THE RELATION BETWEEN THE CREATOR AND THE CREATED WORLD

*God is not only the one who creates but also the God who is love, who comes
into the created world in the form of creative power, and who inspires our
faithful response.*

So far in this chapter we have discussed the relation between the
Creator and the world in terms of dependence and reflection. The world

depends on God for its existence and the world reflects the glory of God. However, there is more to be said about this relation, for dependence and reflection do not speak of God's presence in the world. This presence is the result of the fact that God is love. Love is a matter of entering into the life of someone or something else and identifying with that life. The God who is love comes into the world and identifies with the world.

We can help ourselves think about the God who is love if we represent God's life as a life of movement whereby God comes into the world and dwells as the creative power. The Bible points toward this conviction in its teaching that God sustains life by sending the Spirit into creatures. In these and other ways the Bible testifies to the conviction that God is not simply a being whose command we must obey and whose praise we must offer but is instead the Creator who comes into the world to create fellowship. All this is what we mean when we say that God is love.

But it is not enough to confess that God's life is a movement of creative power into the world, for this divine movement not only comes into the world but also returns to the divine being. It returns in the form of our faithful response to God in praise, confession, and obedience. But how can our response to God be a return of the divine life to God? We find the answer by remembering that our faithful response is inspired by God's creative power. Take praise for instance. Praise is not simply something that we do; it is at the same time something that God does through us. The cry, "Abba, Father," is really an utterance of the Spirit within us (Rom. 8:15-16). This passage and many others tell us that human response to God is brought about by the Holy Spirit. It is the Spirit's working within us. Prayer and confession and obedience consequently take place when we allow ourselves to be incorporated into the movement that is God's life. In this movement the divine life comes into the world as creative power, is embodied in our lives, and finally returns when we, in the power of the Spirit, give to God praise and obedience.

This understanding of God's life as a movement of coming into the world and returning in praise and obedience injects a dynamic note into the idea of the world's order that we discussed previously. If God were merely a being whose perfection the world reflected, then the world's order would be a static order. Features of life such as community, work, and sexuality would be as unchanging as the laws of physics. Our participation in these features would be marked by endless repetition. But because God is the creative power that comes into the world, these features of life are capable of change as we respond to God's call upon us.

In future chapters we will revisit this theme of God's life as a movement to the world and a return from the world. We will see it as the basis of the Church's doctrine of the Trinity.

▶ POSTSCRIPT: THE DOCTRINE OF CREATION AND SCIENTIFIC THEORIES

It is important to observe the difference between the Church's doctrine of creation and the various ways in which Christians have historically understood that doctrine. The doctrine of creation does not depend on or imply any particular scientific or philosophical theory; however, the attempt to understand the doctrine inevitably makes use of scientific and philosophical theories.

A contentious issue in some parts of the Christian world today is the relation between the Christian doctrine of creation and scientific theories that pertain to questions of the universe's origin and processes. In fact, there has been an extended history of contention between some interpretations of Christian doctrine and some spokespersons for the scientific community. Yet in every generation many Christians have found a harmony between doctrine and science, with the conviction that there is no ultimate disagreement between enduring, tested scientific theories and the basic convictions of the Christian faith. Indeed, many Christian disciples have seen scientific knowledge as a gift from God. It is one of the ways in which we fulfill the original command to exercise dominion in the world.

What are the basic convictions of the Christian doctrine of creation? Those convictions are enshrined in documents such as creeds and statements of faith. Here, for example, are excerpts from the Creed of Constantinople (A.D. 381), an important and representative creed:

> We believe in one God, the Father all-governing . . . Creator . . . of heaven and earth, of all things visible and invisible; And in one Lord Jesus Christ . . . through Whom all things came into being. . . . And in the Holy Spirit, the Lord and life-giver.[1]

We notice, first, the brevity of these affirmations. The creed is notable for compressing the essential points of Christian belief about creation into a few words. Later creeds, including those in our tradition, are similarly brief. Second, it is important to note what Christian creeds do not say about creation. Because they are concerned only with setting forth the essential aspects of faith, there is much that they pass over. Notable in this respect is that they take no stand on the relation between the doctrine of creation and scientific theories. This is not to say that this relation is unimportant for the Church. On the contrary, it is important that those who teach within the Church and who guide the Church's understanding should responsibly engage all aspects of human learning, proceeding with the conviction that the Church welcomes all truth that human beings discover by the various modes of inquiry. Nonetheless, scientific discoveries do not supply the content of the Christian faith, which is independent of all systems of human thought, whether ancient or modern. The Church has seen scientific ideas about the universe come and go and long ago decided that what is essential for faith and practice can be stated without using specific scientific and philosophical theories. Scientific theories are not a part of the Christian faith, and accordingly, official statements of faith make no mention of these theories and do not depend upon any particular theory.

However, there is more to be said about the relation between doctrine and scientific knowledge. This is because, besides the Church's role in stating its basic convictions, there is another important task within the Church. This task has traditionally been carried out under the slogan *faith seeking understanding.* This slogan designates the attempt to understand the meaning and implications of Christian doctrines such as the doctrine of creation. This attempt to understand is a vital undertaking for the Church. For example, with the rise of social sciences, the Church has been able to recover more clearly the reality and nature of the corporate dimension of sin. Instead of thinking of sin merely as individual acts of wickedness, the Church is now able to see the ways in which sin infects social structures of all sorts. Similarly, in today's situation we are in a position to appreciate the fact that salvation is not simply the salvation of individuals but also must include the redemption of human institutions and structures.

There is one very important characteristic of the understanding of faith that requires comment. It is that the attempt to understand always makes use of the ideas and assumptions that are available in the intellectual culture in which one lives. In other words, Christians in the fourth century used ideas that were common in the fourth century and Christians in the twentieth century used ideas that were common in their century. As a result, the act of understanding is always relative to a particular time and culture. None of us sees reality from God's perspective; we necessarily see it from our own, culturally limited perspective. The history of the attempt to understand the doctrine of creation provides an excellent illustration of these points.

An examination of the Bible's teaching about creation shows that the biblical writers used concepts that were common in the ancient world. For example, biblical writers utilize the language of chaos and God's control over chaos in Gen. 1:2. Genesis also describes God as creating by separating things ("Let there be a dome in the midst of the waters, and let it separate the waters from the waters" [v. 6]). It was natural for the biblical writers to make use of these ideas of chaos and separation because these were among the principal ideas about creation available in the cultural environment of the biblical writers.

When we look at thinking about creation in the Christian middle ages, we notice that their way of looking at creation and the created world differs from the Bible's in some respects. Christian intellectuals in the middle ages no longer thought in terms of separation and the conquest of chaos. Instead they thought with concepts derived from Platonic, Aristotelian, and Stoic philosophical schools. That meant, for example, that they conceived of the universe as a set of concentric spheres surrounding the earth, with sun, moon, planets, and stars being carried by these spheres. Because of this conception, they wondered whether there were other universes beyond the limits of the outermost sphere. Additionally, they were puzzled by comets, which did not seem to move on any sphere. Christian thinkers in these centuries used these concepts because they had gained wide acceptance in the culture in which the Church developed and because there were no serious alternatives. Virtually all serious thinkers in this culture thought along the lines indicated by the ancient philosophical schools.

In the last several hundred years, the idea of concentric spheres has been discredited and replaced by scientific conceptions of space, time, matter, force, and energy. As a result, some Christians, who seek to understand the doctrine of creation today, think, for example, in terms of big bang cosmology and the general and special theories of relativity. They do so because in our culture the natural sciences provide the dominant concepts for understanding the universe. To these Christians, there are no serious alternatives. They do not think it is possible today to return to ideas such as God creating by overcoming chaos or the universe as a set of concentric circles. Though this theory has support among some Christians, it may be that perhaps someday there will be an alternative to this theory. Though it is important that we think with the tools that are available to us, it is also important for us to be cautious about accepting every scientific theory that is proposed. In the meantime the most responsible thing is to make use of well-established scientific theories, even if we do so tentatively, knowing that some will eventually be proved inadequate and will be replaced by better theories. But in our intellectual context today, it is important for us to think along with contemporary science as we try to understand the created world, even though we do not accept modern science as the ultimate truth about God's creation.

Several points deserve attention. First, the various ways in which Christians have understood this or that part of the Christian faith are not identical with the doctrines that the Church has officially adopted. That is, Christian doctrine consists of those teachings that are essential for Christian belief and practice. These teachings are authoritative for Christians; however, the various ways of understanding the doctrines of the Christian faith are not as such authoritative for belief and practice. The task of understanding is important as the Church seeks to live faithfully in the world but its results do not have the sort of authority for faith and practice that doctrines have.

Second, whereas the doctrines of the faith are remarkably unchanging, the understanding of faith is quite dynamic, for it depends on modes of thinking that change over time. Christians in the middle ages understood the world differently from the way ancient writers understood it. We today understand it differently from the way in which Christians in the middle ages understood it. People in the future may understand it in still other ways. So, whereas the *doctrine* of creation expresses the Church's settled conviction, the *understanding* of that doctrine represents the attempt by Christians in each era to grasp the meaning and implications of that doctrine. As such, the understanding of faith is relative to the intellectual culture in which Christians find themselves.

Third, the doctrines of faith, especially as formally stated in creeds, are normative and authoritative for Christians. They set the parameters for authentic Christian belief and practice. They are, the Church believes, the essential truth that God has for the Church, truth that we cannot ignore without jeopardizing Christian belief and practice. But the various understandings of faith that Christian thinkers have offered over the last 20 centuries are not normative and authoritative. The attempt to understand is an important task for the Church but its results should not be considered authoritative. To make them authoritative would mean treating ideas that are relative to a particular time and culture as essential, normative, and authoritative. To do so would be to treat the ideas of one particular human culture as truths possessing permanent validity. This is a temptation that the Church must constantly resist. It can resist this temptation only by reminding itself that Christian thinkers inevitably borrow ideas from the intellectual cultures that surround them and that, as useful as these ideas may be, none of them has permanent validity.

Consequently, while the Church insists on the normative validity of the doctrines of faith, especially in their creedal expression, we should tolerate a diversity of opinions arising from the attempts at understanding these doctrines as long as they do not contradict basic, creedal convictions.

▶ THE ETHICAL DIMENSION OF FAITH

The doctrine of creation contains an ethical dimension, for the doctrine is about practice as well as belief. Our ethical relation to the world is governed by the concept of dominion, by the fact that the beings of the world have an eschatological destiny, and by the importance of joy and praise in the life of human beings.

It is important to keep in mind that Christian faith is not identical to belief. Belief is a name for the cognitive aspect of Christian faith but besides this cognitive aspect there is an ethical aspect as well. The cognitive dimension of faith denotes the fact that faith is about something and that it can be expressed in the form of statements. The ethical dimension consists in the fact that Christian faith is a matter not only of believing but also of doing.

What do we learn about the ethical dimension of faith from considering the doctrine of creation, especially in its relation to the eschatological end of creation?

We learn that we have an ethical relation to the created world. It may seem odd to say this, for we often think of ethical obligation in terms of rights and it is difficult to sustain the idea that the nonhuman world has rights. However, from a theological perspective we do have an ethical relation to the world, one that is grounded in the fact that we, too, are created. We can see this from an examination of Gen. 1:26: "Let [humankind] have *dominion* over the fish of the sea, and over the birds of the air, and over the cattle, and over all the wild animals of the earth, and over every creeping thing that creeps upon the earth" (emphasis added). The fact that this mandate follows upon the declaration that human beings are created in the image of God means that we exercise dominion precisely because we are created in that image. Our dominion is therefore a delegated responsibility. God is the Lord of all things; however, God has created an image—human beings—to rule on God's behalf: "The heavens are the Lord's heavens, but the earth he has given to human beings" (Ps. 115:16).

However, to avoid getting a distorted understanding of dominion we must see how Genesis joins to dominion the idea of caring for the world: "The Lord God took the man and put him in the garden to till it and keep it" (2:15). *Tilling* and *keeping* help us see that dominion is not simply ruling but is rather exercising God's caring rule. We are reminded that God's rule over the world is not dominating but instead is one of love and provision: "The eyes of all look to you, and you give them their food in due season. You open your hand, satisfying the desire of every living thing" (Ps. 145:15-16). Our dominion, as a delegated responsibility, should likewise be characterized by loving care.

We get more insight into our ethical relation to the world when we consider the world eschatologically. The Bible adamantly proclaims that the world is a part of God's eschatological future. This means that even the nonhuman portion of the universe has a destiny. Admittedly, it is difficult for us to conceive of this destiny. But we have to remember that the universe existed prior to the appearance of humans as indicated in the Genesis account of creation (1:1—2:4). This tells us that God has a relation to the created world besides God's relation to human beings. Everything in the created world bears a relation to God. Accordingly, everything in this world has a destiny with God, a destiny of fellowship with God, even if the nature of that destiny lies beyond our powers of conception. Consequently, we should act toward the world with the knowledge that the world is something for God and not only for us. If the world were only for us—if we owned it—then perhaps we could use and misuse the world in whatever way we wished. But because the world is for God and is a part of God's eschatological future, we are not free to use the world selfishly. Consequently, we should, as an act of devotion, train ourselves to see the world and all things in it in relation to God. We should see the world and everything in it as utterly dependent on the creative power of God. We should regard the world as the object of God's creative power and give praise for God's faithfulness in conquering the power of chaos. We should see the world as the reflection of God's greatness and glory and join the universal symphony of praise.

Finally, we should participate in the features of life—community, work, and sexuality—with joy and praise, in the conviction that these are means by which the creative power of God conserves the world. Of course, we participate in these things in distinctively human ways. Unlike other living beings, we must attend carefully to the ethical obligations associated with these features. We should create and sustain communities with justice. We should work not only for our own benefit but for others' benefit as well. We should engage in sexual activity mindful of its destructive as well as its constructive possibilities. But it is not enough to be aware of our ethical obligations. We should also support those moral communities in which the ethical life can be lived. We must, for example, insist on the importance of marriage as the proper setting for sexual behavior. In short, we should participate in these aspects as beings who are responsible to God, the Creator.

SUMMARY STATEMENTS

1. One of the principal aspects of the doctrine of creation is that the existence of the world and everything in it is utterly dependent upon God's creative power.

2. To say that God is the world's Creator is to say that God is the creative power that conquers chaos and sustains hope.

3. The world that God creates is a world characterized by order.

4. The world as a whole and each thing in the world is an image of God's power and perfection.

5. Chaos and nothingness continue in the world that God created. Accordingly, the doctrine of creation anticipates the doctrine of God's new creation.

6. God is not only the one who creates but also the God who is love, who comes into the created world in the form of creative power, and who inspires our faithful response.

7. It is important to observe the difference between the Church's doctrine of creation and the various ways in which Christians have historically understood that doctrine.

8. The doctrine of creation contains an ethical dimension, for the doctrine is about practice as well as belief. Our ethical relation to the world is governed by the concept of *dominion*, by the fact that the beings of the world have an eschatological destiny, and by the importance of joy and praise in the life of human beings.

QUESTIONS FOR REFLECTION

1. When the Bible teaches about the Creator and the created world, it often uses metaphorical language. What does this suggest about our knowledge of God?

2. The doctrine of creation is independent of scientific and philosophical theories. What does this fact imply about the nature of Christian belief?

3. What does the doctrine of creation imply about our ecological responsibility?

THREE

HUMAN BEINGS MADE BY GOD

OBJECTIVES

Your study of this chapter should help you to:

1. Become acquainted with the Bible's teaching about human beings.

2. Understand the connection between humankind's response to God and God's love and holiness.

3. Become acquainted with important concepts such as the image of God and resurrection.

4. See the importance of thinking about human existence from the perspective of God's eschatological purposes.

5. Understand the connection between the Bible's teaching about human existence and the practice of the Christian life.

KEY WORDS TO UNDERSTAND

Freedom	Resurrection
Image of God	Soul-body dualism

QUESTIONS TO CONSIDER AS YOU READ

1. What are the essential affirmations of the Christian faith regarding human being? What are some of the ways in which Christians have understood human being?

2. What is the connection between the Christian view of human being and the ethical life?

O all-creating God,

At whose supreme decree

Our body rose, a breathing clod,

Our souls sprang forth from Thee;

For this Thou hast design'd,

And form'd us man for this,

To know, and love Thyself, and find

In Thee our endless bliss.

This hymn, first published by the Wesleys in 1763, directs our attention to the Christian doctrine of human being. It tells us that we are created *by* God and that we are created *for* God; it thus captures the essence of the Christian view of humankind. Like everything else in the world, we are totally dependent on God for existence and all else ("our body rose, a breathing clod, our souls sprang forth from Thee"). And like everything else, we have an eschatological destiny, which consists in unhindered fellowship with the Creator ("To know, and love Thyself, and find in Thee our endless bliss").

The purpose of this chapter is to explore in more detail what the Bible says about our being created *by* God and *for* God.

▶ HUMAN BEINGS: MADE BY GOD

OUR PARTICIPATION IN NATURAL PROCESSES

Human beings are a part of the created world and participate in the physical and biological processes in which other creatures participate. Although we participate in these processes in distinctive ways, our being is firmly rooted in the created world.

"The LORD God formed man from the dust of the ground" (Gen. 2:7). This biblical statement conveys the idea that we are made of the same material stuff of which other creatures are made. We are members of the created universe and are subject to all its limitations. With every other physical entity we participate in the laws that determine atomic and chemical relations. We share biological processes with every other living thing. And like other animals, our social life depends on our physiology.

THE DOCTRINE OF CREATION AND SCIENTIFIC THEORIES OF HUMAN ORIGIN

Humankind's participation in physical and biological processes implies the legitimacy of scientific inquiry into human origins, just as the fact that we are social beings implies the legitimacy of social scientific analyses of human existence. This affirmation does not mean that any and every scientific theory of human origins is true. The Church's doctrine of creation does not depend on or imply any particular scientific theory and is compatible with a variety of accounts of origins. Accordingly, the Christian has no objection in principle to scientific attempts to investigate origins, whether of the universe or of human beings. Christians do have a legitimate complaint against the attempt to join scientific inquiry to an atheistic philosophy and with the claim that scientific knowledge requires such a philosophy. Such attempts must be denounced as an improper use of scientific inquiry. In spite of such misuse, Christians are obliged to acknowledge the confirmed results of the sciences.

Although human abilities such as speech and thinking far exceed those of other creatures, we do not transcend the created world. Even our greatest accomplishments remain within the bounds of the created world. Indeed, our abilities and accomplishments are made possible by the things that make us creatures. Our thinking, for example, depends on the way in which the human brain and human community have developed. Without a brain like ours (or some comparable organ) and without some kind of social structure, thinking and reasoned discourse would be impossible. Even the capacity to know and love God depends on brain function and human community. This is because knowing God, like knowing anything, involves the use of conceptions, language, and the formation of beliefs. These activities are functions of our brains. Further, we come to know and love God through the teaching and examples that are given to us in the community of faith, the Church, which shares in the features of all human communities.

Of course, knowing and loving God are not simply the result of chemistry and biology; there is more to human existence than material substance. But it is also important to acknowledge that we relate to God as creatures and by means of capacities that, in some respects, we share with other creatures. To acknowledge this is to acknowledge our essential creatureliness.

THE CONCEPT OF THE SOUL

We are most faithful to the Christian tradition when we think of human beings as embodied creatures existing within social communities. This view contrasts with the popular notion of humans as immaterial, immortal souls.

Because language and thinking arise from the development of an organization of our brains and social communities, it is difficult to accept the widespread idea that human beings are immaterial souls that dwell within bodies. The idea of the soul (which owes far more to Plato's and Rene Descartes's philosophies than to the biblical tradition) is the idea of an immaterial substance, which is the essence of the human person, which dwells temporarily inside a body, and which does not require a body for existence or function. In this view, the soul makes use of the body as an instrument, but it is able to live and think apart from the body. This view is often referred to as *soul-body dualism,* because in it human beings are thought to consist of two substances, the soul and the body.

Although the concept of an immaterial soul is an ancient one that is still held by many people today, it really does not reflect biblical convictions about human nature. The Christian faith affirms instead that human life, like all life, has a material basis and depends on the presence of God's breath or Spirit within us. It is this breath or Spirit, and not an immaterial soul, that is the basis of human life (Gen. 2:7). Further, our eschatological hope is for the resurrection of the body (i.e., the embodied person), not for the immortality of the soul alone.

Besides its lack of biblical support, the concept of the immaterial soul dwelling in the body is untenable on experiential grounds, for it makes little sense in light of phenomena such as Alzheimer's disease and comatose states. People with these afflictions are not souls trapped in malfunctioning bodies. It is more accurate to say that in these cases it is the person himself or herself who is affected. The physical damage caused by Alzheimer's disease to memory and other cognitive functions means that the person, and not only the body, is diminished until finally cognitive functions fall to such levels that the person no longer exists. Likewise, the lack of brain activity in a comatose patient means that the human person either no longer exists or is in such a diminished state that it cannot exist until brain activity resumes. Psychological research provides many other examples of diseases and traumas to the brain that result in a loss of personhood to one degree or another. The appropriate conclusion is that the human person is a complex physical organism in a social environment. When either our physiology or our social environment is adversely affected, we suffer a loss of personhood. In extreme cases the result is death. In light of these considerations, the Bible's concept of the embodied person is superior to the notion of an immaterial soul that inhabits and uses a body.

We can therefore appreciate the Church's historic emphasis on *resurrection.* This is the idea that, in the eschatological end of creation, God will re-create us in the context of the new heavens and the new earth. The popular concept of the soul implies that humans intrinsically possess immortality and that death is only the separation of the soul from the body, allowing the soul to continue its life in an immaterial state. But the Bible has a very different view of human existence. Far from regarding us as immortal, biblical writers never tired of calling attention to the fleeting character of our existence: "For [God] knows how we were made; he remembers that we are dust. As for mortals, their days are like grass; they flourish like a flower of the field; for the wind passes over it, and it is gone" (Ps. 103:14-16). Like grass, our lives have a beginning, a middle, and an end. The middle may be comparatively long or short, but the inevitability of the end looms as a fixed termination not only of our existence but also of the things that give our lives value and meaning. And like the grass, whose time is brought to an end by the hot, drying wind, our lives are brought to an end by forces that lie outside us and over which we have little control. Although, through medical technology, we have a measure of control over various diseases, the unavoidable nature of death is a testimony to the limits of our power. In spite of our efforts, we cannot give ourselves immortality. Even if we could, through technology, indefinitely prolong life, our capacity to die would still make death inevitable.

That is why the Christian faith affirms God's creative power of resurrection as our eschatological destiny. In this affirmation it recognizes the bodily character of human being and grounds our hope in God's creative power. It thus proclaims that our hope and destiny lie in the future of God's new creation, when God will create new heavens and a new earth.

▶ HUMAN BEINGS: MADE FOR GOD

The Christian tradition affirms that even though our brief existence is a small part of the universe, we have been created for God.

Because we are made from dust, the Bible exhibits a frank recognition of the insignificant place of humans in the universe and amazement at the fact that God has any regard for us at all: "O LORD, what are human beings that you regard them, or mortals that you think of them? They are like a breath; their days are like a passing shadow" (Ps. 144:3-4). "When I look at your heavens, the work of your fingers, the moon and the stars that you have established; what are human beings that you are mindful of them; mortals that you care for them?" (Ps. 8:3-4). Two things stand out in these verses: the utter smallness of human beings in comparison to the universe and the fact that, in spite of our smallness, humans are objects of God's love.

The first point contains a helpful corrective to our thinking. We humans have a tendency to regard ourselves as the center of all reality and the summit of all value. We often behave as though we were the reason for the universe's existence and as though we alone mattered. Meditation on this first point reminds us that in comparison with the vast extent of the universe, we are very small and occupy only a brief span of the universe's history.

The second point is important as well, for it tells us that human beings are not only created by God but also created for God and that God is for us. We have an eschatological destiny of fellowship with God. Of course, we should not think that God is for us alone, as though God were not for other creatures. On the contrary, all things have been created for God and God is the God of all creatures.

To be authentically human, then, is to know our smallness and also God's regard for us. It is to acknowledge that our existence is fleeting, that our place in the universe is modest, but also that God knows us and has destined us for fellowship. To be authentically human, in fact, is to be poised between knowledge of our smallness as creatures and our eschatological destiny of fellowship with God.

CREATION IN THE IMAGE OF GOD

The Bible expresses our existence in relation to God with the belief that we are created in the image of God.

One of the ways in which the Bible affirms that we are created for God is the declaration of Gen. 1:26: "Then God said, 'Let us make humankind in our image, according to our likeness.'" Many readers of Gen. 1:26-27 have asked, Which aspect of human nature makes us be in *God's image?* It is natural to assume there is some aspect of the human person that makes us resemble God. But the probable meaning of Genesis is found in the ancient practice of kings placing their images throughout their territories as reminders of their authority. That is why the statement about God creating humankind in the divine image is followed immediately by a word about our "dominion" over the nonhuman world: "Let them have dominion over the fish of the sea, and over the birds of the air, and over the cattle, and over all the wild animals of the earth, and over every creeping thing that creeps upon the earth" (v. 26). Because we have been created in God's image, we are to exercise authority in the world in the name of God, on behalf of God, and in the way in which God exercises authority.

The implication of Gen. 1 is that in order to know truly what we are we must know ourselves in relation to God. We are God's image; our relation, as image, to God is essential to our nature. Because of this relation, we are crowned "with glory and honor" (Ps. 8:5). As God's representatives on earth, exercising God's power, we share in God's glory.

In spite of being crowned with glory and honor, we should remember that we are *only* an image. Our goodness lies in being rightly related to God and not in ourselves. That is why it is important to keep in mind the transitory character of human life. Although we are God's image and serve God by exercising God's authority and although we are crowned with glory and honor, we are still a part of the created world and subject to its limitations. Like other living beings, we experience death and other limitations. To be human, then, is to be a creature that images God, even if sometimes we reflect God poorly. But God has given us the task of being the image by representing God in the world. This task indicates our relation to God and tells us that we are most truly human when we stand before God and, as images, reflect who and what God is.

THE BREATH OF LIFE

The Bible expresses our dependence on God with its teaching about the breath (or Spirit) of God. To receive God's Spirit is to be drawn out of our mundane existence into relation with God.

Besides creation in the image of God, the Bible portrays our relation to and dependence on God in those passages (such as Gen. 2:7) that speak of God's breath or Spirit indwelling us. According to Gen. 2, before God provides the divine breath, humans are nothing more than dust. Although this is a highly metaphorical way of presenting the matter (for God did not literally breathe air into dirt), it dramatically states the fact that we depend upon God in a radical way.

It is not we alone who are dependent on the Spirit of God. All living beings depend on God for their being. In the words of the psalmist, "When you hide your face, [creatures] are dismayed, when you take away their breath, they die and return to their dust. When you send forth your spirit [or, breath], they are created, and you renew the face of the ground" (104:29-30). All creaturely existence is grounded in God's creative power, represented here as Spirit or breath. When God's Spirit goes forth, dust lives. When God's Spirit is absent, death occurs and we relapse into dust.

Of course, this teaching stands alongside the fact, which the biblical writers knew, that creatures come to be by ordinary, natural processes of the sort that the sciences describe. The Bible's teaching is not intended to compete with scientific accounts of creatures and their origin and development. Its purpose is not to give an exhaustive account of the creation of things but is instead to affirm that, within the natural processes that support life, we find the creative activity of God.

God's Spirit is more than a principle of life; it is also the principle by which human beings are drawn out of the limitations of creaturely existence. Without the Spirit of God, dust remains dust and life does not emerge. Similarly, it was by the Spirit that those who built the Tabernacle possessed skill (Exod. 35:30), that Saul fell into a "prophetic frenzy" (1 Sam. 10:6-13), that Ezekiel spoke for God and had visions (Ezek. 2:2), and that Daniel obtained wisdom (Dan. 5:11 and 14).

The Spirit, then, is the creative presence of God that lifts us above our ordinary ways of existence and capacities and gives us extraordinary gifts, such as wisdom and prophecy, in the service of God. The Spirit is the movement of God into the world that draws us into the presence of God. But this capacity to stand in God's presence is grounded in God's grace; in the Bible's picturesque way of speaking, God can take the Spirit away. When this happens the result is death in all of its aspects, for death is the state of being removed from God's presence.

▶ HUMAN RESPONSE TO GOD

Who receives the Spirit's gift? The Bible is clear that in one respect every human being and even animals receive the Spirit (Gen. 1:30; 2:7). Otherwise life itself would be impossible. So, at the most basic level all living creatures share in God's Spirit. But there are other dimensions of receiving the Spirit that are not universal and that depend on our faithful obedience to God. The fullness of the good life is achieved only when we respond faithfully to God's call upon us; such response is our highest good and that which fulfills our created nature.

OUR RESPONSE TO GOD'S LOVE: WISDOM

Human wisdom is a testimony to the wisdom of God's creative power and to the goodness of the created world. But it is also our being incorporated into God's coming into the world.

God's love, which is God's movement into the world that creates fellowship, is disclosed to us as wisdom, righteousness, and faithfulness. God's wisdom is manifest in the creation of a world with a moral order

HUMAN FREEDOM

The importance of humankind's response to God raises the issue of human *freedom.* The creedal statements in our tradition state that our "creation in the image of God included ability to choose between right and wrong" with the result that we are "morally responsible." It is important to note that Christian affirmations of freedom pertain to our capacity to respond to God. They do not, however, pertain to philosophical discussions of free will and determinism or psychological analyses of the motivation and causation of behavior. These are highly significant issues but the Church's focus remains on humankind's ability to respond to God. In the past Christians have vigorously debated the extent to which our response to God is guided by God. Christians in the Reformed (i.e., Calvinist) tradition have affirmed that God actively directs our response in accordance with God's will. Christians in other traditions, including the Wesleyan and the Roman Catholic traditions, have preferred to speak of God's grace enabling us to respond.

that human beings can discern and live by. By living according to this moral order, we attain the good life and fulfill our status as beings created in God's image. Human wisdom is knowing the way in which life is ordered and practicing that way. It is discerning the path that human life should take and living on that path. It is, accordingly, a matter of fitting into the order with which God has created the world. By doing so, humans cooperate with God in keeping the power of chaotic nothingness at bay. By following the way of wisdom, the tendency of human life in society to revert to a state of moral chaos is resisted and the order of God's creation is affirmed.

The path of wisdom is seen in the sorts of virtues that allow one to live well. Wisdom thus embraces prudence, which is the ability to navigate through human affairs, avoiding problems and attaining practical benefits such as peace and contentment. It also embraces diligence and hard work (Prov. 10:4-5); walking with integrity (10:9); love (10:12); cautious speech (10:19); finding pleasure in wise conduct (10:23); honesty (11:1); humility (11:2); kindness (11:17); generosity (11:24-5); loving discipline (12:1); truthfulness (12:17); faithfulness (12:22); being kind to the poor (14:31); and self-control (25:28). Becoming virtuous is a response to God's love because we thereby testify to God's wisdom and affirm the goodness of God and the created world. In becoming wise we reflect God's nature and thus offer praise to the Creator.

More important, wisdom is a response to God's love because through it we are incorporated into the movement of God's life into the world. The God who is love comes into the world, creating fellowship by wisely introducing order. By being wise we not only reflect God's nature but actually share in the divine movement of love. By our wise conduct we conform to God's wise ordering and cooperate with the divine act of creating order. That is why we miss the complete extent of wisdom if we think of it only as a matter of prudently conducting ourselves in the practical affairs of life. It is also a participation in God, who is wisdom itself. The fullness of wisdom therefore requires that we recognize the divine source of wisdom (Prov. 2:5-7). Wisdom is not a human attribute concerned solely with mundane affairs but is a divine reality with a transcendent foundation. As we become wise, we share in this divine reality and thus take part in the movement of God into the world.

OUR RESPONSE TO GOD'S LOVE: RIGHTEOUSNESS AND JUSTICE

For humans, righteousness is a matter of obeying God's commands. Righteousness is made concrete in justice toward our neighbors. Like wisdom, righteousness and justice are our response to God's call upon us. We are enabled to become just and righteous as we are incorporated into God's coming into the world.

When wisdom is understood as God's moral ordering of the world, it blends into the concept of righteousness. Consequently, the wise conduct of human affairs embraces human righteousness: "You will understand righteousness and justice and equity, every good path; for wisdom will come into your heart" (Prov. 2:9-10). Righteousness is the revelation of God's love because it describes God's relation to human beings. It signifies that God is the lawgiver and that human beings are subjects of that law. Obedience to God's law constitutes human righteousness. The proof, for instance, of Noah's righteousness was his simple obedience to God's command to build the ark. Similarly, Abraham was declared to be righteous (Gen. 15:6) because he believed God and because he acted on that belief by forsaking his homeland and journeying to a distant land in response to God's promise.

As obedience, righteousness can be represented in simple terms, as in Ps. 15:

> O LORD, who may abide in your tent? Who may dwell on your holy hill? Those who walk blamelessly, and do what is right, and speak the truth from their heart; who do not slander with their tongue, and do no evil to their friends, . . . who do not lend money at interest, and do not take a bribe against the innocent *(vv. 1-3, 5).*

However, biblical writers also knew that, compared to God's righteousness, human righteousness is negligible: "Do not enter into judgment with your servant, for no one living is righteous before you" (Ps. 143:2). "What are mortals, that they can be clean? Or those born of woman, that they can be righteous? God puts no trust even in his holy ones, and the heavens are not clean in his sight" (Job 15:14-15). These statements, which (as their contexts show) are exaggerations, tell us that no matter how righteous we may be—no matter how faithfully we keep God's commands—we cannot approach God's incomparable righteousness. This is because, whereas God is righteousness itself, we become righteous only by sharing in God's righteousness and being incorporated into God's movement into the world.

Righteous obedience toward God has its counterpart in our just actions toward one another. Deuteronomy conveys the importance of justice: "You must not distort justice; you must not show partiality; and you must not accept bribes. . . . Justice, and only justice, you shall pursue" (16:19-20). Justice is so vital in our response to God that it outweighs sacrifice and other acts of religious devotion: "What to me is the multitude of your sacrifices? says the LORD, I have had enough of burnt offerings of rams and the fat of fed beasts; . . . [Instead] learn to do good; seek justice, rescue the oppressed, defend the orphan, plead for the widow" (Isa. 1:11, 17). As the Bible elsewhere makes clear, sacrifice, fasting, and other acts of devotion are not unimportant; however, without justice these things become hateful to God (see v. 13).

Like wisdom, righteousness and justice are more than human deeds. They are also signs of our being incorporated into God's coming into the world. As the righteous God enters the world, we are called to participate in God's character by practicing righteousness. As we respond positively to this call we are led into obedience to God and into justice toward our neighbors.

OUR RESPONSE TO GOD'S LOVE: HOPE

Hope is our response to God's faithfulness. It is the assurance of God's creative power in the face of affliction and despair. It appears as trust and waiting patiently on God.

God comes into the world as the faithful power that sustains us amid the threat of chaos and nothingness. Our response to that creative power takes the form of hope, which comprises trusting in God and waiting on God.

Hope is based on two contrary experiences. The first is expressed by Ps. 9: "The LORD is a stronghold for the oppressed, a stronghold in times of trouble. And those who know your name put their trust in you, for you, O LORD, have not forsaken those who seek you" (vv. 9-10). Here God appears as the power that sustains us in all the difficulties and traumas of life. The second experience that lies at the basis of hope is found in Ps. 10:1: "Why, O LORD, do you stand far off? Why do you hide yourself in times of trouble?" The Bible testifies to both experiences many times. Biblical writers were convinced that the creative presence of God comes to us as the power that conquers chaos and supports our existence when chaos rises against us. But they acknowledged that we often suffer for lengthy periods of times without deliverance. The Bible has a rich variety of ways of describing the experience of distress: "O God, do not keep silence; do not hold your peace or be still, O God! (Ps. 83:1). "Do not hide your face from me in the day of distress" (102:2). "My God, my God, why have you forsaken me? Why are you so far from helping me, from the words of my groaning? O my God, I cry by day, but you do not answer; and by night, but find no rest" (22:1-2).

In these extended situations of pain, fear, and affliction, the natural temptation is to lose all hope in God and to surrender to despair. Yet, in spite of the overwhelming force of ongoing affliction, the biblical writers could not forget that God is a stronghold in times of trouble. Hope is the experience of affliction together with the belief in God's power: "I wait for the LORD, my soul waits, and in his word I hope; my soul waits for the LORD more than those who watch for the morning, more than those who watch for the morning. O Israel, hope in the LORD! For with the LORD there is steadfast love, and with him is great power to redeem" (130:6-7). Hope is thus structured by the coexistence of two realities in tension: the assurance of God's presence and the experience of God's distance in life's ills. As a result, the life of hope is a tensed life, a life that is pulled between the despair of our pain and our conviction of God's presence.

Hope appears as trust. Trust means that despair does not conquer hope and that in the midst of affliction God's presence abides. Trust signifies that our hope is grounded in a reality that is for us. Hope appears also as waiting on God. Waiting adds to trust the dimension of time. Waiting signals the fact that the presence of God is sometimes taken away, so that we are faced with affliction and nothing but affliction. In these times our horizon seems so filled with pain and trouble that the future seems wholly given over to despair. In this situation, the biblical writers counsel waiting on God: "Be still before the LORD, and wait patiently for him; . . . Wait for the LORD, and keep to his way" (37:7, 34). Waiting is not merely enduring. Waiting is enduring the pain of the present with the steadfast hope that God's creative power will once again come to us and conquer the power of nothingness that threatens.

The connection between hope and God's creative power is expressed in Isa. 40: "The LORD is the everlasting God, the Creator of the ends of the earth. He does not faint or grow weary; his understanding is unsearchable. He gives power to the faint, and strengthens the powerless. . . . Those who wait for the LORD shall renew their strength" (vv. 28-29, 31). This passage tells us that the strength to endure comes from God. But it also tells us something about God, the Creator. If God were only the universe's cause in the way in which physical things are causes, there would be no sense in exercising hope, for a physical cause is indifferent to its effects. But because God is not only the originating cause of the universe but also its covenantal partner, characterized by faithfulness, hope is warranted. To hope in the Creator means to know that the resources for existence are grounded in the Creator, who has come into the world to create fellowship with us. Hope means trusting that the existence of all created things depends, not on an impersonal thing or process, but instead on the God who is faithfully for us.

Of course, neither hope nor God's faithfulness implies uninterrupted blessing. The biblical writers knew very well that disasters come upon us. They also knew that sometimes these disasters are of such magnitude that our existence and our world are crushed. Yet their response to these undeniable facts was to affirm a hope in the Creator who triumphs over the limits of physical existence. Hope, therefore, points us toward humankind's eschatological destiny of fellowship with God.

OUR RESPONSE TO GOD'S HOLINESS: HUMILITY

Humility is the knowledge of the distance that separates us as creatures from God, the holy Creator. Humility implies an awareness of our limitations but also a spirit of thanksgiving.

The God who is love is also the holy God. Holiness signifies God's difference from the created world. Humility, in which we acknowledge our status as creatures, is therefore a response to the greatness and incomparability of God. It is the knowledge that God is great and we are not. It is, in short, a response to God's holiness. But it is also the knowledge that the holy God comes to us in love and is for us. It is, accordingly, an essential requirement of our relation to God. God can be great only for those who are humble. Unless we are humble, we cannot know God as God. We cannot walk with God unless we walk humbly (Mic. 6:8), for God cannot be God for us unless we are humble. With humility we let God be God and we are freed to be creatures who respond to God.

Acknowledging our creaturely status is not always pleasant for us. It means acknowledging that we are limited while God is unlimited: "God knows our thoughts, that they are but an empty breath" (Ps. 94:11). "A mortal, born of woman, few of days and full of trouble, comes up like a flower and withers, flees like a shadow and does not last" (Job 14:1-2).

The experience of limitation is inherently unsettling for it reminds us that we are creatures, created from nothing. It reminds us that our existence is subject to forces over which we have no control and that our lives will come to an end.

And yet our highest good can be attained only by being the creatures that we are and allowing God to be God. This means that we abandon the attempt to be limitless and instead abide in the presence of God as children with their parent: "O LORD, my heart is not lifted up, my eyes are not raised too high; I do not occupy myself with things too great and too marvelous for me. But I have calmed and quieted my soul, like a weaned child with its mother" (Ps. 131:1-2). As a result, humility goes hand in hand with the spirit of thanksgiving. Like praise, thanksgiving is more than a verbal act; it characterizes the entire being of those who dwell in the presence of the holy God. In thankfulness we respond to the Creator by acknowledging our status as creatures. More specifically in thankfulness we acknowledge that we receive our lives from the Creator and that we depend on the processes of the created universe for the sustaining of our lives. As a result, thankfulness is the opposite of being oblivious to God. It is to be aware not only of God but also of our place in the universe, and it is a matter of realizing that we are not self-made but in fact radically dependent on realities outside us and outside our control. To be thankful consists in acknowledging the graced character of all existence. It is to see that all things come from God and find their destiny in God. It is to see that we have received, as a gift of grace, not only the gifts of the Spirit but in fact all things essentially pertaining to human existence.

OUR RESPONSE TO GOD'S HOLINESS: FEAR

The fear of God is grounded in the incomprehensibility of the act of creation and of God's greatness.

God is a source of fear as well as hope. Consider Ps. 33: "Let all the earth fear the LORD; let all the inhabitants of the world stand in awe of him. For he spoke, and it came to be; he commanded, and it stood firm" (vv. 8-9). According to the rules of parallelism in Hebrew poetry, fear is coordinated with awe. The reason for this fear and awe is the great deed of creation—the fact that creation is accomplished by God's Word—and as the result of that deed, the world is standing firm.

We have seen that the proper response to God's holiness is humility. Fear and awe add another dimension to this response, namely that creation is for us something incomprehensible. We understand physical causation, at least well enough to make use of it in everyday knowledge and scientific inquiry. But creation is not physical causation. Even the originating act of creation is not physical causation. Accordingly, the Bible does not attempt to rationally explain creation but instead uses image-laden language: "When [God] established the heavens, I [wisdom] was there, when he drew a circle on the face of the deep, when he made firm the skies above, when he established the fountains of the deep" (Prov. 8:27-28). The Bible's use of images tells us that the act of creation is a divine deed that lies beyond our comprehension. If we could comprehend it, we would dispense with images and instead use the language of precise concepts.

It is the incomprehensibility and sheer unimaginable power of creation that sends the human mind into a state of fear and awe. We recognize in it not just something much bigger than we are but also something that we cannot, in principle, assimilate to our thinking and our power. Physical causation may be for us a puzzle but creation is incomprehensible in a way that no puzzle can be. Even if scientific inquiry sheds light on the physical processes by which the universe has come to be, it will only have solved a puzzle. But creation itself is not a puzzle that can be solved by sustained, diligent thinking. On the contrary, in confronting the act of creation we confront an act that by definition stands outside our thinking, with the result that only poetic images can convey what we mean when we talk about God's creating.

Consequently, the fear and awe that we feel in the face of creation differs significantly from the way these words are ordinarily used. We may say that we fear loud noises or pain but the fear of God is not this sort of fear. In ordinary discourse *fear* signifies a feeling directed toward an object that is dangerous or unpleasant. But to say that we fear God is to say that in God we encounter a reality that is astonishing—a reality that leaves us fearful not because it is dangerous but instead because it cannot be contained by our words or thoughts or actions, a reality that we cannot control or understand.

OUR RESPONSE TO GOD'S HOLINESS: PRAISE

Human beings are called to praise God. Praise is therefore an essential aspect of our eschatological destiny. At the same time, the fear of God brings about human silence in the presence of the holy and incomprehensible God.

As noted in chapter 2, Ps. 148 represents praise as a universal response of creatures to the goodness of God. This is a point to be taken with great seriousness. When Paul wished to give a definitive conclusion to his insisting that Jewish and Gentile Christians live together in harmony, he reminded them that harmony serves a high purpose, namely "so that together you may with one voice glorify the God and Father of our Lord Jesus Christ" (Rom. 15:6). And when the Book of Revelation portrays the heavenly state, in which God's will is unhindered, it presents this state as one of unceasing praise: "Day and night without ceasing they sing, 'Holy, holy, holy, the Lord God the Almighty, who was and is and is to come'" (4:8). The Bible, then, sets forth praise as the normal activity of creatures. However, whereas the rest of the created world praises God spontaneously, simply by virtue of its natural activities, our praise involves decision. Because we are creatures who act on the basis of intention, we do not praise God spontaneously but must instead choose to praise. This means that praise is for us a calling—it is something that God calls us to do. And because praise is something to which we are called, it is our eschatological destiny. The Book of Revelation again makes this clear in its vision of "a great multitude that no one could count, from every nation, from all tribes and peoples and languages, standing before the throne and before the Lamb. . . . They cried out in a loud voice, saying, 'Salvation belongs to our God who is seated on the throne, and to the Lamb!'" (7:9-10). Praise is thus the activity to which God has called us and our eschatological destiny, our highest good, without which human being is incomplete.

The obverse of praise is silence: "The LORD is in his holy temple; Let all the earth keep silence before him!" (Hab. 2:20). Silence is occasioned by the fear of God. This is the message of the final chapters of

Job. Throughout the book, Job has repeatedly asked to be able to meet with God in hopes of asserting his righteousness and protesting the injustices that he has experienced. But in the final chapters, when he finally encounters God, the speech he has been preparing evaporates and, in the face of God's power and inscrutability, Job is reduced to silence, even when God demands a response: "See, I am of small account; what shall I answer you? I lay my hand on my mouth. I have spoken once, and I will not answer; twice, but will proceed no further" (40:4-5). This silence is an extension of the fear of God. The apprehension of God's power and majesty induces in us a sense of our smallness and our unworthiness to stand in God's presence. In this situation, words seem both inappropriate and useless, for in the presence of God our questions are beyond answer and our assertions are out of place. All that we can do is stand before God in a state of awe and fear, like Ezekiel, who, having seen the glory of God, sat stunned for seven days among his comrades (Ezek. 3:15). This explains the inappropriateness of Peter's words on the mountain of transfiguration. Encountering the glorified Jesus, Peter blurted out a desire to build shrines for Jesus, Moses, and Elijah. Mark's commentary is telling: the disciples "did not know what to say, for they were terrified" (Mark 9:6). When (as Luke adds) the voice from heaven commanded them to attend to Jesus, "They kept silent" (Luke 9:36). Peter's words, although intended to be reverential, were in fact out of place.

▶ The Relation Between the Creator and Humankind

Our response is an act of obedience to God's commands but it is also our sharing in God's life that is coming into the world.

God is the holy Lord who infinitely transcends every creature and the whole world. But God is also the one who in love comes into the world as creative power. God is the unity of holiness and love.

Humans are called to respond to God. The fact that we are called to respond means that it is within our power to refuse this response. But the power to respond is not ours alone. On the contrary, our response to God is the work of God within us. We respond to God with wisdom, righteousness, hope, humility, fear, and praise when we allow ourselves to be incorporated into the living God's movement into the world. God comes into the world and returns in the form of our response. Our response in this way completes the circle that is God's life.

As a result, our response to God is our fellowship with God. To have fellowship is to share in something. In wisdom, righteousness, hope, humility, fear, and praise we share in the movement of God's life into the world and its return to God. We share in this movement because our response is the result of God's life coming upon us and drawing us into that life and its movement.

Response to God, therefore, is both a command and a gift. It is a command because we must continually decide to offer this response. It is not automatic or spontaneous. It does not naturally flow from our being. Our social environment does not condition us to give it. Instead it rests on our decision. But it is at the same time a gift, for it is possible only by our being drawn into God's life and allowing that life to live in us. The life of God within us is the anticipation of our eschatological destiny of fellowship with God. The response that we offer to God thus points toward its eschatological fullness in the kingdom of God.

▶ THE ETHICAL DIMENSION OF FAITH

Our response to God must take concrete ethical form in deeds. These deeds are directed toward both God and our neighbor.

Christian teaching about human existence has an ethical dimension. There are two principal aspects of this ethical dimension.

First, our response to God involves action as well as sentiment. Praise, fear, wisdom, righteousness, and the other forms of our response are not passive qualities. On the contrary, in order to be authentic they must be made concrete in specific practices. Praise, for example, is not simply a matter of honoring God in the solitude of our thoughts. Instead, our entire life and every detail of it are to be a praise offered to God. Wisdom is not merely knowing. It is also acting appropriately. The fear of God is not only feeling but also practicing life in the presence of the holy God. Without this concrete and practical aspect, our faithful response to God becomes mere sentiment and overly private.

The second ethical aspect of our response to God is that there is no response to God that is not at the same time an action toward our neighbor. Righteousness toward God, for instance, cannot be obtained without justice toward our neighbors. Having God's wisdom means we act wisely and rightly toward our neighbor. Having hope in God means that we do not put our ultimate trust in finite things. Even fear and silence have an ethical dimension, for their practice means that we acknowledge our essential creatureliness. Doing so implies that we take our place alongside other human beings and other creatures and do not exalt ourselves in pretended transcendence. Humility toward God is matched by meekness toward one another. In short, to respond to God is to live rightly in relation to our fellow human beings.

SUMMARY STATEMENTS

1. Human beings are a part of the created world and participate in the physical and biological processes in distinctive ways.

2. We are most faithful to the Christian tradition when we think of human beings as bodily creatures existing within social communities. This view contrasts with the popular notion of humans as immaterial, immortal souls.

3. The Christian tradition affirms that even though our brief existence is a small part of the universe, we have been created for God.

4. The Bible expresses our existence in relation to God with the belief that we are created in the image of God.

5. The Bible expresses our dependence on God with its teaching about the breath (or Spirit) of God. To receive God's Spirit is to be drawn out of our mundane existence into relation with God.

6. Human wisdom is a testimony to the wisdom of God's creative power and to the goodness of the created world. But it is also our being incorporated into God's coming into the world.

7. Human righteousness is a matter of obeying God's commands. Justice toward our neighbors is the result of this obedience to God.

8. Hope is our response to God's faithfulness. It is the assurance of God's creative power in the fact of affliction and despair. Hope appears in the forms of trust and waiting patiently on God.

9. Humility is the knowledge of the distance that separates us as creatures from God, the holy Creator. Humility implies an awareness of our limitations but also a spirit of thanksgiving.

10. The fear of God is grounded in the incomprehensibility of the act of creation and of God's greatness.

11. Human beings are called to praise God. Praise is therefore an essential aspect of our eschatological destiny. At the same time, the fear of God brings about human silence in the presence of the holy and incomprehensible God.

12. Our response is something that God commands but it is also our sharing in God's life that is coming into the world.

13. Our response to God must take concrete ethical form in deeds. These deeds are directed toward both God and our neighbor.

QUESTIONS FOR REFLECTION

1. What is involved in thinking about human existence in a distinctively Christian way? How is it different from and in what ways is it compatible with other ways of thinking about human existence?

2. What do disciplines such as philosophy and the sciences have to contribute to our understanding of human existence?

3. What are the practical and ethical implications of the Bible's teaching about humankind?

UNIT 2

THE COMING OF GOD INTO THE WORLD

FOUR

THE REVELATION OF GOD TO ISRAEL

OBJECTIVES

Your study of this chapter should help you to understand:

1. The meaning of God's holiness and human holiness.
2. The paradoxical nature of God's revelation.
3. The purpose of God's coming into the world.
4. The concepts of election and covenant.

KEY WORDS TO UNDERSTAND

Consecration	Love
Covenant	Mediation
Election	Paradox
Glory of God	Righteousness
Law	Revelation

QUESTIONS TO CONSIDER AS YOU READ

1. What does it mean to say that Israel is the people of God?
2. How does God's holiness differ from the holiness of human beings and other created things?
3. What does *revelation* mean?

Holy as thee, O Lord, is none!
Thy holiness is all thy own;
A drop of that unbounded sea
Is ours, a drop derived from thee.

And when thy purity we share,
Thy only glory we declare;
And humbled into nothing, own
Holy and pure is God alone.

Sole self-existing God and Lord,
By all thy heavenly hosts adored,
Let all on earth bow down to thee,
And own thy peerless majesty.

Thy power unparalleled confess,
Established on the Rock of peace,
The Rock that never shall remove,
The Rock of pure, almighty love!

This hymn by the Wesleys, published in 1762, affirms that nothing is as holy as God, for God's holiness is God's own, whereas our holiness is derived from God's. As a result, we are humbled and glorify God. Finally, it reminds us that God's holiness stands in a close relation to God's love. The purpose of this chapter is to expound on the themes of this hymn. In this chapter we will focus on the revelation of God's holiness and love to Israel and describe the way in which Israel was to respond to this revelation, which is essential to a proper Christian perspective on these themes.

▶ INTRODUCTION

Chapters 1-3 set forth the Christian faith respecting the Creator, the created world, and human beings. In this chapter and the following chapters we will look at the revelation of God in the concreteness of human history, beginning with God's revelation to Israel to gain a fuller knowledge of the movement of the holy God into the world.

▶ HOLINESS IN THE OLD TESTAMENT

THE HOLINESS OF CREATED THINGS

Created things are holy when they are devoted to God's service.

The Old Testament describes the physical instruments used in worship, including the ark of the covenant, the table of the bread of presence, altars, and various utensils used in the sacrifice of animals (see Num. 4:1-15). These physical instruments are said to be holy. Other physical things are likewise holy: the tithes that Israel was to bring to God (Lev. 27:30) and the seventh day of the week, the Sabbath (Exod. 20:11).

For modern people, holiness tends to designate moral goodness so that regarding things like the Sabbath, tithes, and utensils as holy seems to be a misuse of the word. But we will be overlooking something of great importance if we fail to understand why the Old Testament regards these things as holy. They were holy because they had been reserved for God's exclusive purposes. Take, for example, an orchard. Its fruit has no special qualities that make it holy. But the first tenth of those fruits was reserved for God and therefore was holy. The holiness of the fruit resulted from its standing in a special relation to God, a relation that the remaining 90 percent did not have. The same is true of the Sabbath. As a day it is like every other; it has no intrinsic properties that make it holy. But it is holy, because God selects it for special purposes. The utensils used in worship were like every other utensil except that they had been devoted to exclusive service in the worship of God. By being reserved for this special purpose, they thereby became holy. God, therefore, is the source of whatever holiness created things possess. They become holy when they are reserved for God's service.

To understand the holiness of created things it is helpful to take note of the Old Testament's distinction between things that are holy and things that are common. As already mentioned, things become holy when they are brought into relation to God. The realm of the common is simply everything that has not been brought into this special relation. One day in seven, the Sabbath, is holy; the others are common. One land, Israel, is holy; other lands are common. And so on. Common, therefore, does not have a negative connotation. It does not mean wicked or evil or defiled. It just signifies that something has not been devoted to God's service but is instead available for ordinary use.

THE HOLINESS OF GOD

God is holiness itself. God's holiness is the majestic power that distinguishes God from the created world.

Created things become holy when they stand in relation to God; however, God does not need to become holy. God is holy and the source of all holiness.

God's holiness signifies God's greatness. To speak of God's holiness is to speak of God's infinity—God's difference from the world and every-thing in the world. This aspect of holiness is articulated in those biblical passages that recount the awe-inspiring presence of God. Consider Deut. 5:23-26, which describes Israel's experience of God:

> When you heard the voice out of the darkness, while the mountain was burning with fire, you approached me . . . and you said, "Look, the LORD our God has shown us his glory and great-ness, and we have heard his voice out of the fire. Today we have seen that God may speak to someone and the person may still live. So now why should we die? For this great fire will consume us; if we hear the voice of the LORD our God any longer, we shall die. For who is there of all flesh that has heard the voice of the living God speaking out of fire, as we have, and remained alive?"

This dramatic narrative gives testimony to the conviction that God's greatness is such that human beings can barely exist in its presence. Even when God is indirectly present, as in the darkness and the fire of Mount Sinai, human beings can scarcely abide in the presence of the holy God.

It is important to distinguish the awe caused by experiencing God from the terror caused by God's judgment. Only the wicked feel this ter-ror; however, the sense of awe is felt by everyone who experiences the holy presence of God. Moses, for instance, on learning that he is standing on holy ground in the presence of God, "hid his face, for he was afraid to look at God" (Exod. 3:6).

The sense of awe reflects the fact that God is experienced as a pow-er that is not under our control and whose workings we do not fully understand. There is, in these narratives, a sense of wonder about this power and an anxiety because it is not subject to our wishes. Two classical narratives in this regard are Exod. 19:21-22 and 2 Sam. 6:6. The former relates events surrounding the Israelites' encounter with God at Sinai: "Then the LORD said to Moses, "Go down and warn the people not to break through to the LORD to look; otherwise many of them will perish. Even the priests who approach the LORD must consecrate themselves or the LORD will break out against them.""

Second Samuel 6:6 relates the fate of the unfortunate man who touched the ark of the covenant in an attempt to steady it:

> Uzzah reached out his hand to the ark of God and took hold of it, for the oxen shook it. The anger of the LORD was kindled against Uzzah; and God struck him there because he reached out his hand to the ark; and he died there.

God in these strange stories seems out of character. It is difficult to imagine the God who is love lashing out in hot anger against seemingly minor infractions. But the point of these stories is that God is a power that we do not control. Creatures cannot approach the holy God casually and without preparation. That is why, in Exodus 19, the priests had to consecrate themselves. Without acts of purification, they would not have the degree of holiness necessary to allow them to stand in the presence of God safely. These narratives teach us, accordingly, that God is a majestic, awe-inspiring power.

Because God is holy, Israel was obliged to act in such a way that God's holiness was not compromised. That is the message of Exod. 20:7 ("You shall not make wrongful use of the name of the LORD your God"). Israel was to use God's name in ways that were consistent with God's holiness. Conversely, it was not to use God's name in the ways in which common words and names are used. Lev. 19:12 gives concrete illustration of this prohibition: "You shall not swear falsely by my name, profaning the name of your God." This law shows us that using God's name in order to back up a false statement is wrong because it means that God's name is being used in the same way in which common words are used. Israel, accordingly, was required to think of God as the holy one, who should never, under any circumstances, be treated as something in the common realm.

▶ THE HOLY GOD IN THE WORLD

God's love is God's act of coming into the world to create fellowship with creatures and to call us into responsive faithfulness. God's coming into the world is also the revelation of God. In it God is revealed to us as the one who is always both present and distant. God is therefore the one who, although revealed, is never fully disclosed.

If the Bible affirmed only that the holy, majestic God dwells in heaven and is far removed from the created world, we would not be surprised. Holiness, after all, signals the distance between the transcendent God and creatures. But the Bible affirms also that the holy God comes into the created world and dwells with us and for us.

The word that expresses God's coming into the world is *love,* because love is a matter of sharing in another's being and because it is through the movement of God into the world that we share in God's Trinitarian being. God is love thus means that God comes into the world and allows us to share in the divine life. As we will see in subsequent chapters, the doctrine of the Trinity is the Church's doctrine about God's movement into the world.

The Christian faith, then, is the affirmation that the God who is holy, who is distinct from the world and utterly different from the world, is also the God who is love, who comes into the world and draws creatures into that love. God is God because God can come into the world of creatures and draw creatures into the divine life without ceasing to be holy and transcendent. God is God because the holiness of God does not contradict the loving movement of God into the world.

This means that in order to think rightly about God we must simultaneously affirm God's nearness and God's difference from the world. To speak in this way is to use the language of *paradox,* which is a matter of affirming two things that are normally not thought to go together. In the words of Hosea, God is "the Holy One in your midst" (11:9). God is both holy and love, distant and near. If we affirm only God's nearness and God's love, then we will lose sight of God's greatness and power. We will instead fashion a picture of God that is comfortable for us and will worship it. If on the contrary we affirm only the holiness of God and

God's distance, then we will not know the God who is for us and is with us. The Christian faith requires that we think of God as coming into the world and yet in such a way that the distance between God and the world is preserved. God is utterly distinct and infinitely different even as God is with us.

The movement of God into the world—God's love—is also the *revelation* of God. Revelation means unveiling, uncovering. It is the act by which the presence of something becomes known. God's movement into the world is such an act. In this entrance into the world God comes to be present with us and known by us.

REVELATION AND INSPIRATION

Revelation is sometimes confused with inspiration. The latter refers to the Bible's quality of being the "Spirit-breathed" expression of God's Word. Revelation refers to every way in which God is disclosed to us. Revelation is sometimes regarded as God's act of communicating truth to us. In this view, God miraculously conveys to us important truths that we otherwise would not possess. But this view of revelation falls far short of the Bible's understanding of revelation. In the Bible, revelation is the act whereby God comes to be present with us. God's revelation is not a matter of supplying information that we lack but is instead the act of drawing near to the created world.

In thinking about God's revelation we must once again use the language of paradox to affirm ideas that do not seem to belong together. This is because the Bible presents revelation as the disclosure of the God who remains hidden in the act of revelation. The best way to see this point is to consider some biblical examples.

Take, for instance, Deut. 5:4, which narrates the encounter with God at Sinai: "The LORD spoke with you face to face at the mountain, out of the fire." This passage is suggestive because of the way it sets together the face-to-face encounter and the fact that God spoke from the fire. God was present ("face to face") but in such a way as also to be hidden (in the fire). Israel "heard the sound of words but saw no form: there was only a voice" (4:12) yet Israel witnessed God's "glory and greatness" (5:24). God was revealed (they saw God's "glory and greatness") but the revelation was such that this face-to-face encounter did not involve seeing any form.

Similarly, Ezekiel's vision of God was in one sense quite direct: "The heavens were opened, and I saw visions of God" (1:1). But at the same time this vision was rather indirect, a point we gather from Ezekiel's way of describing the vision:

> Above the dome . . . there was *something like* a throne, in *appearance like* sapphire; and seated above the *likeness* of a throne was something that *seemed like* a human form. Upward from what *appeared like* the loins I saw *something like* gleaming amber, something that *looked like* fire enclosed all around; and downward from what *looked like* the loins I saw something that *looked like* fire, and there was a splendor all around. *Like* the bow in a cloud on a rainy day, such was the *appearance* of the splendor all around. This was the *appearance* of the *likeness* of the glory of the LORD *(1:26-28, emphasis added).*

In Ezekiel's vision God was present but also hidden in the concrete images: something like a throne that was like sapphire, something like a human form that seemed like amber and fire. Ezekiel even denied that he had seen God's glory, indicating instead that he had seen the *likeness* of God's glory. Passages like this tell us that we receive God's revelation through concrete things in the world that simultaneously reveal and conceal God.

These passages point us to the idea of **mediation.** Mediation refers to the way in which God's revelation—God's presence—is given to us by means of some part of the created world. Created things thus mediate to us the presence of God while at the same time veiling God. The idea of mediation helps us see the importance of the prophets. In prophecy, human words reveal God. In them God is present but at the same time concealed; God is present in the words. Mediation, then, is an essential aspect of God's revelation. God comes into the world by means of concrete things in the world, whether human beings such as prophets or natural phenomena such as clouds and thunder.

METAPHORICAL LANGUAGE

Our observations about the paradoxical character of God's revelation remind us that our language about God is not direct and literal but instead metaphorical. Our language is adapted to things in the world and objects of ordinary experience. Things in the world are either revealed or concealed but are not both at once. Likewise, they are either present or distant but not both present and distant at the same time. But with God it is different. Therefore, talk about God requires us to stretch our language and use it outside its customary applications. We must use the language of paradox, metaphor, and other nonliteral modes of discourse.

One of the Bible's symbols for the presence of the holy and distant God, the God who is simultaneously revealed and concealed, is God's *glory*. The glory is often represented as something bright, either fire (Exod. 24:17) or light (1 Tim. 6:16). The theology of God's glory receives classical expression in Exod. 33, in which Moses asks for something extraordinary: "Show me your glory, I pray" (v. 18). But God's response shows that Moses did not know what he was asking for: "I will make all my goodness pass before you, and will proclaim before you the name, 'The LORD' . . . But . . . you cannot see my face; for no one shall see me and live" (vv. 19-20). God then fulfilled Moses' request as far as was possible: "While my glory passes by I will put you in a cleft of the rock, and I will cover you with my hand until I have passed by; then I will take away my hand, and you shall see my back; but my face shall not be seen" (vv. 22-23).

This extraordinary narrative says that the knowledge of God is always indirect. Moses could not see God's face, the fullness of the glory. All that Moses could have is a brief glimpse of God's back as the glory passed by. God was revealed to Moses but at the same time remained concealed and hidden. God was present yet remained distant and transcendent. So, we are not surprised when Ezekiel describes his vision of God with an abundance of images. The glory of God, then, is a concrete symbol of God's presence and God's revelation.

▶ THE END OF GOD'S COMING INTO THE WORLD

God comes into the world to create fellowship and to fulfill the eschatological destiny of creatures. In relation to Israel, this coming into the world appears as God's election of Israel to be the people of God.

The God who is love comes into the world creating fellowship. For human beings, this fellowship embraces our faithful response in the forms of wisdom, righteousness, hope, humility, fear, and praise. To these general comments drawn from the doctrine of creation we can now add a fuller understanding of God's end in coming into the world, one drawn from God's revelation to Israel.

The theological term that designates God's coming to Israel in creative power is **election.** Election signifies God's choosing Israel to be the people of God:

THE DOCTRINE OF ELECTION

The doctrine of election has been one of the most controversial doctrines in Christian history and Christians have for centuries debated its implications in a highly contentious way. One complicating factor is that election is often associated with predestination, another doctrine of considerable complexity. Another factor is that election has usually been understood quite individualistically, as though God elects individuals. But the Bible portrays election primarily as God's choosing and creating Israel, not individual Israelites. Similarly, God has chosen the Church, the Body of Christ and the new Israel, but this does not imply that God selects individuals for eternal salvation. Because the doctrine of election has been associated with predestination and because of individualistic interpretations, the creedal statements in our tradition do not make affirmations about election. Nonetheless, election is an important biblical teaching that students of the Christian faith should know.

> Although heaven and the heaven of heavens belong to the LORD
> your God, the earth and all that is in it, yet the LORD set his heart
> in love on your ancestors alone and chose you, their descendants af-
> ter them, out of all the peoples (Deut. 10:14-15).

Election is more than choosing; it is also creating. Before election, Israel
did not exist as a people. Election brought Israel into existence as "a
priestly kingdom and a holy nation" (Exod. 19:6). The Book of Isaiah repeatedly represents God as Israel's Maker (45:9 and 11) and the one who
formed Israel in the womb (44:2 and 24). Election, therefore, is simply
another instance of the creative power of God, calling into being realities
that do not exist. Election is God's coming into the world, forming a
people and calling them into a relationship of faithful response.

Because election is an act of creation it is not a reward for anything
that Israel had accomplished. Election creates Israel as a people; therefore,
it could not be based on anything that Israel had done. Accordingly, "it is
not because of your righteousness or the uprightness of your heart that
you are going in to occupy [the] land" (Deut. 9:5). Just as the originating
act of creation that brings forth the universe was preceded by nothing
other than God, so the creative and creating act of election is preceded by
nothing other than God's intention to fulfill the world's eschatological
destiny. Consequently, election is grounded solely in God's love and
grace: "It was because the LORD loved you and kept the oath that he
swore to your ancestors, that the LORD has . . . redeemed you from the
house of slavery" (Deut. 7:8). Election, then, is the creative power of God
forming a people so that God's purpose—creating fellowship with the
world—might be fulfilled. It is God's coming to the world in love in order to draw human beings into a relation of responsive obedience.

▶ ELECTION AND ISRAEL'S HOLINESS

*Israel was holy because of election. Election signifies God's creation of Israel as
a holy people. God's act of electing Israel called for Israel to consecrate itself to
God in response. Consecration meant that Israelites were to conduct themselves in an ethically responsible way.*

As we have already seen, created things become holy when they are
devoted to God's exclusive use and when they serve God's purposes. It is

no different with Israel. Israel is a holy people because it has been drawn into the sphere of divine holiness and reserved for God's purposes. The act by which Israel becomes a holy people is election.

Deuteronomy 7:6 is an important witness to the connection between holiness and election: "You are a people holy to the LORD your God; the LORD your God has chosen you out of all the peoples on earth to be his people, his treasured possession." Election thus forms a people that are God's and that have been created expressly to serve God's purposes. This is not to say that other people in the world are in no sense God's or that God has no regard for them. The doctrine of creation shows us that God is for everyone and that every human being, like every created thing, is for God. But, as the partial fulfillment of God's promise to Abraham, Israel stands in a special relation to God's end of creating fellowship with the world. Israel is God's chosen instrument for drawing human beings into a relation of responsive obedience. That is what it means to say that Israel is collectively a holy people.

It is important to note that the holiness due to election is the holiness of a collective people, not the holiness of individual Israelites. Holiness, therefore, is first of all a statement about Israel's collective relation to God and its status as "a priestly kingdom and a holy nation" (Exod. 19:6). Individual Israelites may, in their conduct, have been quite far from a holy life. But Israel as a people was holy because it had been created by God for a special role in God's movement into the world. Although individual Israelites were required to live a holy life, the holiness of Israel as a people depended only on election and its special role in God's purpose.

God's election of Israel called for a response. While election forms the people of Israel and establishes them as holy, Israel was nonetheless required to respond to God's act of election. Israel was called upon to live as a holy people. Without Israel's faithful response to God the purpose of election remains unfulfilled. So, although election is an act of God's creative power, it calls for a response that fulfills the purpose of election.

The word that designates this response is *consecration.* Consecration is that act by which something is made fit to stand in the presence of the holy God. Exodus 19 gives us an example of consecration, describing the preparation that Israel must make before encountering God: "The

LORD said to Moses, 'Go to the people and consecrate them today and tomorrow. Have them wash their clothes and prepare for the third day, because on the third day the LORD will come down upon Mount Sinai in the sight of all the people'" (vv. 10-11). This passage illustrates the nature of consecration. Human beings cannot without preparation stand in the presence of the holy God. An act of consecration is required. Even the priests, who are to minister before God and who dwell in a special state of holiness, had to engage in special consecration: "The priests who approach the LORD must consecrate themselves or the LORD will break out against them" (Exod. 19:22).

It was not only Israel that must be consecrated. The altar, for instance, on which the priests were to offer sacrifices, had to be made holy through an act of consecration (Exod. 29:36-37). Apart from the act of consecration, the altar was nothing special; it was just another physical thing. But, when consecrated, the altar became holy and qualified for God's use. The same was true of other things associated with the Temple:

> The LORD spoke to Moses: . . . [make] a holy anointing oil. With it you shall anoint the tent of meeting and the ark of the covenant, and the table and all its utensils, and the altar of incense, and the altar of burnt offering with all its utensils, and basin with its stand; you shall consecrate them, so that they may be most holy. . . . You shall anoint Aaron and his sons, and consecrate them, in order that they may serve me a priests *(Exod. 30:22, 25-30).*

Consecration, therefore, was a vital aspect of Israel's holiness. Like the utensils of the Temple, Israel had to be in a state of consecration if it was to remain the holy people of God.

The consecration that makes Israel holy results in ***righteousness.*** In contrast to the utensils and furniture used in the Temple, which were consecrated by acts of ritual purification, Israel's consecration took the form of righteous conduct toward God and neighbor. Leviticus 19 is instructive in this regard. It begins with the command "You shall be holy, for I the LORD your God am holy" (v. 2). It then tells us how Israel is to be holy by setting forth many ethical prescriptions, including:

- Revering parents (v. 3)
- Keeping the Sabbath (v. 3)

- Not making images of God (v. 4)
- Leaving some unharvested crops in the field so that the poor can have food (vv. 9-10)
- Refraining from stealing, lying and dealing falsely (v. 11)
- Not swearing falsely by God's name (v. 12)
- Not defrauding one's neighbors (v. 13)
- Paying day laborers in a timely way (v. 13)
- Not reviling the deaf or putting a stumbling block in front of the blind (v. 14)
- Acting with justice (v. 15)
- Refraining from slander (v. 16)
- Avoiding hate (v. 17)
- Forbearing vengeance and not holding grudges (v. 18)
- Loving one's neighbor (v. 18)

By adhering to these and other ethical admonitions Israel would obey God's command to "consecrate yourselves therefore, and be holy. . . . [And to] keep my statutes, and observe them" (20:7-8).

▶ ELECTION AND COVENANT

Election becomes historically concrete in God's covenant with Israel. The covenant contained stipulations that Israel was to obey. Obedience was to be a heartfelt response to God's acts of deliverance.

God's election of Israel means that God enters into a **covenant** with Israel. The covenant adds an element of historical specificity to the idea of election by connecting election to the details of Israel's history and by linking Israel's status as the people of God to its faithfulness to the covenant.

The covenant is grounded in God's faithfulness, which is manifested by God's blessings on the world. The same divine faithfulness is the basis of God's covenant with Israel. In the words of Deuteronomy: "The LORD your God is God, the faithful God who maintains covenant loyalty with those who love him and keep his commandments" (7:9). "The LORD your God is a merciful God, he will neither abandon you nor destroy you; he will not forget the covenant with your ancestors that he swore to them" (4:31). However, the covenant requires a response from

Israel in the form of faithful obedience to God's commands. These commands constitute the *law*, often referred to as the law of Moses. The terms *obedience* and *law* require comment. When we hear the word *law*, we are apt to think of more or less arbitrary stipulations that are imposed on us. We often cannot see the logic behind such laws. For example, suppose the speed limit is 65 miles per hour. There seems to be no good reason why it is 65 and not 60 or 70. In the Bible, however, the law has a different character. The word for law is *torah*, which also means *instruction* in wisdom. When, for instance, Proverbs counsels "Hear, my child, your father's instruction, and do not reject your mother's teaching" (1:8), we see the close connection between law and wisdom. As Ps. 119 expresses it, "Your commandment makes me wiser than my enemies, for it is always with me. I have more understanding than all my teachers, for your decrees are my meditation. I understand more than the aged, for I keep your precepts" (vv. 98-100). The law, then, is not a set of arbitrary rules but is instead the wisdom of God and the path to the good life: "You must follow exactly the path that the Lord your God has commanded you, so that you may live, and that it may go well with you, and that you may live long in the land that you are to possess" (Deut. 5:33).

The concept of obedience likewise requires comment. We are likely to regard obedience to the law as something onerous and unpleasant. No one particularly enjoys driving at 65 miles per hour since driving faster would be more convenient. It is easy to imagine Israelites chafing under the burden of the law and grumbling about having to obey it. But we get a very different picture from the Bible. Consider Ps. 119: "I find my delight in your commandments, because I love them" (v. 47). "Oh, how I love your law! It is my meditation all day long" (v. 97). Verses such as these show us that, when law is understood as instruction in God's wisdom, obedience is no burden but instead a cause of blessing.

Deuteronomy elaborates this point by showing us that the obedience that God wants is a heartfelt response, not a grudging and coerced conformity: "You shall love the LORD your God with all your heart, and with all your soul, and with all your might. Keep these words that I am commanding you today in your heart. Recite them to your children and talk about them when you are at home and when you are away, when you lie down and when you rise" (6:5-7). The biblical writers wanted Israel to internalize the law, so that obedience would be not only a matter of behavioral conformity but also a sincere response of love toward God. As a response of love, obedience to the law can be summarized briefly and simply: "O Israel, what does the LORD your God require of you? Only to fear the LORD your God, to walk in all his ways, to love him, to serve the LORD your God with all your heart and with all your soul" (Deut. 10:12). The words that describe obedience to the law (loving, walking, and holding fast) help us to see that the obedience that God wants is a loving response.

THE LAW, JESUS, AND PAUL

It is easy to become confused about the nature of the law because the Old Testament's positive approach to the law contrasts with Jesus' harsh denunciations of the Pharisees and with Paul's remarks about the law in Romans. In subsequent chapters we will look at the law from the perspective of the New Testament. For now we can note several things. First, the New Testament has a complex relationship to Moses' law, with the result that it cannot be summarized briefly or explained easily. Second, Jesus' criticism of the Pharisees did not mean his rejection of the law. Third, it is important to see that Jesus' debates with the Pharisees were debates between Jews about the proper interpretation of the law. It is historically inaccurate to represent Jesus as rejecting the ideals of the Pharisees, who stood for faithfulness to the covenant. Fourth, Paul's negative remarks about the law have to be balanced by his positive remarks, such as Rom. 7:22 and Phil. 3:6.

The loving response that the Bible values includes exclusive faithfulness to God. This meant, first of all, that Israel must worship no gods besides God. But it signified also that Israel was to seek wisdom in God, to see God alone as the source of blessing and to set their hope only in God.

Israel's response to God was also to be characterized by remembering what God had done. Obedience, accordingly, was a thankful response to God's acts of deliverance and blessing:

> Take care and watch yourselves closely, so as neither to forget the things that your eyes have seen nor to let them slip from your mind all the days of your life; make them known to your children and your children's children *(Deut. 4:9).*

This remembrance consisting in looking back and seeing the hand of God in history and, in response, obeying the law that God had set forth: "Your ancestors went down to Egypt seventy persons; and now the LORD your God has made you as numerous as the stars in heaven. You shall love the LORD your God, therefore, and keep his charge, his decrees, his ordinances, and his commandments always" (Deut. 10:22—11:1). The word *therefore* in this passage is significant. It tells us that Israel was being called to obey not an arbitrary set of rules but instead the God who had created and delivered Israel. It tells us also that the motivation for obedience, consequently, was found in Israel's history with God: "When your children ask you in time to come, 'What is the meaning of the decrees and the statutes and the ordinances that the LORD our God has commanded you?' then you shall say to your children, 'We were Pharaoh's slaves in Egypt, but the LORD brought us out of Egypt with a mighty hand'" (Deut. 6:20-21). Faithfulness to God, therefore, requires not only a future orientation—hope—but also a recollection of the past, for the future that gives us hope is grounded in the history of God's movement into the world.

There is a final aspect of the covenant, its conditionality. The covenant is grounded in God's faithfulness but depends as well on Israel's obedience. In contrast to God's covenant with the created world (Gen. 9:8-17), the covenant with Israel came with conditions: "If you do forget the LORD your God and follow other gods to serve and worship them, I solemnly warn you today that you shall surely perish. Like the nations that the LORD is destroying before you, so shall you perish, because you would not obey the voice of the LORD your God" (Deut. 8:19-20). Deuteronomy as well as the prophets thus held out the prospect of Israel's destruction if it failed to be faithful to God.

▶ THE ETHICAL DIMENSION OF FAITH

It is not enough to be aware of God's covenant with Israel and its demand for a faithful, obedient response. It is even more important to see that the movement of God that created Israel has created the Church as well. Consequently, the Christian life is characterized by the same realities that characterized Israel. In particular, our lives should be marked by a faithful, obedient response to God's command. And, we live between the remembrance of God's coming into the world in the past and the hope of the fulfillment of God's coming into the world in the future. Only as we live faithfully and with remembrance and hope do we truly know the Bible's teaching about Israel and Israel's God.

SUMMARY STATEMENTS

1. Created things are holy when they are devoted to God's service.
2. God is holiness itself. God's holiness is the majestic power that distinguishes God from the created world.
3. God's love is God's act of coming into the world to create fellowship with creatures and to call us into responsive faithfulness. God's coming into the world is also the revelation of God. In it God is revealed to us as the one who is always both present and distant. God is therefore the one who, although revealed, is never fully disclosed.
4. God comes into the world in order to fulfill the eschatological destiny of creatures. In relation to Israel, this coming into the world appears as God's election of Israel to be the people of God.
5. Israel was holy because of election. Election signifies God's creation of Israel as a holy people. God's act of electing Israel called for Israel to consecrate itself to God in response. Consecration meant that Israelites were to conduct themselves in an ethically responsible way.
6. Election becomes historically concrete in God's covenant with Israel. The covenant contained stipulations—laws—that Israel was to obey. Obedience was to be a heartfelt response to God's acts of deliverance.

QUESTIONS FOR REFLECTION

How is our view of God affected if we think of:

1. God's coming into the world as God's love?

2. God as simultaneously present and distant, simultaneously revealed and concealed?

3. God's holiness as God's majestic distance from the created world?

FIVE

SIN

OBJECTIVES

Your study of this chapter should help you to understand:

1. The Christian doctrine of sin.

2. The difference between sin and finitude.

3. The various forms that sin takes.

KEY WORDS TO UNDERSTAND

Christian Freedom	Infirmities
Conscience	Sins of commission
Finitude	Sins of omission
Hubris	Temptation

QUESTIONS TO CONSIDER AS YOU READ

1. How is our understanding of sin affected if we begin with the premise that humankind's highest good is found in faithfully responding to God?

2. What is the significance of the fact that the Bible and the Christian tradition present a variety of ways of portraying sin?

Jesu, in whom the weary find
    Their late, but permanent repose,
Physician of the sin-sick mind,
    Relieve my wants, assuage my woes;
And let my soul on thee be cast,
Till life's fierce tyranny be past.

Loosed from my God, and far removed,
    Long have I wandered to and fro,
O'er earth in endless circles roved,
    Nor found whereon to rest below:
Back to my God at last I fly,
For Oh! the waters still are high!

Selfish pursuits and nature's maze,
    The things of earth, for thee I leave;
Put forth thine hand, thine hand of grace,
    Into the ark of love receive,
Take this poor flutt'ring soul to rest,
And lodge it, Saviour, in thy breast.

Fill with inviolable peace,
    'Stablish and keep my settled heart;
In thee may all my wand'rings cease,
    From thee no more may I depart;
Thy utmost goodness called to prove,
Loved with an everlasting love.

This hymn by the Wesleys speaks of our sinful condition. It describes our being loosed from God and wandering here and there seeking rest. It notes our selfish pursuits. It compares us to the dove in the story of Noah, which flew about looking for a place to rest and having to return to the ark because the flood had not abated. It reminds us that our striving for rest is futile until we return to the God who created us. By using the imagery of the flood, the hymn also reminds us that the power of chaos stands at the periphery of God's creation and that sin is a manifestation of this power.

▶ INTRODUCTION

The holy God comes into the world in love. The God who is distant comes near while remaining distant; the God who is hidden is revealed while remaining hidden. The movement of the holy God into the world calls forth response from us: wise conduct in response to God's wisdom; righteousness and justice in response to God's righteousness; hope and trust in response to God's faithfulness; and humility, fear, and praise in response to God's holiness. Our response—our sharing in God's coming into the world—is our fellowship with God and an anticipation of our eschatological destiny.

But humankind has not responded to God as we ought. We do not share in God's coming into the world and do not accept fellowship with the holy God. This is our sin. Human existence, consequently, is a tensed life, poised uneasily, dramatically and untenably between the call to respond to God's coming into the world and our failure to respond as we should. Consequently, human existence is a world of sin.

▶ A PRELIMINARY MEDITATION ON SIN

Chaos and nothingness appear in the form of sin. Because we are created from nothing, we are incomplete. Our existence is characterized by a striving for completion. We can find such completion only by faithfully responding to God. But instead of dwelling in the world that God creates, we create a world for ourselves, a world of sin.

Sin is the revival of chaos. In creation God overcomes the power of chaos and thus fashions a world for our existence. But chaos is not utterly destroyed; it is only kept at bay, lurking around the edges of God's creation, always ready to burst forth and mar God's creation. Sin is the power of chaos manifesting itself in human being, resisting and distorting the creative power of God's coming into the world. It is the spirit of the antichrist (1 John 4:3) and the mystery of lawlessness (2 Thess. 2:7). It is human being in a distorted, chaotic form.

Why do we not faithfully and obediently respond to God? Why do we inhabit the world of sin? Why are our lives characterized by chaotic power? A variety of legitimate answers to these questions can be given.

We can point to the fact that people willfully and knowingly rebel against God's will. We can note that unjust social relations and dysfunctional institutions permit and encourage wickedness. We can observe the destructive effects that social conditioning has upon us. These and other informative analyses help us understand in empirical terms the various forms that wickedness takes and the ways in which human beings come to be malformed. But we can understand the ultimate origin of sin only by inquiring into our created being.

In asking about the origin of our sin, we are not asking about the historical beginnings of sin. We are not, for example, asking about the connection Paul drew (in Rom. 5:12-21) between our sin and the events narrated in Gen. 3. We are similarly not asking about the fall of Satan and its connection to human sin. Historical explanations have a place in theology but they do not get to the heart of the matter. What is required is a different sort of analysis, one that begins with our created nature and finds in it the possibility of sin.

We, like everything else in the world, are created from nothing; consequently, we depend on God in a radical way. As a result, our existence is a being in relation to God. To be authentically human is to be oriented toward God. Without this orientation we are a distorted version of our true being. Because we are made for God, our existence is complete and sound only as we are oriented toward God.

Our creation from nothing and our orientation toward God means that we are creatures who require and seek completion. We are not complete in ourselves and are radically needy and empty. So, to say that we are created from nothing is to say that human existence, considered apart from our orientation to God, is a void and that we become truly human only as we exist in orientation to God. Unless we are oriented toward God, our existence reverts to the nothingness from which we are created.

Because we are created from nothing we are finite (i.e., limited) beings. But *finitude* is not our sin. Bacteria and galaxies are finite and they are not sinful. Our finitude does not make us sinful. It creates the possibility of sin, for our finite, incomplete nature induces a striving within us that can turn us away from God. And yet finitude does not necessitate sin. We can imagine beings like us who, though finite, gratefully consented to dwell in the world that God's creates and to participate in God's coming into the world. Finitude, therefore, creates the possibility but not the actuality of sin.

Because of our finitude we are afflicted with various *infirmities.* Our knowledge is little. Our judgment is impaired. Our memory fails. Our patience weakens. And yet these failings are not sin; they are simply the inevitable results of our finitude. They may be joined to our sin, as when we become short-tempered because of a difficult physical condition or become harshly judgmental because of a lack of knowledge. But in themselves they are not sin.

WESLEY ON FINITUDE

John Wesley (1703-1791) discussed the limitations of our finite nature in some detail. He observed that Christians are susceptible to a wide range of nonsinful infirmities: ignorance about matters both great and small; frequent mistakes about facts; errors in judgment and in the interpretation of the Bible; and physiological frailties.

It is important as well to distinguish sin from *temptation* although, as with finitude, there is a close relation. Being tempted is not sin. It is not even a sign of sin. It is, on the contrary, a sign of our finitude. Temptation is feeling the possibility and desirability of wrongdoing; however, it signals only that we have been presented with the possibility of wrongdoing and can see advantages in pursuing that wrongdoing. Of course, sometimes a particular temptation follows upon our sin and thus presupposes our sin. A thief who is caught may be tempted to lie in order to get free. This temptation occurs in the context of prior sin and so it is easy to confuse sin and temptation. Nonetheless, temptation in itself is not sin and does not necessarily presuppose sin.

If sin is neither finitude, nor infirmities, nor temptation, what is it? It is the event of turning away from God and the resulting state of being without our orientation to God. It is our failure to faithfully and obediently respond to God, and it is our life in a disordered and disorienting fallen world.

But why is sin even possible? Why are we not created in such a way that we spontaneously and unfailingly respond to God and abide in our orientation to God? The answer is that to be human is to be creatures characterized by emptiness and lack. Because of our inherent emptiness, we necessarily seek fullness and completion. Our good is found in finding our completion in God; however, sin can occur because of the unavoidable possibility that we will seek completion and fullness in realities other than God.

▶ The Forms of Sin

Sin mimics and distorts the world that God creates. We can see this in the ways in which it presents us with a distorted image of the response that God's coming into the world calls for. God's coming into the world in love expresses itself as God's wisdom, righteousness, and faithfulness. It calls for our response in the forms of wise conduct, righteousness and justice, and hope. Sin is the distorted image of these forms: foolishness, unrighteousness and injustice, and trusting creatures instead of God. God's holiness calls for our response in the forms of humility, fear, and praise. Sin therefore appears as *hubris,* over-familiarity with God, and idolatry.

FOOLISHNESS

Sin appears as foolishness, the opposite of wisdom. Foolishness is a mode of existence that takes no account of God.

The Bible sometimes portrays foolishness as acting stupidly, as when it describes the regrettable results of gluttony (Prov. 23:20-21). It also portrays foolishness as a departure from sound ethical prescriptions. But there is still more to sinful foolishness than stupidity and ethical failure. As Ps. 14 observes, foolishness is ultimately grounded in our disengagement from God: "Fools say in their hearts, 'There is no God.' They are corrupt, they do abominable deeds; there is no one who does good" (v. 1). This verse clearly connects ethical malfeasance with foolishness and being heedless of God. The fool is corrupt and fails to do good precisely because the fool says there is no God and is ethically and spiritually disengaged from God.

Foolishness has a corporate dimension. It is a part of the sinful reality that humankind creates in its disorientation from God. Foolishness is thus an ethical world in competition with God's created world. Like the world of God's creation, it has a prescribed way of life based on norms and experiential wisdom. But the ethical world of foolishness is a distorted version of God's wisdom and creation, for its paths lead to death, not to life: "The iniquities of the wicked ensnare them, and they are caught in the toils of their sin. They die for lack of discipline, and because of their great folly they are lost" (Prov. 5:22-23). The fool does not abide in the moral and practical world that God is creating but instead dwells in the world that we have collectively made, a world in which there is no orientation to God and in which God's wisdom is alien.

As we become disengaged from God and create our own world, the foolish wisdom of our world opposes God's wisdom. As the Book of James asserts,

> If you have bitter envy and selfish ambition in your hearts, do not be boastful and false to the truth. Such wisdom does not come down from above, but is earthly, unspiritual, devilish. . . . The wisdom from above is first pure, then peaceable, gentle, willing to yield, full of mercy and good fruits, without a trace of partiality or hypocrisy *(3:14-15, 17)*.

This passage clearly points to the difference between God's wisdom and the wisdom that we devise when we create a world heedless of God. Even more striking in this vein are Paul's remarks in 1 Corinthians. Here Paul forcefully asserted that God's values are inversion of our world's values: "God chose what is foolish in the world to shame the wise; God chose what is weak in the world to shame the strong; God chose what is low and despised in the world, things that are not, to reduce to nothing things that are" (1:27-28). In its dealing with Jesus Christ, the world's foolish wisdom was thoroughly incongruent with God's wisdom. The world, falling back on its own scarce moral resources, could resolve the incongruity only by violence against the one who "became for us wisdom from God" (v. 30).

UNRIGHTEOUSNESS AND INJUSTICE

Unrighteousness is breaking God's law and failing to offer God our heartfelt, obedient, and faithful response. Unrighteousness in relation to God goes hand in hand with injustice toward our neighbor.

Although these terms are close in meaning, *unrighteousness* suggests disobedience to God and *injustice* suggests acting wrongly toward other human beings.

Like foolishness, unrighteousness and injustice occur on several levels. In the most basic and overt sense, unrighteousness is breaking the law of God.

DEFINITION OF SIN

John Wesley is well known for asserting that sin "properly so called" is a "voluntary transgression" of a law of God. This definition reflects the character of sin in the form of unrighteousness. This is an important aspect of sin; however, Wesley did not intend for this definition to be a complete or adequate definition. As we have seen and will see in the remainder of this chapter, the multidimensionality of sin means that no brief definition of sin can be adequate. There is much to sin besides voluntarily transgressing the command of God. It is therefore a mistake to think that the Wesleyan view of sin is principally about voluntary transgressions of God's law.

The Bible is a voluminous compendium of the variety of ways in which human beings can and have broken God's law. However, sin is more than breaking God's law through outward behavior. This is because of the importance of inwardness in obeying God, who is interested not only in observation of the commandments but also in heartfelt obedience.

This was the prophets' message. Hosea indicted Israel for its lack of faithfulness and loyalty to God (4:1-2), its forgetting God's law (4:6), its having forsaken God (4:10), its false heart (10:2), its having forgotten God in the midst of its prosperity (13:6), and its rebellion against God (13:16). Isaiah likewise noted that Israel's heart was far from God (29:13) and Jeremiah frequently drew attention to Israel's stubborn and rebellious heart (for instance, 5:23 and 7:24). Unrighteousness, then, is disobedience to God and also the attitude of the heart from which disobedience arises.

SINS OF COMMISSION AND OMISSION

Sin in the form of unrighteousness encompasses **sins of commission** and **sins of omission.** The former are deeds that transgress God's law. The latter are deeds that are commanded by God and that we fail to perform. For example, if God commands us to be merciful to our neighbor and we fail to act mercifully, we have committed a sin of omission.

The world of sin is a world that we create, a world that in a distorted way mimics God's creation. How does seeing sin as unrighteousness help us understand the character of sin as a distorted world? It does so by reminding us that being in a world is about having loyalties. Many things in life deserve our loyalty. These include family, friends, and worthy institutions. But God demands loyalty of a different sort. The loyalty that we give to family, friends, and institutions is relative. We should be loyal to our family, but that loyalty is not absolute, for our loyalty to a friend could conceivably take precedence over loyalty to a member of our family. God, however, demands absolute loyalty; nothing should take precedence over our loyalty to God. In the world that God creates and in which God calls us to live, loyalty to God is the highest form of loyalty. Deuteronomy expressed this truth in the command that Israel was to make no covenant with the inhabitants of the land that they were to occupy (7:2). A covenant would mean that Israel had accommodated itself to the culture and religion of these people.

Unrighteousness goes hand in hand with injustice toward our neighbor. This was a subject of great concern to the prophets. Amos, for example, denounced Israel's injustice in great detail: "They sell the righteous for silver, and the needy for a pair of sandals—they who trample the head of the poor into the dust of the earth" (2:6-7). "I know how

many are your transgressions, and how great are your sins—you who af-
flict the righteous, who take a bribe and push aside the needy in the gate"
(5:12). As with righteousness, the demand for justice is grounded in Israel's historical memory: "You shall not deprive a resident alien or an orphan of justice; you shall not take a widow's garment in pledge. Remember that you were a slave in Egypt and the LORD your God redeemed you
from there" (Deut. 24:17-18).

There is, then, a close connection between righteousness and justice. For the biblical writers, obedience and loyalty to God require that
we act justly toward our neighbor. So it is not surprising that Jesus proclaimed love of God and neighbor to be the greatest of the commandments (see Matt. 22:37-39).

It is important to recognize that not everything that seems to be a
violation of God's command is so. This is because we may be mistaken
about the scope of God's law. For example, in Romans 14 Paul was dealing with two sorts of Christians, the "weak" (who had many religious
scruples) and the "strong" (who had fewer such scruples):

> Some [i.e., the strong] believe in eating anything, while the weak
> eat only vegetables. Those who eat must not despise those who ab-
> stain, and those who abstain must not pass judgment on those who
> eat. . . . Let all be fully convinced in their own minds. . . . Those
> who eat, eat in honor of the Lord, since they give thanks to God;
> while those who abstain, abstain in honor of the Lord and give
> thanks to God *(vv. 2-3, 5-6)*.

The weak saw eating meat in certain circumstances as a religiously significant matter and regarded the strong as being disobedient. Understandably, the strong had a very different view of God's law.

Paul's view was that God's law does not extend to matters such as
eating and observing days. Keeping in mind the importance of pursuing
"what makes for peace and for mutual upbuilding" (14:19), Paul
nonetheless held that faith, not law, is the critical issue in these matters:
"The faith that you have, have as your own conviction before God. . . .
Those who have doubts are condemned if they eat, because they do not
act from faith; for whatever does not proceed from faith is sin" (vv. 22-
23). Consequently, he felt that we should exercise caution in these mat-

ters (see v. 10), for what we believe to be an aspect of God's law may lie outside the scope of that law.

Our concern for righteousness, therefore, must be balanced by an appreciation of *Christian freedom*—the principle that Christians are free to practice or not practice according to *conscience* in matters that are outside the scope of divine law. Of course, the principle of freedom is not absolute. Some matters are subject to God's command. Moreover, as noted, freedom must be tempered by the well-being of fellow Christians: "If your brother or sister is being injured by what you eat, you are not walking in love. Do not let what you eat cause the ruin of one for whom Christ died" (v. 15). Further, conscience is not an infallible guide, for it can be distorted by our evil desires and can be malformed by improper or inadequate moral education. As a result, the voice of conscience must be confirmed by and subject to correction by the collective wisdom of the community of faith. Nonetheless, it is vital that we recognize the distinction between things that God has commanded and things that are left to the discretion of individuals, subject to the conditions that we have discussed.

MISPLACED TRUST

In the world of sin, we place our hope and trust in created things instead of in God. Such misplaced trust is characterized by destructive emotions such as anxiety and fear. Ironically, the objects of our trust, being created things, cannot save us.

A lack of hope and trust in God results from foolishness. This is because, in a state of foolishness, our lives lack a divine center. By creating a moral and practical world as a substitute for the world that God is creating, we seek well-being and goodness in realities other than God. This is what it means to fail to trust in God. We do not trust God and instead put our trust in worldly realities. They become surrogate gods, for a god is anything that we look to for well-being and goodness and anything that is our source of hope. Failure to trust God, therefore, is really a matter of misplaced trust, for trust and hope are essential aspects of human existence. We necessarily have an object or objects of trust and hope—if not God then something else.

Like foolishness, misplaced trust operates in several dimensions of human life. At its most basic level, it generates undesirable attitudes: "Do not fret over those who prosper in their way, over those who carry out evil devices" (Ps. 37:7). "Why should I fear in times of trouble, when the iniquity of my persecutors surrounds me?" (49:5). "I was envious of the arrogant; I saw the prosperity of the wicked" (73:3). "My soul was embittered" (73:21). Each of these passages describes the temptation to lose hope in God and to place trust in something besides God, generating painful and destructive emotions: anxiety, fear, envy, and bitterness.

At another level, misplaced trust signifies our disengagement from God and our seeking fullness and completion in created realities. Once again, the Psalms provide illustration: "Some take pride in chariots, and some in horses" (20:7). "Happy are those who make the Lord their trust, who do not turn to the proud" (40:4).

The essential problem of misplaced trust is that we set our hope on things that cannot save us. The Psalms belabor the pointlessness of such hope, since the things that we trust are as transitory as we are: "Do not be afraid when some become rich, when the wealth of their houses increases. For when they die they will carry nothing away; their wealth will not go down after them" (49:16-17). "Do not put your trust in princes, in mortals, in whom there is no help. When their breath departs, they return to the earth; on that very day their plans perish" (146:3-4). From the perspective of the biblical writers, misplaced trust makes no sense, because the things that we trust are inherently untrustworthy, not because they are evil but because they are created things and therefore incapable of being the God whom we need.

HUBRIS

Hubris is the opposite of humility. It is substituting ourselves in the place of God as the source of our well-being and highest good. In hubris we think of ourselves as possessing all the resources necessary for finding the completion that we seek.

Hubris is a Greek word. It was used by ancient writers to describe the attitude of human beings who overstepped the natural boundaries of mortals and arrogated to themselves the prerogatives of the gods. Hubris, therefore, is the sinful substitute for the humility that should be our response to God. In contrast to idolatry, hubris is our aspiring to be divine. In hubris we ascribe holiness to ourselves and not to God. It is therefore an instance of hubris when in Genesis Adam and Eve disobey God's command, for in doing so they assume the right to determine which laws should be obeyed and which ignored. In effect, they establish themselves as the lawgivers in place of God.

Hubris is illustrated in several prophetic oracles. Isaiah, for example, denounced the ruler of Babylon thus: "You said in your heart, 'I will ascend to heaven; I will raise my throne above the stars of God; I will sit on the mount of assembly on the heights of Zaphon; I will ascend to the tops of the clouds, I will make myself like the Most High'" (14:12-14). This is clearly a metaphorical mode of discourse. No human being would literally think of raising his or her throne above the stars. Isaiah's point, however, is that the ruler's actions betrayed the spirit of hubris. They showed that he was not humble toward God and thought of himself as answerable to no higher reality or power.

Ezekiel wrote in a similar vein about the king of Tyre:

> Your heart is proud and you have said, "I am a god; I sit in the seat of the gods, in the heart of the seas," yet you are but a mortal, and no god, though you compare your mind with the mind of a god. . . . You were the signet of perfection, full of wisdom and perfect in beauty. . . . [But] your heart was proud because of your beauty; you corrupted your wisdom for the sake of your splendor *(28:2, 12, and 17).*

Passages such as these tell us that in the state of hubris we believe that we possess within ourselves the resources needed to achieve fullness and completeness of being. The quest to overcome the lack that characterizes beings made from nothing consequently begins and ends with us. The solution to our deepest problem lies within us. This is what it means to aspire to divinity and to say, "I will make myself like the Most High."

FAMILIARITY

Familiarity with God is the opposite of fear and awe. In the world of sin we do not fear God because we fashion a picture of God that is convenient for us, a picture of a being who accepts and affirms us just as we are. In this way, we feel comfortable with God and have no sense of divine judgment.

As we saw in chapter 4, the Bible portrays the presence of God as something terrifying. The Bible's ways of representing God's presence, such as the glory of God, evoked for biblical writers the sense of an awe-inspiring and uncontrollable power. The anxiety generated by the presence of God was provoked by the experience of something unconsecrated standing before the holy and majestic God. It was provoked as well by the sense of power associated with the divine presence. Consequently, the biblical writers were adamant that God could not be approached casually and familiarly. The psalmists may have exhibited great boldness in voicing their complaints to God, but they never forgot that human beings cannot stand in the presence of God without preparation and consecration.

Israel, however, did not always honor God's glory or feel an appropriate sense of fear. On the contrary, at times they felt an overwhelming sense that God existed for their benefit. They were fond of proclaiming "This is the temple of the LORD" (Jer. 7:4) while failing to render obedience to God (see vv. 1-10). They said, "We are wise, and the law of the LORD is with us" (8:8) in spite of their ignorance of God. In short, they did not feel the distance between them and God and consequently felt quite familiar with God.

Our situation today is not much different. Popular American television programs, for instance, present God's presence as something common and not at all terrifying. In these programs and elsewhere God is often represented as a loving being who inspires insight into life's problems and provides ways of helping us in the task of becoming mature, well-adjusted people. There is much to like about this picture of God; however, it does not encourage the fear of God and does not do full justice to the Bible's portrait of God. Nonetheless, it is pervasive. Public opinion polls routinely show, for example, that an overwhelming majority of Americans believe in God and engage in religious practices such as prayer. But it is worthwhile to ask about the character of the God in which they believe. Judging from what is portrayed in the media, modern people appear to believe that God is our Creator and is a power available to help us. What is lacking is a sense of the distance between us and the holy God. In other words, people today feel very comfortable with God and relate to God on casually familiar terms.

Familiarity with God rests on the conviction that God accepts and affirms us just as we are. Now there is an important sense in which God does affirm and accept all creatures in their created state, for each thing in the world reflects God's wisdom and glory. However, God's acceptance and affirmation of humankind is contingent on our responding to God with praise, righteousness, and other forms of obedience. The contingency of God's acceptance is a measure of the distance between us and the holy God. But according to popular thinking, because God has created each of us with the physical and emotional features that we possess, God must therefore approve of us as we are. Consequently, confident of God's approval and acceptance, modern people feel little distance from God and, as a result, the concept of the fear of God has little meaning in today's culture.

In familiarity, then, we rob God of divine holiness by fashioning a picture of a God who is convenient for us and who makes few demands upon us. In familiarity we construct a world for ourselves around a God of our own making, a God who accepts us without question or criticism. But this God is not the holy God. A holy God is a demanding God. A holy God requires that we undergo preparation before entering the divine presence. A holy God insists on high standards of ethical conduct and devotional practice. But in a fast-food world that seeks maximum convenience and minimal demands, a familiar God is preferable to a holy God.

IDOLATRY

Idolatry is withholding praise from God and directing our worship to created things. But it is also the attempt to control God's revelation and to secure the presence of God. Accordingly, idolatry is not limited to representing God in physical form, although it always involves our choosing some created thing as the means by which to secure God's presence.

Because we are creatures, we are created for God and our well-being consists in praising God. Praise is a part of our eschatological destiny for it is one of the ways in which we have fellowship with God. But in the world of sin, we withhold our praise and in its place we fashion idols.

The creation of idols has to do with our quest for revelation. Because of God's hiddenness and our desire for God, we fashion idols in order to assure ourselves of God's presence and to bring about revelation. We find an illustration of this in Exod. 32: "When the people saw that Moses delayed to come down from the mountain, the people gathered around Aaron, and said to him, 'Come, make gods for us, who shall go before us'" (v. 1). The Israelites became anxious when Moses, who was to deliver God's revelation to them, did not appear. In their anxiety and their desperation for revelation and God's presence, they took matters into their own hands. Refusing to wait for the genuine revelation of God, they created idols that would guarantee the presence of God among them. This episode gives us an important insight into idolatry. It tells us that idolatry arises out of our need to be in the presence of God and that it occurs when we do not wait for revelation but instead try to find ways of bringing it about. In this way we implicitly think of God as something that we can manipulate and whose presence we can bring about by our own means. This amounts to thinking of God as something finite and subject to our power. As a result, we rob God of holiness and infinity.

Sometimes idolatry takes the form of physical representations of God—idolatry in the literal sense. For the biblical writers this sort of idolatry is objectionable because the element of human activity in bringing about revelation is to manifest: "The iron smith fashions [the idol] and works it over the coals. . . . The carpenter stretches a line, marks it out with a stylus, fashions it with planes, and marks it with a compass; he makes it in human form, with human beauty, to be set up in a shrine" (Isa. 44:12-13). The problem with physical idols, then, is that they are obviously human attempts to secure the presence of God and to control God's revelation.

However, not all idolatry involves physical representations of the divine. Ephesians 5:5, for instance, states that "no . . . one who is greedy (that is, an idolater), has any inheritance in the kingdom of Christ and of God." Here, greed is said to be a form of idolatry. The things that the greedy person desires have become that person's god, or, more exactly, they have become for the greedy person a means of access to the holy and the infinite. What is true of greed is true of many other human obsessions such as sexuality and politics. In each case we seek fullness and completeness of being in order to fill the lack that is characteristic of every being created from nothing. But in these obsessions we seek completeness of being not by sharing in God's coming into the world but instead by pursuing created things. These created things, then, whether material goods or sexual pleasure or power, mediate to us (we believe) the fullness and completeness that we innately seek. We are attracted to this subtler form of idolatry because, as with idolatry in the literal sense, we are able to control the things that provide access to the holy and the infinite. However, experience shows that in fact these things soon control us, with the result that idolatry inevitably becomes slavery. Far from delivering fullness and completeness, the things that we pursue only reveal our own emptiness and compound that emptiness by hindering us from seeking out God.

Idolatry, then, whether in its literal form or in other forms, is about our attempts to control God's presence and to create for ourselves means by which God can be revealed to us. In idolatry we insist that God be available to us on our terms and by means of our making. We thus refuse to allow God to be the holy one who is hidden in revelation and distant even when present and who is never at our disposal. This is the God who "has said that he would dwell in thick darkness" (1 Kings 8:12) and who "dwells in unapproachable light, whom no one has ever seen or can see" (1 Tim. 6:16). These verses tell us that we cannot come to know God by searching but instead can know God only through the vehicles of revelation that God has appointed. Idolatry, accordingly, plays its part in the inverted world of sin that we create. It mimics the world of God's creation by seeing that revelation requires the mediation of created things. It sees, rightly, that God comes to us through things in the created world such as the Temple, the priests, and the ark of the covenant. But idolatry is a distorted version of God's world because for it the things that mediate revelation are things that human beings have made or chosen and that are subject to our control.

▶ The Ethical Dimension of Faith

To affirm the doctrine of sin is more than merely understanding what sin is. It is also to know ourselves to be sinners—people whose deeds fashion the world of sin and who have been content to dwell in that world; people who have been foolish, unrighteous, and unjust; who have trusted in created things, and who have exhibited hubris, familiarity, and idolatry. It is to feel the force of God's judgment on the world of sin and to know that our alienation from God is a matter of our own doing. But to know ourselves as sinners is at the same time to know ourselves to be creatures of God and called by God to participate in God's movement into the world and in the fellowship that God is creating. This is because we can know ourselves as sinners only as we are brought by God's grace into the presence of the holy God. Only thus can we come to know our sin.

SUMMARY STATEMENTS

1. Chaos and nothingness appear in the form of sin. Because we are created from nothing, we are incomplete. Our existence is characterized by a striving for completion. We can find such completion only by faithfully responding to God. But instead of dwelling in the world that God creates, we create a world for ourselves, a world of sin.

2. Sin appears as foolishness, the opposite of wisdom. Foolishness is a mode of existence that takes no account of God.

3. Unrighteousness is breaking God's law and failing to offer God our heartfelt, obedient, and faithful response. Unrighteousness in relation to God goes hand in hand with injustice toward our neighbor.

4. In the world of sin, we place our hope and trust in created things instead of in God.

5. Hubris is the opposite of humility.

6. Familiarity with God results from a lack of fear and awe.

7. Idolatry is withholding praise from God and directing our worship to created things.

QUESTIONS FOR REFLECTION

1. What light does the doctrine of sin shed on our understanding of human existence?

2. How does the doctrine of sin help us understand the character of God?

3. What are the implications of the doctrine of sin for living the Christian life?

SIX

THE WORLD OF SIN AND ITS EFFECTS

OBJECTIVES

Your study of this chapter should help you to understand:

1. The Christian doctrine of original sin.

2. Different ways of understanding original sin.

3. The results of existence in the world of sin.

KEY WORDS TO UNDERSTAND

Alienation	Original sin
Apocalyptic literature	Outward sin
Corruption	Spiritual Death
Depravity	Vice
Flesh	Wickedness
Inward sin	World
Judgment	

QUESTIONS TO CONSIDER AS YOU READ

1. What does the doctrine of original sin say about human existence?

2. What are the implications of original sin for the doctrine of salvation?

O great mountain, who art thou,
Immense, immovable?
High as heaven aspires thy brow,
Thy foot sinks deep as hell!
Thee, alas, I long have known,
Long have felt thee fixed within;
Still beneath thy weight I groan;
Thou art Indwelling Sin.

Thou are darkness in my mind,
Perverseness in my will,
Love inordinate and blind,
That always cleaves to ill;
Every passion's wild excess,
Anger, lust, and pride, thou art;
Thou art sin and sinfulness,
And unbelief of heart.

These verses from a hymn by the Wesleys describe original sin, here called "indwelling sin" because it seems to arise from the depths of the human heart. They compare sin to a great and immovable mountain, a reference to the intractability of sin and the futility of our efforts to overcome its effects. They testify that sin is something that we know and feel within us and something under whose oppressive weight we groan. They also point to the effects of this sin: darkness of mind, perverseness of will, the disordered character of our love, the excess of our passion, the unbelief of the heart. Original sin is all this and more.

▶ THE WORLD OF SIN

Sin organizes itself into a world that is the distorted image of God's created world.

The destructive power of chaos does not result in sheer annihilation. Sin does not efface God's creation so far that literally nothing remains. Instead sin is the distortion of God's creation and perversely creates an alternative world. Sin thus has a creative dimension that mimics God's creative power. But whereas God's creative power draws us into God's life and orients us to God, sin disorients us by disengaging us from God.

Sin, therefore, is a created world in which the power of chaos reigns; it is not simply a name for acts of human wickedness. It is not a second world besides God's world; it is God's world existing in a distorted form under the power of chaos. And it remains God's world in spite of the reign of chaos.

Because sin is a world, it is more than ego-centrism. Placing ourselves at the center of things in place of God is a manifestation of sin but it is not the only form that sin takes. As Christian feminist theologians have observed, for many women sin is manifested not so much in ego-centrism but instead in a lack of self-assertion and in being dominated by others. Such women have placed not their egos but others at the center of reality in place of God. So, it is better to think of sin as creating a world in which we are oriented toward created things (whether self or other realities), instead of being oriented to God.

▶ BIBLICAL AND TRADITIONAL PORTRAITS OF THE WORLD OF SIN

THE WORLD OF SIN IN APOCALYPTIC LITERATURE

The apocalyptic literature of the Bible portrays the world of sin in terms of cosmic powers that stand opposed to God. It thus testifies to the corporate character of sin and the experience of the demonic in personal form.

Apocalyptic literature is a genre of Jewish and Christian writings, some of which (e.g., Daniel and Revelation) are biblical and some of which (such as 2 Esdras) are found outside the Bible. One of the features of this literature is its portrait of cosmic powers and their role in the world of sin.

Consider the New Testament's conviction that "the whole world lies under the power of the evil one" (1 John 5:19) and that "our struggle is not against enemies of blood and flesh, but against the rulers, against the authorities, against the cosmic powers of this present darkness, against the spiritual forces of evil in the heavenly places" (Eph. 6:12). These passages tell us that sin organizes itself into a rebellious, demonic world distinct from the sinful deeds of individual human beings. Sin is thus a world into which we are born and which distorts our nature.

The apocalyptic impulse in the Bible reminds us that sin cannot be adequately analyzed in terms of human wickedness. It tells us that sin forms a system of existence that encompasses us and facilitates our own sin. It shows us, consequently, that the salvation of individual human beings is not a total solution of the problem of sin, for those individuals still dwell in the world of sin and experience its corrupting effects. It shows us the extent of sin's distortion of God's good creation.

THEORIES ABOUT SATAN AND DEMONS

Theories about Satan and demons are speculative but not idle. They are not idle because experience of the demonic is a part of humankind's experience. Nearly every age and culture has testified to the experience of evil in a personal form. Even though it is rare for people in technologically advanced societies to experience evil as a personal but non-human force, we have to take seriously the reality of this experience in other cultures and in other historical eras. However, theories about the demonic are inevitably speculative, for we have no adequate concepts for evil that is personal but not human. An adequate concept would be one that provided a full measure of understanding and that could be meaningfully related to other areas of human knowledge such as biology and sociology. As it is, we do not have a concept adequate to the experience of this sort of evil. Instead we have images and symbols that designate this experience. These images and symbols should be taken with great seriousness, even if we do not take them literally.

THE WORLD OF SIN IN JOHN'S GOSPEL AND LETTERS

In the Johannine literature, the central concept for understanding sin is the world. Within this literature, world means both God's creation and also the system of sin that humans inhabit and that is opposed to the revelation of God.

The conception of sin as a corporate reality appears quite clearly in the concept of the *world* in the Gospel and Letters of John. Even though the world is the creation of God and is therefore the object of God's love (John 3:16), under the power of sin, the world does not know God (1 John 3:1) and in fact hates God (John 15:18). This literature powerfully captures the ambivalent character of the world—created by God yet dominated by sin. By their repeated use of the phrase *the world* the Gospel and Letters compel us to see the world of sin as an alternative way of being, an organization of human existence.

This helps us understand the situation of Jesus' antagonists, who in perplexity ask, "Surely we are not blind, are we?" (John 9:40). They are blind but they are not aware of their blindness, for they are of the world. Because they dwell in the world of sin, they are blind to God's revelation: "The works that I do in my Father's name testify to me; but you do not believe, because you do not belong to my sheep. My sheep hear my voice" (10:25-27). To be of the world, therefore, is to be unable to hear the voice of God and to recognize the revelation of God.

THE WORLD OF SIN IN PAUL'S LETTERS

In Paul's theology, the central concept for understanding sin is flesh. Under the condition of sin, flesh signifies the root of wickedness and the rebellious condition of existence in the world of sin, experienced as a power over which we have no control.

Paul's favorite term for portraying the corporate character of sin is *flesh*. Immediately, however, we must pause and note that in Paul's thought the flesh is not the same as the body. It is instead Paul's symbol for the universal power of sin. It signified for him what *world* signified for John—that dimension of sin that precedes the individual and that, by encompassing us, shapes our thinking and acting.

It is important to note as well that the flesh is not simply a collective name for wicked deeds. It is true that there is a close connection between the flesh and wicked deeds, for Paul considered things such as fornication, strife, and jealousy as "works of the flesh" (Gal. 5:19-21). At the same time, the flesh really signifies a corporate mode of existence that is contrary to God: "What the flesh desires is opposed to the Spirit, and what the Spirit desires is opposed to the flesh" (v. 17).

The flesh is a power that determines the existence of those who dwell in the world of sin:

> I am of the flesh, sold into slavery under sin. . . . For I do not do what I want, but I do the very thing I hate. . . . In fact it is no longer I that do it, but sin that dwells within me. For I know that nothing good dwells within me, that is, in my flesh. . . . I see in my members another law at war with the law of my mind, making me captive to the law of sin that dwells in my members *(Rom. 7:14-15, 17-18, 23).*

This passage says several things. First, being in the flesh is like being a slave. It is a condition from which we cannot free ourselves. Second, being in the flesh involves a contradiction between our true, created selves and our sinful selves: "I do not do what I want, but I do the very thing I hate. . . . In fact it is no longer I that do it, but sin that dwells within me." To be in the flesh, therefore, is to be possessed by an alien power that opposes and distorts our true existence in the presence of God. Third, being in the flesh is like being ruled by a law that controls our actions without our consent.

The flesh, accordingly, is the world of sin experienced as a corrupting power over which we have no control. It points to the fact that the world of sin is a trans-individual reality that controls the individual: "It is no longer I who do [wrong], but sin dwells within me" (7:17). The sin that dwells within me is the same power of sin at work in everyone. It is the power of chaos that transcends the individual.

SOME MODERN INSIGHTS INTO THE WORLD OF SIN

Christian theologians have, over the centuries, offered numerous ways of understanding the corporate dimension of sin. In the modern era two theological movements, the Social Gospel and Liberation Theology, have offered helpful and suggestive insights into the corporate aspect of sin. Both have asserted that, just as salvation pertains to every aspect of our being, so sin must be understood not only individualistically but also corporately.

Throughout the centuries the Church has gained more insight into the corporate nature of sin. One powerful development has been in the application of social scientific analysis. An early example of this is found in the works of the American Social Gospel Movement. This movement arose in the last half of the 19th century in response to evils such as slavery and the degradation of life and society resulting from the rapid rise of industrialization. It began as a movement of reform, aiming to root out social forms of sin by charitable works, legislation, and other forms of action. The leaders of this movement soon realized that, because we are social beings, the conversion of individuals, although critically important, was not the sole solution to sin. The solution, they saw, required that our social world be changed so that deeds commensurate with the kingdom of God would be encouraged and deeds contrary to the Kingdom would be shunned. For example, they realized that trying to use moral persuasion in order to get industrialists to eliminate child labor and to introduce safety into the workplace was fruitless as long as profit and competition made such exploitation inevitable. If, however, laws could be enforced that negatively sanctioned such exploitation, then conditions agreeable to the kingdom of God could be brought about. The same argument was applied to slavery, the alcohol business, and many other undesirable features of industrial America.

The Social Gospel was based on an understanding of the kingdom of God as a reality that manifests itself in society as well as in the human heart. It presumed as well that sin is a reality that transcends the deeds and intentions of individuals. These insights were taken up in the various forms of Liberation Theology in the 20th century. Like the Social Gospel, liberation theologies rest on the conviction that salvation has often been thought of too individualistically. Because human existence takes place on a multitude of axes—the physical, the social, the political, and so on, salvation must be the redemption of all of these axes. A one-sided focus on individual salvation is inadequate because it leaves untouched most of the axes of life. Liberation theologians were also convinced of the corporate nature of sin. They were particularly appalled by the way in which in the 1960s, '70s, and '80s political oppression went hand in hand with economic injustice, a condition clearly at odds with the kingdom of God.

The point of this review of the Social Gospel and Liberation Theology is to provide illustrations of the ways in which theologians have penetrated further into the corporate nature of sin. Of course, these theologies (like all theologies) have serious shortcomings but we can use their analyses to understand more clearly that sin is more than the wicked acts of individuals. It constitutes itself as a world in opposition to God. Just as salvation embraces and transforms every aspect of human life so the world of sin corrupts and distorts every aspect of human life.

EVANGELICAL CHRISTIANS' UNDERSTANDING OF CORPORATE SIN

Evangelical Christianity has made its own contribution to our understanding of corporate sin. For instance, evangelicals were in the forefront of the antislavery movement and other reforming movements of the 19th century. Alongside of their commitment to individual repentance and faith, evangelicals have struggled against entrenched social structures that create the conditions for many forms of sin.

▶ THE WORLD OF SIN AND THE DOCTRINE OF ORIGINAL SIN

The doctrine of original sin affirms the corporate dimension of sin as well as the depth and extensiveness of human depravity. It is a statement about the universality of human sin and the fact that sin organizes itself into a world that is opposed to the world of God's creation. The social nature of human beings helps us understand why sin has a corporate dimension and why we are all born into the world of sin.

The corporate dimension of sin has traditionally been expressed in the doctrine of **original sin**. Discussions about original sin often focus on the biblical story of Adam and Eve. However, original sin is more than the first sin. *Original* means *universal.* The originality of sin is found in the fact that all have sinned and all fall short of God's glory. The originality of original sin is that each of us is born into a world that is sinful and into a sinful human nature and that, even before we become responsible moral and spiritual agents, we participate in this sinful world and receive the consequences of such participation.

PELAGIUS-AUGUSTINE: DEBATE ON ORIGINAL SIN

One of the earliest debates on original sin was occasioned by the teaching of Pelagius (died sometime after A.D. 418) and his theological supporters. Pelagius, who was a popular teacher, set forth the view that Adam's sin affected only Adam, so that each person coming into the world is in the same condition in which Adam was created. As a result, to speak of sin is to speak only of voluntary transgressions. Opposed to Pelagius was Augustine of Hippo (A.D. 354-430). Augustine argued that Adam's sin resulted in the **corruption** of human nature, so that everyone coming into the world possesses a nature that is already sinful before acts of sin are committed. Pelagius was concerned that Augustine's teaching meant that human beings are not free. Augustine believed that Pelagius' teaching overlooked the devastating effects of sin and the consequent necessity of God's grace for salvation. The creedal statements in our tradition follow Augustine's views, affirming that original sin "is not simply the following of Adam's example" but is instead the "corruption of the nature of all the offspring of Adam."

Paul taught that "by the one man's disobedience the many were made sinners" (Rom. 5:19). How should we understand the connection between the universality of sin and the sin of this individual?

Consider Paul's contrast between Adam and Christ: "Just as by the one man's disobedience the many were made sinners, so by the one man's obedience the many will be made righteous" (Rom. 5:19). Or, as he stated elsewhere, "'The first man, Adam, became a living being'; the last Adam became a life-giving spirit" (1 Cor. 15:45). Paul was saying that the sin of this individual created the corporate world of sin by fashioning a new mode of existence, marked by disobedience and unrighteousness. Our humanity is thus distorted into the sinful condition in which we now share. We participate in that sinful humanity and, in turn, contribute to it by our own sins. Jesus Christ, however, exemplified and created for us a new mode of existence, characterized by obedience and righteousness, and thus began the re-creation of God's world. Those who by faith come to be in Christ share in his obedience and righteousness and are enabled to live righteously.

We bear, in Paul's words, "the image of the man of dust" (1 Cor. 15:49) because we are social beings and because our social being has been determined by the world of sin. Every aspect of this world—its individuals and its structures—is immersed in sinfulness. This sinful world and everything in it determines our being. Before we are conceived, this world has already fashioned a distorted human nature. From the beginning of our existence we participate in this distorted humanity. Each individual person is this distorted humanity existing in historical particularity. We bear the image of the man of dust because we participate in the fallen humanity that sin has created.

If we dwelled not in the world of sin but in the world that God creates, then the members and social structures of that world would all mediate to us the knowledge of God. However, in the world of sin, they do not mediate this knowledge. On the contrary, they inculcate sin and ignorance of God. This is not to say that every aspect of the world is overtly evil. Even in the condition of sin, the features of the world feebly mediate God's revelation. Nonetheless, our world and its elements have become self-serving instead of God-serving. As a result, we who dwell in this world share in the world's self-serving character and its alienation from God.

The doctrine of original sin, then, affirms that the features of the world that constitute human nature are sinful. It states that from the beginning of our existence we are under the control of forces that are hostile to God and that, without God's intervention, we will continue under sin's domination. We are shaped by a world of sin that corrupts the nature we share. We then make our own contribution to the world of sin by acts of wickedness and by perpetuating the sinful features of our world. As a result, sin is inescapable for those who dwell in this world.

This analysis provides us with a way of understanding the traditional concept of depravity. As previously noted, sin encompasses more than our acts of wickedness. It includes also the fact that we are turned away from God, that our desires are not God's desires, and that we persistently walk contrary to God's ways. The theological term for this fact is ***depravity,*** sometimes called the sinful nature. The sinful nature is the state of human existence as it dwells in the world of sin. In contrast to our created nature, which was oriented toward God, our sinful nature is our orientation away from God and the resulting life of alienation and wickedness. The sinful nature exists before we do; we are born into it. As we develop as humans, the sinful character of the world has a formative effect on us. Having been born into this world of sin, it is the only world we have known. Consequently, it is like the air that we breathe. We are so accustomed to it that we cannot imagine an alternative. Moreover, the pervasiveness of the world of sin means that we cannot by our efforts and without God's help escape from it and its destructive effects.

▶ THE CONSEQUENCES OF LIVING IN THE WORLD OF SIN

ALIENATION

Existence in the world of sin means alienation from God, encompassing spiritual death and liability to God's judgment. It also means alienation (in the form of injustice) from other members of the human community and from our physical environment. This signifies that, because of our sin, the physical world does not function in relation to us as it should.

As we have already seen, the world of sin is a world that subsists in ***alienation*** from God. The Bible has many ways of expressing this alienation, such as Paul's observations that "the mind that is set on the flesh is hostile to God" (Rom. 8:7) and that those in the world "are darkened in their understanding, alienated from the life of God because of their ignorance and hardness of heart" (Eph. 4:18).

Alienation manifests itself as ***spiritual death***. Two New Testament passages, Rom. 8:6 ("to set the mind on the flesh is death") and John 17:3 ("This is eternal life, that they may know you, the only true God") are especially pertinent. The first clearly identifies life in the flesh, that is, the world of sin, with death. This life is a death because it is the distorted image of true life in God's created world. The second passage reminds us that eternal life is essentially a matter of knowing God. It tells us that spiritual death is the state of those who do not know God. By turning away from God and failing to receive God's revelation, they have consigned themselves to a state of living death, for although they continue to exist in the world of sin, they are as separated from God as a corpse is from the living.

Alienation manifests itself also as *judgment*. Judgment implies a separation, as in the gospel affirmation about the eschatological separation of the wicked from the righteous "as a shepherd separates the sheep from the goats" (Matt. 25:32). Judgment means that in the eschatological future those who have faithfully responded to God will "shine like the brightness of the sky" (Dan. 12:3). Those, however, who remain "enemies of the cross of Christ" (Phil. 3:18) will face "the punishment of eternal destruction, separated from the presence of the Lord" (2 Thess. 1:9).

But judgment is more than an act of separation. It is also the revelation of the world's sinful character: "This is the judgment, that the light has come into the world, and people loved darkness rather than light because their deeds were evil" (John 3:19). God's judgment is actualized in the sending of Jesus Christ, the light, into the world to reveal humankind's love of the darkness. Without the light, our love of darkness is not manifest, for all is dark in the world of sin. But when the light appears in the midst of the darkness, our love of darkness and our fear of the light become evident. Judgment, therefore, is God's revelation and God's coming into the world. The presence of God in the world throws into clear relief the human impulse to dwell in the dark and to shun the light. Making this impulse manifest is God's judgment on the world of sin.

The alienation that characterizes our existence extends beyond estrangement from God. As noted previously, faithful response to God issues forth in justice between human beings. Injustice, accordingly, is a measure of our alienation from each other. It results from one part of the human community having no regard for another part of that community and separating itself from the good of that part and of the whole community.

We are also alienated from our physical environment. Ideally, that is, in the world that God creates, the physical world around us mediates to us the knowledge of God. Careful meditation on the things around us would lead our thoughts to God. But in the world of sin, physical things do not mediate the knowledge of God, at least not very well. On the contrary, they stand before us mute, saying nothing or little about God. This is not because something has happened to the physical world. It is because we exist in a state of alienation from God. Because of our alienation from God, we are alienated as well from the created world that tells of God.

CORRUPTION

Another result of sin is the corruption (or depravity) of our created nature. Corruption manifests itself in wrong desire, loss of true freedom, distortion of our thinking and ethical conduct, and in wickedness.

In the world of sin we are alienated from God, from other members of the human community, and from the rest of the created world. We are also alienated from our true selves. The true self is a life of obedient response to God, a life characterized by wise conduct, righteousness and justice, hope, humility, fear, and praise. But as we dwell in the world of sin we distance ourselves from that life. In its place we substitute a life that is disengaged from God and in which the power of chaos rules.

The traditional term for this alienation is depravity, which we now consider in terms of its manifestations in life.

ORIGINAL SIN IN THE WESLEYAN TRADITION

The creeds in our tradition uniformly describe original sin as the corruption of human nature from its created state.

One term (used by John Wesley) for depravity is *inward sin*, which denotes evil thoughts and tempers such as pride, anger, self-will, and jealousy. Inward sin is thus distinguished from *outward sin*, which is overt acts of wickedness. Simply put, inward sin consists of sins of the heart; outward sin consists of wrongful deeds. More carefully stated, inward sin describes our inclinations, affections, passions, appetites, and thoughts as they are determined by the world of sin. It signifies that the motivations of our actions are grounded not in the love of God but in the twisted love for creatures, in the desire for sensual pleasure, and in anything else that is contrary to our faithful response to God.

Corruption manifests itself as wrong desire. Because we are created from nothing our existence is characterized by a fundamental lack of being. Human existence is consequently marked by a restless searching for fullness and satisfaction. This searching manifests itself in desire. Ideally, our desire would be for God. But existence in the world of sin means that we are "slaves to various passions and pleasures, passing our days in malice and envy . . . hating one another" (Titus 3:3). Instead of faithfully responding to God's holiness and love, our desires are directed entirely toward ourselves and other things in the created world. That is why we are counseled to "renounce impiety and worldly passions" and instead to "live lives that are self-controlled, upright, and godly" (2:12).

It is important to remember, however, that neither the self nor other things in the created world are evil. Even desire and passion are not evil. They are, after all, an essential aspect of our created existence. But it is characteristic of our existence in the world of sin that our desire has lost its rightful object, God, and that we desire created things in the place of God. Sin, then, lies not in the objects of desire but in the fact that we desire created things instead of God. We have forsaken the object of desire that alone can give us completion of being and satisfaction and have come to desire instead things that cannot give us this completion. The result is that our desire is corrupted and we exist in a state of alienation from that vital aspect of our being.

Corruption results in loss of freedom. In the world of God's creation, human freedom means that every aspect of our existence is a faithful response to God. However, in the world of sin, corrupted desire signals the loss of freedom. We are, on the contrary, "slaves to various passions and pleasures." Of course the loss of this freedom does not mean that human beings are automatons who lack choice. We exercise choice every day, from choosing which brand of toothpaste to buy to deciding whether or not to go to work. But this element of choice is not the freedom that would be ours in the world of God's creation. It is a pale imitation of that freedom, and because we are slaves to passion, in important respects it is no freedom at all. Above all, it is not the freedom to respond faithfully to God. The Christian tradition has emphatically held that in ourselves, that is, in so far as we live in the world of sin, we lack the capacity to respond to God.

WORLD OF SIN AND THE LOSS OF FREEDOM

The creeds in our tradition affirm our lack of freedom by stating that those in the world of sin "are unable in their own strength to do the right. . . . [And] cannot of themselves even call upon God or exercise faith for salvation" and that they "are unable by their own strength and work to restore themselves in right relationship with God and to merit eternal salvation."

Corruption shows itself also in the distortion of thought. This does not refer to the natural limitations of knowledge and understanding that result from our finitude. These limitations are inescapable features of our creaturely existence. The sinful distortion of thought is another name for our ignorance of God. In the words of Ephesians, those in the world of sin "are darkened in their understanding [and are] alienated from the life of God because of their ignorance and hardness of heart" (4:18). Of course, this sort of ignorance does not mean that people in the world of sin are all atheists. They certainly may believe that there is a God. But this kind of belief is not the proper knowledge of God, for it is not a faithful response to God. It is instead an opinion that people hold, a notion that enters their thoughts in moments of crisis or happiness. That is why ancient people, although "they knew God, they did not honor him as God or give thanks to him, but they became futile in their thinking, and their senseless minds were darkened" (Rom. 1:21). In the world of God's creation human thought would find its natural object in God and God's work. But in the world of sin a haze hangs over our thoughts so that we know nothing except for the finite realities around us and our own distorted notions.

Finally, corruption extends to our ethical existence. Humans are able to discern enough of God's wisdom to establish the rule of law and systems of practical ethics. However, in the world of sin, human ethical conduct is disengaged from God. Although this does not mean that all human systems of ethics are wicked, it does mean they are seriously incomplete and flawed, for (like other institutions in the world of sin) they instill God-forgetfulness. Systems of ethics, then, and ethical conduct generally suffer from the effects of original sin. That is why the Christian tradition has held that even admirable ethical conduct has the character of sin. It is not that such conduct is overtly evil or even that it proceeds from evil motivations. The point is that these works, no matter how good in motivation and consequence, are lodged within the world of sin and are disengaged from God.

OUR DEEDS WHILE IN THE WORLD OF SIN

The creeds in our tradition assert that our deeds while in the world of sin participate in that sin by noting that "we have no power to do good works, pleasant and acceptable to God." They thus teach that, while we can and should do works that are good when judged by human standards, we cannot, while under the power of sin, do works that constitute a proper and faithful response to God.

The corruption of our ethical existence shows itself in *wickedness.* This is Paul's argument in Rom. 1. Having argued that humankind "did not see fit to acknowledge God" (v. 28), he offered a list of resulting *vices:* covetousness, malice, envy, murder, strife and so on (see vv. 29-31). The important point here is that although people customarily think of sin as misdeeds, or vices, of the sort that Paul enumerated, it is more accurate to think of these vices as the *result* of sin. Sin is principally a matter of dwelling in the world of sin that we have created as an alternative to the world of God's making. One consequence of our creating our own world is that we depart not only from the knowledge of God but even from human systems of ethics and fall into overt acts of wickedness.

ORIGINAL SIN AND WICKEDNESS

The creeds in our tradition note the connection between original sin and wickedness when they state that original sin is that "whereby man is very far gone from original righteousness, and of his own nature inclined to evil, and that continually."

The importance of this distinction between sin and wickedness or vice is that it reminds us that even those who live blamelessly according to human systems of ethics are not thereby responding to God with the fullness that God requires. Our ethical conduct may be flawless (in the sense of avoiding all vice), but if we inhabit the world of sin, we fail to offer God praise and we trust in realities other than God. This distinction, then, reminds us that while ethical conduct is important, faithful response to God is something different. The former can be instilled in us by family and education; the latter is ours only through God's grace.

▶ THE ETHICAL DIMENSION OF FAITH

To believe in the doctrine of original sin means that we live mindful of the way in which our lives are shaped by the world of sin. It means also that we take responsibility for our contribution to the world of sin. It is to realize in our thoughts and conduct the pervasiveness of sin and its effect upon us. In short, this doctrine is an invitation to all who live in the world of sin to embrace the world of God's creation through repentance, faith, and hope in the grace of God.

SUMMARY STATEMENTS

1. Sin organizes itself into a world that is the distorted image of God's created world.

2. The apocalyptic literature of the Bible portrays the world of sin in terms of cosmic powers that stand opposed to God and thus constitute the realm of the demonic. It thus testifies to the individual-transcending character of sin and the experience of the demonic in personal form.

3. In the Johannine literature, the central concept for understanding sin is the *world*. Within this literature, *world* means both God's creation and also the system of sin that humans inhabit and that is opposed to the revelation of God.

4. In Paul's theology, the central concept for understanding sin is *flesh*. Under the condition of sin, flesh signifies the root of wickedness and the rebellious condition of existence in the world of sin, experienced as a power over which we have no control.

5. Christian theologians have, over the centuries, offered numerous ways of understanding the corporate dimension of sin. In the modern era two theological movements, the Social Gospel and Liberation Theology, have offered helpful and suggestive insights into the corporate aspect of sin. Both asserted that, just as salvation pertains to every aspect of our being, so sin must be understood not only individualistically but also corporately.

6. The doctrine of original sin affirms the corporate dimension of sin as well as the depth and extensiveness of human depravity. It is a statement about the universality of human sin and the fact that sin organizes itself into a world that is opposed to the world of God's creation. The social nature of human being helps us understand why sin has a corporate dimension and why we are all born into the world of sin.

7. Existence in the world of sin means alienation from God, encompassing spiritual death and liability to God's judgment. It also means alienation (in the form of injustice) from other members of the human community and from our physical environment. This signifies that, because of our sin, the physical world does not function in relation to us as it should.

8. Another result of sin is the corruption (or depravity) of our created nature. Corruption manifests itself in wrong desire, loss of

true freedom, distortion of our thinking and ethical conduct, and in wickedness.

QUESTIONS FOR REFLECTION

1. What is the significance of the fact that there are multiple ways of portraying original sin?

2. Why is the doctrine of original sin important in the system of Christian doctrine? How does it affect other doctrines, such as the doctrine of creation and the doctrine of salvation?

SEVEN

THE TRIUMPH OF GRACE

OBJECTIVES

Your study of this chapter should help you to understand:

1. The connection between divine judgment and redemption.

2. The character of God's grace.

3. The relation between the doctrine of God and the doctrine of grace.

KEY WORDS TO UNDERSTAND

Common grace	Prevenient grace
Discipline	Redemption
Grace	Repentance
Hope	Wrath

QUESTIONS TO CONSIDER AS YOU READ

1. How is God's judgment related to God's mercy?

2. How do the biblical passages that describe the restoration of Israel anticipate the New Testament?

3. How is grace a manifestation of God's creative power?

Glory to God, whose sovereign grace
  Hath animated senseless stones;
Called us to stand before his face,
  And raised us into Abraham's sons!

The people that in darkness lay,
  In sin and error's deadly shade,
Have seen a glorious gospel day,
  In Jesus' lovely face displayed.

Thou only, Lord, the work hast done,
  And bared thine arm in all our sight,
Hast made the reprobates thine own,
  And claimed the outcasts as thy right.

Thy single arm, almighty Lord,
  To us the great salvation brought,
Thy word, thy all-creating word,
  That spake at first the world from naught.

For this the saints lift up their voice,
  And ceaseless praise to thee is giv'n;
For this the hosts above rejoice,
  We raise the happiness of heaven.

For this (no longer sons of night)
  To thee our thankful hearts we give;
To thee, who call'dst us into light,
  To thee we die, to thee we live.

Suffice that for the season past
  Hell's horrid language filled our tongues,
We all thy words behind us cast,
  And lewdly sang the drunkard's songs.

But, Oh! the power of divine grace!
  In hymns we now our voices raise,
Loudly in strange hosannas join,
  And blasphemies are turned to praise!

This hymn by the Wesleys, written in 1740, draws our attention to several important aspects of God's grace, which is God's creative power and God's act of saving us from sin. First, it ascribes sovereignty to this grace by expressly connecting it with God's creative power: "Thy Word, the all-creating Word, that spake at first the world from naught." In this way, the hymn helps us see that the creation of the world and God's gracious *redemption* are not utterly distinct acts of God but instead intimately related to each other in the ongoing divine movement into the world that aims at our eschatological destiny, fellowship. The hymn introduces this destiny by noting that grace has "called us to stand before [God's] face." In grace God comes to us, draws into a relation of faithful obedience, and thus fulfills our created purpose. The hymn then expands on the notion of sovereign grace by asserting that "Thou only, Lord, the work [of redemption] hast done." To say that God's grace is sovereign is to say that God is the sole source of our redemption. Even our faithful response to God has its ground in God's sovereign grace. Finally, the hymn shows us what redemption consists in. It means that God reclaims the reprobates and outcasts. It also means that these former reprobates and outcasts are enabled to offer a response to God in the form of praise, rejoicing, and thankful hearts.

▶ INTRODUCTION

Grace is the creative power of God, manifested as judgment and redemption in the world of sin.

The holy God comes into the world for the purpose of creating fellowship with creatures. This is God's love for the world and the revelation of God in the world. This creative, loving and revealing movement of God appears in the world as acts of creation and election. But in the world of sin this movement appears also as judgment and redemption.

It is important to think of judgment and redemption together. Judgment is not contrary to God's love and creative power. It is, on the contrary, a manifestation of that love and power. Accordingly, we must guard against the easy assumption that wrath and punishment come from God's holiness and that redemption comes from God's love. This could be true only if holiness and love were distinct realities. However, they are not two realities but are an indivisible unity in the one God. They seem to us to be opposed to one another because in our experience human beings often exercise judgment in ways that contradict redemption and often seek redemption without justice. But in God's providence judgment aims at redemption and redemption presupposes justice. Judgment and redemption are, therefore, not opposed. They are instead the movement of the holy God into the world of sin for the purpose of creating fellowship with us. Of course, we have to recognize that sometimes God's purposes are frustrated, with the result that judgment does not attain its redemptive purpose.

The word *grace* denotes God's movement into the sinful world. Grace, therefore, is simply another name for the creative power of God, for God's revelation in the world, and for God's love. As such, grace embraces both judgment and redemption.

▶ GOD'S JUDGMENT ON ISRAEL'S SIN

THE GOD WHO JUDGES

In the world of sin, God's holiness is experienced as alienation from the holy God. God's wisdom is experienced as discipline. God's righteousness is experienced as God's wrath. And God's faithfulness becomes God's commitment to renew the covenant with Israel.

God's holiness means that, even in revelation, God remains hidden and transcendent. But in the world of sin, Israel experienced the holiness of God as terrible *wrath* and experienced the hiddenness of God as alienation: "Your iniquities have been barriers between you and your God, and your sins have hidden his face from you so that he does not hear" (Isa. 59:2). But the prophets wanted to say more than that Israel's sin had created alienation. They asserted as well that, in response to sin, God had deliberately turned away from Israel: "I will return to my place until they acknowledge their guilt and seek my face. In their distress they will beg my favor" (Hos. 5:15). "You have hidden your face from us, and have delivered us into the hand of our iniquity" (Isa. 64:7). In these and similar passages the hiddenness of God is no longer simply a result of God's holiness and otherness. It is instead a result of God's wrath and, consequently, becomes destructive as God deliberately hides from Israel. God is still experienced as the holy one, but now, in judgment, becomes a "devouring fire" (Deut. 4:24).

Like the experience of God's holiness, the experience of God's wisdom undergoes change in the world of sin. In the world of God's creation divine wisdom is experienced as the way in which the world, especially the moral world, works. But in the world of sin, God's wisdom is manifested as *discipline.*

God's disciplinary wisdom normally appears when the wicked come to their end through the inevitable fruit of foolishness: "A babbling fool will come to ruin" (Prov. 10:8); "the wicked fall by their own wickedness" (11:5). Just as a righteous life will bring about blessing so an unrighteous life will bring disaster according to the usual relation of act and consequence in the world's moral order.

But with respect to Israel, discipline assumed a different character. With Israel, God's discipline is not a matter of sin's inevitable consequences. Discipline for Israel had a more personal character, as in the relation between parent and child: "Know then in your heart that as a parent disciplines a child so the LORD your God disciplines you" (Deut. 8:5). Jeremiah likewise cast rebellious Israel in the role of a child refusing to accept discipline: "In vain I have struck down your children; they accepted no correction" (2:30). "This is the nation that did not obey the voice of the LORD their God, and did not accept discipline" (7:28).

The familial character of discipline makes clear that God's punishment has a remedial and corrective purpose, for it aims at restoring fellowship that has been severed by sin. Thus, judgment experienced as discipline is the expression of God's grace. It always takes place within the context of God's eschatological purpose, the creation of fellowship. This helps us understand Isaiah's belief that God will both punish and eventually redeem Egypt: "The LORD will strike Egypt, striking and healing; they will return to the LORD, and he will listen to their supplications and heal them" (Isa. 19:22). Passages such as this show us that God's discipline ("striking") must always be understood alongside God's redemption ("healing"), even if, because of human obstinacy, judgment does not lead to redemption. Both are moments in God's ongoing movement of grace that creates fellowship with creatures.

The remedial and gracious character of God's discipline is seen also when the prophets present Israel's destruction and exile as a refining process: "I will turn my hand against you; I will smelt away your dross as with lye and remove all your alloy" (Isa. 1:25). "See, I have refined you, but not like silver; I have tested you in the furnace of adversity" (48:10). Although this refining process involved great destruction and loss of life, the prophets were clear that its goal was positive—the purifying of Israel and the restoration of its fellowship with God.

In the world of God's creation, God's righteousness appears as God's lawfulness and covenant faithfulness, which we are to imitate. But in the world of sin, God's righteousness is experienced also as wrath. God, who upholds justice, judges human sin. God, who is righteous, becomes the standard against which our unrighteousness is measured (Ps. 96:13).

Accordingly, biblical writers affirmed God's rightness in judging and condemning Israel: "The LORD kept watch over this calamity until he brought it upon us. Indeed, the LORD our God is right in all that he has done; for we have disobeyed his voice" (Dan. 9:14). For the biblical writers, it could not be otherwise, for God is inherently just and righteous (Deut. 10:17-18).

And yet, wrath, like discipline, is an expression of grace, for wrath shows that Israel still stands in a covenantal relation to God. Although in its sin Israel was alienated from God, this alienation was not complete. God did not utterly abandon Israel. On the contrary, wrath resulted from God's covenantal stipulations. Israel was still God's partner in covenant and the recipient of God's grace. The fact that God's wrath is an expression of God's judgment means that it can be understood only in the context of the covenant with Israel, whereby God pledged to be faithful to Israel and Israel pledged to be obedient to God's command. God's wrath and judgment, therefore, are ultimately the result of God's covenantal faithfulness.

To speak of God's faithfulness with Israel is to speak of God's steadfast determination to come into the world and establish fellowship by overcoming Israel's sin. Judgment, including alienation, discipline, and wrath, is an essential component in overcoming that sin. But it is only one component and therefore must be seen in relation to the totality of God's movement into the world of sin. In other words, God's justice serves God's faithfulness and, ultimately, God's eschatological purpose, fellowship.

▶ THE REDEMPTION OF ISRAEL

INTRODUCTION

The doctrine of redemption is grounded in the conviction that God's unalterable eschatological purpose for humankind as a whole will not be thwarted by human sin, even if some members of the human race remain in the world of sin by refusing to respond to God's grace. God will not abandon us in our sin. For this reason, the doctrine of sin must always be understood in the context of God's grace. As a result, sin is not the true and final state of human existence. It is, on the contrary, the state that contradicts our created purpose and our eschatological destiny.

In this section we will have a look at the principal aspects of the doctrine of redemption: the God who redeems, repentance, and the various aspects of Israel's restoration.

THE GOD WHO REDEEMS: HOLINESS

The doctrine of grace affirms that the holy God comes into the world of sin in order to create and to re-create fellowship.

Because holiness denotes God's transcendence, majesty, and distance, we may at first not connect it to God's sovereign and redeeming grace. However, the connection is easier to make when we recall that God is present even while distant and revealed even while hidden. It is the holy God who is with us, even as the redemptive power of grace in the world of sin. This, indeed, is one of the central paradoxes of the Christian faith—that the holy God enters the world of sin and comes to us while remaining the holy, distant God. The idea of grace points us to the distance that God traverses by coming into our world of sin and redeeming us.

If God were a part of the created world, then redemption would be notable but it would not be a miracle. It is a miracle because it involves the paradox of the holy saving the sinful. We may be grateful but are not surprised if a compassionate person delivers us from our troubles. After all, that is what compassionate people do. But it is a matter of surprise if the majestic, distant, and holy Creator enters a sinful world in an act of re-creation. It is a surprise if the inherently hidden God makes the divine presence known in the midst of a world that practices God-forgetfulness. The idea of grace points us to the miraculous and unexpected character of redemption.

The fact that the holy God comes into the world of sin signifies additionally the priority of God's grace. God's creative power, whether in creation or new creation, is always prior to human action; our response to God is just that—a response to God's prior movement toward us. To speak of grace, then, is to speak the language of initiative and response, a language in which God is always the initiator who calls upon humankind to respond with faithfulness.

THE GOD WHO REDEEMS: WISDOM, RIGHTEOUSNESS, AND FAITHFULNESS

The doctrine of grace affirms that redemption is grounded in the wisdom, righteousness, and faithfulness of the God who in love comes into the world of sin.

Redemption is an expression of God's wisdom. As we have seen, God's wisdom is the establishing of a practical and moral order in the created world. In the world of sin, wisdom is distorted and foolishness takes its place. But in redemption, God begins recreating the world according to wisdom. Isaiah, for instance, looked forward to the messianic king who would exhibit wisdom, understanding, knowledge, and the fear of God (11:2). Redemption, therefore, is not only deliverance from God's wrath and from sin's effects but also the restoration of the wise ordering of God's creation.

Redemption is grounded as well in God's righteousness. It is common to think that God's righteousness is contrary to mercy because, being righteous, God must punish sin. But for the biblical writers, righteousness is doing what is right and creating justice. Sometimes righteousness appears as destructive judgment. More often it appears as saving deliverance: "Zion shall be redeemed by justice, and those in her who repent, by righteousness" (Isa. 1:27). God's righteousness thus manifests itself as mercy and redemption because God's eschatological purpose is fellowship with humankind. Therefore, all of God's acts that serve to bring about this fellowship are acts of righteousness—they are God's act of creating what is right. Righteousness, accordingly, shows itself as redemption.

Redemption is also an expression of God's faithfulness. In the world of sin, God's faithfulness appears in judgment, because God is faithful to the terms of the covenant. But it appears also in redemption, for God is rich in mercy. Faithfulness to the covenant, in other words, does not limit God's mercy, for the covenant is an instrument of God's eschatological purpose. In the words of Deuteronomy, "Because the LORD your God is a merciful God, he will neither abandon you nor destroy you; he will not forget the covenant with your ancestors that he swore to them" (4:31). In the prophetic writings, God's mercy and faithfulness are expressed in the concept of the eternal covenant: "I will make an everlasting covenant with them, never to draw back from doing good to them; and I will put the fear of me in their hearts, so that they may not turn from me" (Jer. 32:40). Convinced that mercy is rooted in God's faithfulness, the prophets believed that God's redeeming activity would overcome Israel's sin.

THE GOD WHO REDEEMS: FORGIVENESS AND MERCY

Mercy, not wrath and judgment, is the final word in God's relation with Israel.

In the wake of wrath and judgment, God came to Israel in mercy and renewed the covenant relationship. Three points deserve attention.

First, God's grace limits the divine wrath and does not allow the full extent of its destruction: "For my name's sake I defer my anger, for the sake of my praise I restrain it for you, so that I may not cut you off" (Isa. 48:9). This restraint is an expression of God's freedom. Although God may seem sometimes to act with uncontrolled fury, in fact God is free from the necessity of judgment. Stated differently, God's wrath is an instrument of God's purposes: "For the sake of my praise I restrain it for you." God's wrath is controlled by God's compassion: "I will not continually accuse, nor will I always be angry; for then the spirits would grow faint before me, even the souls that I have made" (57:16). As this passage shows, God does not allow judgment to negate creation. Judgment may be destructive, but it is not so destructive that there is nothing left to redeem.

Second, although God is righteous, God is not bound by an abstract standard of justice that requires the necessary and complete application of punishment; consequently, God is quick to forgive and slow to punish: "If you, O LORD, should mark iniquities, Lord, who could stand?" (Ps. 130:3). "He does not deal with us according to our sins, nor repay us according to our iniquities. . . . As a father has compassion for his children, so the LORD has compassion for those who fear him. For he knows how we were made; he remembers that we are dust (103:10, 13-14). The God of grace uses justice as an instrument of redemption.

Third and most important, compassion follows judgment. The biblical writers used several striking metaphors to affirm this. One is the image of a woman's love for her child: "Can a woman forget her nursing child, or show no compassion for the child of her womb? Even these may forget, yet I will not forget you" (Isa. 49:15). Another metaphor is that of a husband's love for his wife: "For the LORD has called you like a wife forsaken and grieved in spirit, like the wife of a man's youth when she is cast off, says your God. For a brief moment I abandoned you, but with great compassion I will gather you" (Isa. 54:6-7). These familial metaphors show us that compassion, not wrath, has the final word in God's relation to Israel.

ISRAEL'S RESPONSE TO GOD'S GRACE: REPENTANCE

Israel's redemption required its repentance, which embraces amendment of life.

God's compassion is everlasting and unconditional; however, God's forgiveness required Israel's **repentance:**

> When all these things [i.e., God's punishment] have happened to you, . . . if you call them to mind among all the nations where the LORD your God has driven you, and return to the LORD your God, and you and your children obey him with all your heart and with all your soul . . . then the LORD your God will restore your fortunes and have compassion on you *(Deut. 30:1-3).*

Forgiveness required more than Israel's confession and sorrow for its sin. It required also that Israel change its ways and obey God with undivided heart and soul: "If the wicked turn away from all their sins that have committed and keep my statutes and do what is lawful and right, they shall surely live, they shall not die. None of the transgressions that they have committed shall be remembered against them" (Ezek. 18:21-22). Amendment of life meant that Israel had to abandon its devotion to other gods and had to practice justice, especially toward the poor, the widowed and orphaned, and resident foreigners.

THE REDEMPTION OF ISRAEL: A NEW CREATION

The redemption of Israel was the exercise of God's creative power. Redemption, accordingly, is a new act of creation by the God of grace.

Israel's restoration was a new creation—a renewed exercise of God's creative power. God was declaring "new things" that would prompt Israel to sing to God a "new song" (Isa. 42:9-10). Israel was accordingly urged to forget its immediate past—the past of God's judgment—and instead to behold the new thing that God was about to do (43:18-19). Above all, the restoration of Israel to its land was understood to be a prelude to a more extensive act of new creation: "I am about to create new heavens and a new earth; the former things shall not be remembered or come to mind. But be glad and rejoice forever in what I am creating; for I am about to create Jerusalem as a joy, and its people as a delight" (65:17-18). The prophet saw the redemption of Israel as the first stage in a universal restoration of all things, a critical moment in God's gracious movement into the world of sin, creating and recreating fellowship.

Because this restoration is a new creation, it is a victory over the power of chaos. When the prophet looked forward to Israel's return from Babylon, it was natural to portray this event in terms of overcoming chaos: "Awake, awake, put on strength, O arm of the LORD! Awake, as in days of old, the generations of long ago! Was it not you who cut Rahab in pieces, who pierced the dragon?" (Isa. 51:9). Redemption is the reversal of the effects of chaos, a reversal in which the creative power of God saves Israel from the destructive power of chaos and restores Israel to its national existence.

THE REDEMPTION OF ISRAEL: THE RENEWAL OF ELECTION

The grace of God—God's redemptive movement into the world of sin—restored Israel's status as the elect people of God and renewed the covenant with Israel.

Another aspect of Israel's redemption was the renewal of Israel as the chosen and holy people of God. Divine punishment threatened Israel with loss of its status as God's people. Redemption, accordingly, meant the restoration of Israel to its former status. This was especially important in the midst of and after the exile, for in this period Israel was no longer a sovereign nation. It was instead incorporated into a series of foreign empires. Its identity as the holy, elect people of God was consequently of paramount importance. This helps us see the force of Isa. 41:8-10: "You, Israel, my servant, Jacob, whom I have chosen, . . . you whom I took from the ends of the earth, and called from its farthest corners, saying to you, 'You are my servant, I have chosen you and not cast you off'; do not fear, for I am with you, do not be afraid, for I am your God." This passage, with its strong language of election, affirms that Israel is God's chosen people and the object of God's calling. On that calling rested the promise of God's presence and the assurance that Israel would remain the people of God.

ISRAEL'S REDEMPTION: THE MESSIANIC KING AND THE RULE OF GOD

The new creation effected by the God of grace would culminate in God's Lordship over the world through a hoped-for messianic king.

An important part of Israel's redemption was the hope for a king who would exemplify faithful obedience and would ensure that justice and righteousness prevailed in the restored Israel. In the words of Isaiah, "His authority shall grow continually, and there shall be endless peace for the throne of David and his kingdom. He will establish and uphold it with justice and with righteousness from this time onward and forevermore" (9:7). The rule of the messianic king would be characterized by peace and blessings. He would exhibit the traits of wisdom and understanding, for he would fear God. He would establish justice and righteousness in the land and be an example of righteous conduct. Above all, he would embody the ideal characteristics of redeemed Israel.

In Israel's hoped-for future, the messianic king would be the physical presence and instrument of God's rule, which would have a universal scope: "In days to come . . . Many peoples shall come and say, 'Come, let us go up to the mountain of the LORD, to the house of the God of Jacob; that he may teach us his ways and that we may walk in his paths.' . . . He shall judge between the nations, and shall arbitrate for many peoples" (Isa. 2:2-4). This important passage shows us that the restoration of Israel was, in the prophetic conception, merely a prelude to the universal rule of God, a rule that would be characterized by worldwide justice and peace. Along with this hope went the expectation that the Gentiles would come to obey and worship God: "In those days ten men from nations of every language shall take hold of a Jew, grasping his garment and saying, 'Let us go with you, for we have heard that God is with you'" (Zech. 8:23). Gentiles would no longer be excluded from the worship of God simply because they were non-Israelites. On the contrary, the worship of God would know no national boundaries:

> The foreigners who join themselves to the LORD, to minister to him, to love the name of the LORD, and to be his servants, . . . these I will bring to my holy mountain, and make them joyful in my house of prayer; their burnt offerings and their sacrifices will be accepted on my altar; for my house shall be called a house of prayer for all peoples *(Isa. 56:6-7).*

ISRAEL'S REDEMPTION: THE RESTORATION OF FAITHFUL RESPONSE TO GOD

The hoped-for redemption of Israel included the restoration of its response to God. Restored Israel would exhibit wisdom, righteousness and justice, trust, humility, fear, and praise.

All of these aspects of Israel's redemption—renewal of election, the messianic king, the new covenant, and so on—culminate in the restoration of Israel's faithful response to God's grace. As noted in previous chapters, faithful response appears as wisdom, righteousness and justice, trust, humility, fear, and praise. In the world of sin, this response becomes distorted. Wisdom degenerates into foolishness. Trust becomes misplaced. Humility becomes hubris. Israel's redemption meant not only the restoration of its existence in the land and the rebuilding of Jerusalem and its temple, but also the restoration of its faithful response to God.

For this restoration it was not enough that God renew the covenant. Israel had disregarded the demands of the original covenant and might do so again. For this reason, the renewed covenant would have to be accompanied by a more direct act of God's creative grace. In the hoped-for future, Israel would have to be transformed. In the words of Jeremiah,

> The days are surely coming, says the LORD, when I will make a new covenant with the house of Israel and the house of Judah. It will not be like the covenant that I made with their ancestors. . . . But this is the covenant that I will make with the house of Israel after those days, says the LORD: I will put my law within them, and I will write it on their hearts *(31:31-33)*.

> I will give them one heart and one way, that they may fear me for all time, for their own good and the good of their children after them. I will make an everlasting covenant with them, never to draw back from doing good to them; and I will put the fear of me in their hearts, so that they may not turn from me *(32:39-40)*.

Jeremiah saw that the redeemed Israel would need a different sort of covenant, one accompanied by the transforming power of God's creative grace. Israel's hope, therefore, lay in a work of God whereby each member of the community would have a heartfelt and God-given desire to obey God's command. In this work, God would write the law on Israel's heart and give Israel an undivided heart that would fear God forever.

In Ezekiel's writings, the promise of a new heart was accompanied by the promise of a new spirit:

> I will sprinkle clean water upon you, and you shall be clean from all your uncleannesses, and from all your idols I will cleanse you. A new heart I will give you, and a new spirit I will put within you; and I will remove from your body the heart of stone and give you a heart of flesh. I will put my spirit within you, and make you follow my statutes and be careful to observe my ordinances *(36:25-27)*.

This promise looks forward to the day when God's Spirit would not only give life but also transform God's people so that they would willingly and unfailingly obey God's command. In that day, God would provide Israel with an obedient heart by imparting this new spirit. Obedience would no longer depend solely on human decision but would be inspired directly by God's Spirit. In the giving of this new spirit, God's grace would prove itself sovereign over humankind's inclination to disobey.

The restoration of Israel's faithful response to God meant the triumph of wisdom over foolishness. Foolishness, we recall, is not simply practical stupidity or even moral depravity. It is human existence that is out of step with the moral and practical order that God creates. In redemption Israel would live according to the knowledge and fear of God. The victory of wisdom over foolishness would mean the restoration of the created world's moral order and humankind's renewed harmony with creation.

Israel's redemption implies also the victory of righteousness and justice over wickedness and injustice. "As the earth brings forth its shoots, and as a garden causes what is sown in it to spring up, so the LORD God will cause righteousness and praise to spring up before all the nations" (Isa. 61:11). As we have seen, wisdom and righteousness are closely related, for both involve obedience to God. But righteousness has a special connection to the idea of covenant. The renewal of Israel's status as the elect and covenant people of God would result in a renewed demand for righteousness and justice. But, as we have also seen, this righteousness and justice would be the result of grace in the gift of the new heart and spirit. By this heart and spirit, Israel would be able to practice righteousness and justice and would delight in practicing them.

Israel's redemption would also bring about a renewal of Israel's faithful trust in God. Formerly, Israel's trust had often been placed in foreign gods. But in the hoped-for future, God's sovereign grace would bring about the elimination of those gods and would direct Israel's trust back to God. Moreover, not only Israel but the entire world would be summoned to place trust in God: "Turn to me and be saved, all the ends of the earth! For I am God, and there is no other" (Isa. 45:22). Trust, in Israel's future, then, would rest on the conviction that Israel's God alone is God and that nothing else is divine. Previously Israel had been tempted to put its trust in idols because of the belief that they represented true divinities. But redeemed Israel would come to know that God alone is divine and that only Israel's God is a suitable object of trust.

God's grace would also return Israel to a spirit of humility. In the words of Zephaniah, "On that day . . . I will remove from your midst your proudly exultant ones, you shall no longer be haughty in my holy mountain. For I will leave in the midst of you a people humble and lowly" (3:11-12). We notice in this passage that Israel's humility will, like other aspects of its renewed response to God, be the result of God's sovereign grace. It is God who will bring humility to Israel.

The obverse of humility is thankfulness. The same redemption that would transform Israel's pride into humility would give it a spirit of thanksgiving: "You will say in that day: I will give thanks to you, O LORD, for though you were angry with me, your anger turned away, and you comforted me. . . . And you will say in that day: Give thanks to the LORD, call on his name" (Isa. 12:1, 4). After judgment, Israel would again render thanks to God. But in that day thanks would be offered because of the redemption that God had accomplished.

Alongside the renewal of humility and thankfulness is the restoration of the fear of God. As previously noted, in the world of sin, fear is replaced by an overfamiliarity with God. This goes hand in hand with the idolatrous tendency to try to control the revelation of God. By worshiping a god that is familiar to us, we control that god. We are thus able to live comfortably in the world of sin that we have created. Redemption signifies that Israel would once again fear God and would once again experience God as the holy one who even in revelation is hidden. The Book of Isaiah persistently identifies Israel's redeemer as the holy one (41:14, 16, 20, and elsewhere). It also announces that in the restoration "They will sanctify my name; they will sanctify the Holy One of Jacob, and will stand in awe of the God of Israel" (29:23). After the redemption, Israel would again have a lively sense of awe and would again regard God as a holy reality.

The restoration of Israel would also renew Israel's capacity to praise God. As we have seen, praise is an essential part of our faithful response to God. But in the world of sin, praise becomes distorted as we set our love on created things so that we can secure for ourselves God's presence and revelation. Israel's redemption would mean more than just the elimination of its idols. It meant additionally that Israel would no longer try to control the revelation of God by its own efforts. On the contrary, in the hoped-for future, God would freely reveal the divine presence. As a result of the renewed revelation of God and its purification from idolatry, Israel would once again praise God and glorify God: "Sing to the LORD a new song, his praise from the end of the earth! Let the sea roar and all that fills it, the coastlands and their inhabitants. . . . Let them give glory to the LORD and declare his praise in the coastlands (Isa. 42:10, 12).

▶ ISRAEL'S HISTORY AND HOPE

The promised redemption was not completely fulfilled in the course of Israel's history. As a result, hope is an essential aspect of the doctrine of grace.

The prophets of Israel's exile and redemption painted a vivid picture of Israel's future and of the effects of God's sovereign grace. However, their prophecies were only partially realized in Israel's history. Israel was indeed freed from its exile in Babylon. The Persian empire, which conquered the Babylonians, allowed those Israelites who wanted to return to the land of Israel to do so. Jerusalem and the Temple were rebuilt and Israel resumed an existence in its own land. However, the more far-reaching expectations were not realized. Israel had a measure of autonomy but was subject to the Persian and subsequent empires. In the sad words of Ezra, "God . . . has left us a remnant, and given us a stake in his holy place, in order that he may brighten our eyes and grant us a little sustenance in our slavery. For we are slaves" (9:8-9). The Temple was rebuilt; however, it was not the glorious building that Ezekiel envisioned. Contrary to expectations, the nations did not come to Jerusalem to worship God and they did not bring their wealth into the Temple. Israel remained a small, poor part of succeeding empires.

The fact that Israel's history did not conform to the prophets' promises led Israel to the principle of *hope* and gave its faith an orientation to the future. Jeremiah, for instance, announced: "Surely I know the plans I have for you, says the LORD, plans for your welfare and not for harm, to give you a future with hope" (29:11). This verse states briefly the doctrine of grace. God's grace is the creative power that, in the world of sin, creates a hopeful future. In exile, Israel was tempted to look back to the destructive judgment of God. But the message of grace is that God is not only a wrathful judge but also the power that re-creates us and gives us a future.

The principle of hope means that, although sin corrupts the good creation of God, it does not have the final word, for God is the one who makes all things new (Rev. 21:5). As we have noted, God's creative activity is not only about the beginning of the world but also about accomplishing God's end, which is fellowship. Hope, therefore, is an essential aspect of the Christian faith, for it reminds us that the God who is love, who wills fellowship with us, is the creative presence among us and re-creates our world after the devastation of sin, even if we do not experience the full extent of that re-creation in our lifetime.

Hope anticipates the restoration of creation. The flood story of Gen. 8—9 provides us with a prototype of the world's ultimate redemption. In this story, God allows the created world to revert to a chaotic state as the water overcomes the dry land and life is extinguished. But after this chaos-inducing judgment, God brings about a re-creation. Once again a mighty wind blows over the waters as in Gen. 1, causing the water to subside (8:1) and dry land to appear. Once again God renews the mandate to be fruitful and multiply (8:17; 9:1) and blesses the creation (8:22). We can see this pattern repeatedly in the Bible: out of chaos resulting from sin and judgment, God creates the world anew.

Hope thereby signals the ultimate demise of the world of sin. For the Book of Revelation the new heaven and earth are the end of alienation between God and humankind: "See, the home of God is among mortals. He will dwell with them; they will be his peoples, and God himself will be with them" (21:3). The new creation, then, is about the eschatological triumph of God's creative activity and sovereign grace in the world and the destruction of the world of sin that we have made for ourselves.

▶ THE EXTENT OF GOD'S GRACE

Grace is freely given to every human being as God seeks to create fellowship.

So far we have been discussing the revelation of God to Israel and the triumph of God's grace over Israel's sin. However, it is important to note that God's revelation and grace are not restricted to Israel, even though, understandably, Israel is the primary focus of the Bible's witness to God.

Every nation and every human being is the object of God's grace; there are no limits to God's will to fellowship. Isaiah, for instance, foresaw a day when "Israel will be the third with Egypt and Assyria, a blessing in the midst of the earth, whom the LORD of hosts has blessed, saying "Blessed be Egypt my people, and Assyria the work of my hands, and Israel my heritage" (19:24-25). This was an extraordinary promise, for in Isaiah's day the northern portion of Israel was destroyed by Assyria and the southern portion nearly destroyed. Yet Isaiah saw that God's will to fellowship extended even to Israel's historic enemies.

The Christian tradition has two terms for describing the universality of God's grace. One is *common grace.* This term has been articulated in the Reformed tradition, represented today by the Presbyterian and other churches. *Common grace* signifies the presence of God's grace in the entire world, as God moves every human heart and thus prevents us from doing as much evil as we otherwise would. It signifies also that God's grace enables human beings to overcome, to some extent, the destructive effects of sin and to create societies and cultures that, although flawed by sin, allow human life to take place. The term *common grace* reminds us that human achievements for good should be understood in the context of God's grace and not merely as the result of human striving.

The other term, one favored by churches in the Wesleyan tradition, for describing the universality of grace is *prevenient grace. Prevenient* is based on the Latin word for *preceding.* Prevenient grace encompasses much of what the Reformed tradition has affirmed about common grace. Prevenience signifies that God's grace always precedes human action. In seeking fellowship, God always takes the initiative with human beings; we, in turn, respond to God. The idea of prevenient grace ensures that we see the fulfillment of our eschatological destiny as a work of God to which we have responded and not as a human accomplishment.

The prevenience of grace means also that grace enables us to faithfully respond to God. God is always seeking to draw us into fellowship by eliciting our faithful response. Often human beings turn away from God and refuse to respond. Nonetheless, God's grace makes it possible for us to respond and draws us into response. That is why it is more appropriate to speak of free grace than of free will. The idea of free will tells us that human response to God is an authentic act of the human person and is not forced upon us by God. But it is more important to emphasize that our response to God is elicited and made possible by God's grace. Our freedom, in other words, is a gift of God's grace. Our response is neither an act that we initiate nor an act that we accomplish on the basis of our human capacities.

PREVENIENT GRACE IN THE WESLEYAN TRADITION

The creeds in our tradition assert that "we have no power to do good works, pleasant and acceptable to God, without the grace of God by Christ preventing [i.e., preceding] us, that we may have a good will, and working with us, when we have that good will;" that "through Jesus Christ the prevenient grace of God makes possible what humans in self-effort cannot do;" and that "grace of God through Jesus Christ is freely bestowed upon all people, enabling all who will to turn from sin to righteousness."

The universality of grace explains how it was possible for Jesus to speak of the good Samaritan. This person was not a Jew and, of course, not a Christian. Yet the Samaritan "was moved with pity" (Luke 10:33). Although outside the community of Israel, he nevertheless acted rightly and thus exhibited a faithful response to God's grace. Likewise, Acts portrays Cornelius as "a devout man who feared God with all his household; he gave alms generously to the people and prayed constantly to God" (10:2). Cornelius was neither a Jew nor a Christian. He was a Roman soldier. Yet his life shows us that he had responded faithfully to God's grace. It was possible for the Samaritan and Cornelius to be faithful to God because God's grace is given to everyone and seeks to elicit from everyone a faithful response to God. As a result, "God shows no partiality, but in every nation anyone who fears him and does what is right is acceptable to [God]" (10:34-35).

Every human being, therefore, is in a state of grace. Not everyone is in a state of saving grace, for not everyone responds faithfully to God. But no one is completely cut off from God's grace, which is the creative power of God that comes to everyone, seeking to create fellowship.

DEBATE OVER GRACE IN THE CHRISTIAN TRADITION

Although the churches of the Christian tradition agree on the necessity of grace, Christian history has seen considerable debate on some aspects of the doctrine of grace. As early as the 4th century, theologians were debating about the best way of expressing the relation of grace to human responsibility. Pelagius and his supporters thought of grace as helping us to be faithful to God's command. He believed that human beings had the capacity to obey God but that grace made it far easier for us to obey. Augustine argued that humans have no capacity to obey God and that any good we do is strictly the result of God's grace working in us. In the middle ages theologians used the language of operating and cooperating grace. By this distinction they meant that God's grace initially operates on us without our cooperation, for (agreeing with Augustine) they believed that sin has destroyed our capacity to respond to God. Once grace has become effective in us, they argued, we can then cooperate with God's grace as we mature in the Christian life. In the era of the Reformation, Protestants thought that the Church was putting too much emphasis on cooperation and not enough on operating grace. Accordingly, some Protestants developed a concept that has come to be called irresistible grace. This is simply the concept of operating grace with a reduced emphasis on cooperation. Wesleyan theologians have historically sought to find a balance between operating grace and human cooperation with God's grace.

▶ THE ETHICAL DIMENSION OF FAITH

The doctrine of grace is not only an object of belief but also a truth to be practiced. We practice it by offering to God our faithful response, by cooperating with God in the work of creating fellowship, and by living hopefully.

Because Christian faith is both doctrine and practice, it is important to ask about the ethical dimension of the doctrine of grace.

For one thing, we practice the doctrine of grace by responding to God. It is not enough to believe that God is gracious. It is essential as well to allow God's grace to be effective in our lives. This means exhibiting faithful obedience to God and offering praise and thanksgiving to God.

Second, practicing the doctrine of grace means that we cooperate with God in the task of fulfilling the eschatological destiny of creation, fellowship. Although the fulfillment of this destiny is the work of God, it does not happen without us, for we participate in this fulfillment as we offer to God a faithful response of obedience. But we participate in it also by becoming mediators of God's grace in the world. God's grace comes to us through various media, including the Bible, preaching, and sacraments. But it also comes to us through the mediation of other human beings who have become vehicles of divine grace. We are obliged, therefore, to mature in our faithfulness so that we become channels of God's grace to others.

Finally, we practice the doctrine of grace by living with hope. The Christian faith has an inescapably eschatological character because the promise of redemption, made to Israel, still awaits its complete fulfillment. The grace of God, the creative power of God that seeks to create fellowship, is still at work. To practice this grace is to overcome despair with the hope that God's sovereign grace will indeed triumph and transform the world of sin into the world of God's creation.

SUMMARY STATEMENTS

1. Grace is the creative power of God, manifested in the forms of judgment and redemption in the world of sin.

2. In the world of sin, God's holiness is experienced as alienation from the holy God. God's wisdom is experienced as discipline. God's righteousness is experienced as God's wrath. And God's faithfulness becomes God's commitment to renew the covenant with Israel.

3. The doctrine of grace affirms that redemption is grounded in the wisdom, righteousness, and faithfulness of the God who in love comes into the world of sin.

4. Mercy, not wrath and judgment, is the final word in God's relation with Israel.

5. Israel's redemption required its repentance, which embraces confession and amendment of life.

6. The redemption of Israel was the exercise of God's creative power. Redemption, accordingly, is a new act of creation by the God of grace.

7. The grace of God—God's redemptive movement into the world of sin—restored Israel's status as the elect people of God and renewed the covenant with Israel. As a new creation, this renewal looked forward to the transformation of the peoples' hearts.

8. The new creation effected by the God of grace would culminate in God's Lordship over the world through a hoped-for messianic king.

9. The hoped-for redemption of Israel included the restoration of its response to God. Restored Israel would exhibit wisdom, righteousness and justice, trust, humility, fear, and praise.

10. The promised redemption was not completely fulfilled in the course of Israel's history. As a result, hope is an essential aspect of the doctrine of grace.

11. Grace is the creative power of God that overcomes sin. It is freely given to every human being as God seeks to create fellowship.

12. The doctrine of grace is not only an object of belief but also a truth to be practiced. We practice it by offering to God our faithful response, by cooperating with God in the work of creating fellowship, and by living hopefully.

QUESTIONS FOR REFLECTION

1. How is God's judgment manifested in the world today?

2. With respect to redemption, what is the relation of Israel to the Christian Church?

3. How does defining grace as the creative power of God affect our understanding of the doctrine of creation?

UNIT 3

THE NEW CREATION

EIGHT

JESUS AND THE KINGDOM OF GOD

OBJECTIVES

Your study of this chapter should help you to understand:

1. The way in which Jesus Christ fulfilled Israel's hope of redemption.

2. How Jesus Christ's message was a message of both judgment and good news.

3. How, in the ministry of Jesus, the kingdom of God was both a present and a future reality.

KEY WORDS TO UNDERSTAND

Age of the Spirit

Kingdom of God

Messiah

Messianic king

QUESTIONS TO CONSIDER AS YOU READ

1. To what extent should we think of Jesus as a first-century Jew speaking to other first-century Jews?

2. In what ways was Jesus' message a continuation of the Old Testament and in which ways was it a departure from the Old Testament?

3. What is the kingdom of God?

O Come, thou radiant Morning Star,
Again in human darkness shine!
Arise resplendent from afar!
Assert thy royalty divine:
Thy sway o'er all the earth maintain,
And now begin thy glorious reign.

Thy kingdom, Lord, we long to see:
Thy scepter o'er the nations shake;
T'erect that final monarchy,
Edom for thy possession take;
Take (for thou didst their ransom find)
The purchased souls of all mankind.

Now let thy chosen ones appear,
And valiantly the truth maintain;
Dispread thy gracious kingdom here;
Fly on the rebel sons of men;
Seize them with faith divinely bold,
And force the world into thy fold!

This hymn by the Wesleys speaks of God's kingdom. It is a prayer that God's rule will be extended to every corner of the earth. As we saw in chapter seven, the idea of the kingdom of God was a central part of Israel's redemption and hope. This hymn similarly locates God's rule in the context of redemption, as it refers to human souls ransomed by God. These redeemed souls are a sign of God's rule, for they represent a part of the created world that obeys God and "valiantly the truth maintain[s]." The hymn also reminds us ("force the world into thy fold") that God's kingdom is an expression of God's sovereign grace and that creation's destiny will be fulfilled.

▶ INTRODUCTION

Israel's prophets looked forward to Israel's full redemption. In the future, they proclaimed, God would re-create Israel, renew its covenant and its status as the holy, elect people, rule the earth through the messianic king, and restore Israel's faithful response. Jesus Christ is the fulfillment of this prophetic promise.

The life, death, and resurrection of Jesus Christ was an act of God's grace and was the revelation of God in the world of sin; for in Jesus Christ the holy and loving God came into the world. God did not come into the world in a general way but instead appeared in the world in Jesus of Nazareth, a Jew from Galilee. Because he was a first-century Jew, the grace and revelation of God took shape in Jesus' preaching about Israel's hope of redemption. In particular, Jesus Christ came preaching about the **kingdom of God** (Mark 1:15). This preaching was the announcement of good news—the gospel.

▶ THE KINGDOM AND THE NEW CREATION

In Jesus Christ God came into the world to create fellowship in a new act of creation and redemption. The kingdom of God is this new creation.

The Book of Isaiah had spoken of God creating new heavens and a new earth and of doing a new thing. For the gospel writers, this hope for a new creation was fulfilled in Jesus' preaching about the kingdom of God. The kingdom was such a radically new reality, that, like new wine, it could not at all be contained by the old reality (Mark 2:22).

This stark contrast between the old and the new helps us understand Jesus' saying: "Among those born of women no one has arisen greater than John the Baptist; yet the least in the kingdom of heaven is greater than he" (Matt. 11:11). Jesus was saying that, in a way, even John belonged to the old order. He announced the kingdom as a prophet but was still embedded in the old order.

The contrast between the old and the new also explains Jesus' harsh words to his family:

> They said to him, "Your mother and brothers and sisters are outside, asking for you." And he replied, "Who are my mother and my brothers?" And looking at those who sat around him, he said, "Here are my mother and my brothers! Whoever does the will of God is my brother and sister and mother" *(Mark 3:32-35).*

The newness of the kingdom meant that even family relations had to be rethought—one's biological family differed from the new family that one would have in the kingdom: "There is no one who has left house or brothers or sisters or mother or father or children or fields, for my sake . . . who will not receive a hundredfold now in this age—houses, brothers and sisters, mothers and children" (10:29-30).

The newness of the kingdom meant also that one's responsibility to God's command would change: "You have heard that it was said . . . 'You shall not murder'; . . . But I say to you that if you are angry with a brother or sister, you will be liable to judgment" (Matt. 5:21-22). Although Moses' law continued in force, the newness of the kingdom brought about a radical reinterpretation of the law's significance.

▶ THE KINGDOM AND THE RENEWAL OF ELECTION

The kingdom of God in Jesus' preaching was an affirmation of Israel's status as the elect people of God; however, it was also an extension of God's grace and mercy to the entire world.

The kingdom of God was a part of Israel's hope for a secure, on-going national existence. This point is confirmed by Zechariah's song, which describes Jesus' significance for Israel:

> Blessed be the Lord God of Israel, for he has looked favorably on his people and redeemed them. He has raised up a mighty savior for us in the house of his servant David, as he spoke through the mouth of his holy prophets from of old that we would be saved from our enemies and from the hand of all who hate us. Thus he has shown the mercy promised to our ancestors, and has remembered his holy covenant, the oath that he swore to our ancestor Abraham (*Luke 2:68-73*).

The ministry of Jesus was grounded in the covenant with Israel; it thus confirmed Israel's status as the elect people of God. So, we are not surprised to hear the disciples asking the resurrected Jesus, "Lord, is this the time when you will restore the kingdom to Israel?" (Acts 1:6). This was a completely reasonable question because the kingdom of God meant the full restoration of Israel. This restoration was predicated on Israel's election.

However, Jesus was quite critical of any misunderstanding of Israel's election. He told the parable of the vineyard (Matt. 21:33-41), the message of which is that "the kingdom of God will be taken away from you and given to a people that produces the fruits of the kingdom" (v. 43). Being a part of the elect people of God, therefore, did not guarantee entry into the kingdom of God. On the contrary, only those who exhibited good fruit would be accepted. As Jesus said, "Many are called but few are chosen" (22:14).

The emphasis on fruits signaled that the Kingdom was open to everyone, even those who are not a part of the elect people: "Many will come from east and west and will eat with Abraham and Isaac and Jacob in the kingdom of heaven, while the heirs of the kingdom will be thrown into the outer darkness" (Matt. 8:11-12). The Kingdom thus welcomes everyone who exhibits the fruits of the Kingdom, as when the Roman centurion demonstrated faith in Jesus' power and was commended by Jesus (Luke 7:9). For entrance into the Kingdom, repentance and faith were more important than being an Israelite.

▶ The Kingdom and Israel's Holiness

The kingdom of God in Jesus' preaching meant the renewal of holiness; however, Jesus' preaching about holiness emphasized the centrality of righteousness, mercy, and justice.

As we have seen in previous chapters, Israel's corporate holiness as a people was grounded in their status as the elect people of God. The holiness and purity of Israel was accordingly an important matter in the ministry of Jesus. He criticized the commerce taking place in the Temple precincts (Mark 11:15-16) because he perceived it to be a desecration of the Temple's holiness.

However, Jesus directed the impulse toward holiness in a new direction when he declared "There is nothing outside a person that by going in can defile" (Mark 7:15). Mark's Gospel drew the obvious conclusion from this saying: "Thus he declared all foods clean" (v. 19). Jesus, in other words, had declared the food laws and the purity laws of the Old Testament null and void. Neither eating with unwashed hands nor consuming unclean animals would make one impure. On the contrary, "It is what comes out of a person that defiles. For it is from within, from the human heart, that evil intentions come" (vv. 20-21). Regarding purity and impurity in this way, Jesus had no compunction about touching lepers and corpses in the act of healing. Jews would normally strive to avoid such contact, for it would render them unclean. But Jesus saw that physical contact with lepers or unclean animals does not transmit impurity.

Like every faithful Jew, therefore, Jesus was greatly concerned about holiness and purity. However, the holiness and purity demanded in the Kingdom differed from that required by the law of Moses. Holiness and purity in the Kingdom meant freedom from "fornication, theft, murder, adultery, avarice, wickedness, deceit, licentiousness, envy, slander, pride, [and] folly" (Mark 7:21-22).

▶ THE KINGDOM AND THE BLESSINGS OF THE NEW AGE

The kingdom of God in the preaching of Jesus brought with it the blessings that the prophets foretold.

The prophets had looked forward to an age when the curse of war would be past and when prosperity and health would be enjoyed by all. The kingdom of God in Jesus' ministry was God's response to those prophetic longings.

It is no accident that Matthew's Gospel presents Jesus' first sermon as an announcement of the blessings of the new age: "Blessed are the poor in spirit, for theirs is the kingdom of God" (5:3). The approach of the Kingdom meant that the poor in spirit, the meek, the merciful, and others were already in a state of blessedness. They were blessed precisely because they were participating in the kingdom of God, which was God's rule of peace, health, and prosperity for Israel and the world.

There were various aspects of the blessings of the Kingdom. One aspect was the casting out of demons and other forms of healing. At one level, this was a humanitarian gesture, aimed at relieving human suffering. But at another and more important level this miracle signified the liberation of human beings from the evil spiritual powers that gripped humankind. That is the meaning of the parable of the strong man: "No one can enter a strong man's house and plunder his property without first tying up the strong man; then indeed the house can be plundered" (Mark 3:27). In the parable Jesus is the thief who has bound Satan—the strong man—and proceeds to plunder Satan's goods by liberating those who were oppressed by evil powers. Casting out the demons, therefore, signi-fied the defeat of Satan. By binding the strong man and effecting libera-tion for humankind, Jesus had in principle secured the blessing of free-dom from oppression.

Another blessing of the kingdom was found in eating. The Book of Isaiah had proclaimed that "On this mountain the LORD of hosts will make for all peoples a feast of rich food" (Isa. 25:6). Jesus' ministry did not provide a literal fulfillment of this promise. But, in miraculously feeding the multitudes, Jesus did provide an anticipation of the great banquet. In feeding the 4,000 and the 5,000, Jesus was performing an act that looked forward to the fulfillment of Isaiah's vision. Although Jesus did not feed the world in these acts, they announced that the great ban-quet of the Lord was in the process of being fulfilled.

The Kingdom also signaled the end of unnecessary social distinc-tions. The Kingdom, for instance, meant a new freedom for women. In contrast to the customs of his society, Jesus accepted women as disciples and accepted their support (Luke 8:1-3). Women made the journey to Jerusalem with Jesus and the Twelve (Luke 23:49) and were witnesses of the resurrection (Luke 24:1-10).

Finally and above all, the blessings of the kingdom included for-giveness of sin. By forgiving sin, Jesus erased people's alienation from God and prepared them for the judgment that would accompany the Kingdom. Nothing better illustrates the extravagant grace and blessings of the Kingdom than the way in which Jesus freely announced forgive-ness with no condition except repentance.

However, it is important to keep in mind that the blessings of the Kingdom were good news only to those who embraced the Kingdom with faith, repentance, and humility. They were not good news for those who would not embrace the Kingdom; the obverse of the good news was strife as the Kingdom encountered resistance: "Do not think that I have come to bring peace to the earth; I have not come to bring peace, but a sword. For I have come to set a man against his father, and a daughter against her mother" (Matt. 10:34-35). The good news of the Kingdom, therefore, was an instrument of judgment, for it compelled people to de-cide for or against it and thus was a cause of division.

▶ THE KINGDOM AND THE AGE OF THE SPIRIT

The kingdom of God in the preaching of Jesus signaled the arrival of the age of the Spirit foretold by the prophets.

As we saw in chapter seven, the prophets looked forward to the day when God's Spirit would be bestowed on Israel, enabling God's people to render perfect obedience to God and to love God with an undivided heart. The ministry of Jesus and the approach of the kingdom of God signaled the fulfillment of this hope.

The preaching of the Kingdom was thus the dawning of the age of the Spirit. Luke's Gospel describes this dawn: John the Baptist was filled with the Spirit before birth (1:16). His parents were likewise filled with the Spirit (vv. 41, 67). Simeon, a righteous and devout person, knew by the Holy Spirit that he would not die before seeing the messianic king (2:26). In these examples Luke's Gospel shows that the *age of the Spirit* was approaching with the coming of the Kingdom.

JESUS: CONCEIVED BY THE HOLY SPIRIT, BORN OF THE VIRGIN MARY

The creeds in our tradition affirm that Jesus was "conceived by the Holy Spirit, born of the Virgin Mary." It is easy to misunderstand the significance of Jesus' virginal conception. First, it should not be confused with the idea of the immaculate conception, which is the Roman Catholic teaching that Mary was conceived without the guilt and depravity caused by original sin. Second, it is not the basis of Jesus' sinlessness; the Church affirms Jesus' sinlessness because of his identity as God. Third, it does not in any way compromise Jesus' full humanity. It is not the belief that Jesus was partially divine and partially human. The idea of the virginal conception is principally the New Testament's affirmation that the entirety of Jesus' life, including his conception, transpired in and through the power of the Holy Spirit.

Above all, it was Jesus Christ who represented the age of the Spirit. His conception involved the Spirit's power: "The Holy Spirit will come upon you, and the power of the Most High will overshadow you; therefore the child to be born will be holy; he will be called Son of God" (Luke 1:35). Through him Israel would receive the Spirit, for he would "baptize you with the Holy Spirit and with fire" (3:16). Most important, Jesus' ministry was conducted in the power of the Spirit. This is part of the significance of the Spirit's descending on Jesus in his baptism (Luke 3:21-22). By this anointing with the Spirit, Jesus received the power by which "he went about doing good and healing all who were oppressed by the devil" (Acts 10:38). In short, it was by the power of the Spirit that Jesus actualized the Kingdom (Matt. 12:28).

And yet, as with the preaching of the Kingdom, the dawn of the age of the Spirit was a sign of judgment, for it compelled decision and divided Jesus' hearers into two groups—those who recognized the coming age of the Spirit and those who did not. Some did not recognize the Spirit, for they believed that Jesus derived his miraculous power from Satan (Matt. 9:34). The approach of the age of the Spirit was not, then, apparent to all. Like the kingdom of God, the age of the Spirit was hidden even as it was revealed in the words and deeds of Jesus. It could be mistaken for a demonic reality by those who were not disposed to believe in Jesus.

▶ THE KINGDOM AND THE MESSIANIC KING

Jesus fulfilled Israel's hope for a messianic king; however, his embodiment of this hope did not conform to common expectations about the messianic king.

Israel's hope was intimately connected to the idea of a future **messianic king** who would rule over a kingdom of peace, righteousness, and justice. Jesus was the fulfillment of that hope. As the angel announced to Mary, "He will be great . . . and the Lord God will give to him the throne of his ancestor David. He will reign over the house of Jacob forever, and of his kingdom there will be no end" (Luke 1:32-33).

However, Jesus' messianic kingship contradicted the expectations of many in his society. John the Baptist, for instance, wondered whether Jesus really was the **Messiah,** for the reports that he received of Jesus' activity did not correspond to his concept of the messianic king (Luke 7:18-19).

Similarly, Peter reacted strongly and negatively when Jesus began talking about suffering and dying in Jerusalem (Mark 8:31-32). The problem was that the Kingdom that Jesus was announcing was a peculiar sort of kingdom. For one thing, unlike ordinary kingdoms it could not be physically perceived: "The kingdom of God is not coming with things that can be observed; nor will they say, 'Look, here it is!' or 'There it is!'" (Luke 17:20-21). For another thing, the working of the Kingdom differed from ordinary kingdoms, with their bureaucracies and armies. Everyone in the ancient world knew how ordinary kingdoms operated. But no one could know how the kingdom of God worked: "The kingdom of God is as if someone would scatter seed on the ground, . . . and the seed would sprout and grow, he does not know how" (Mark 4:26-27). The kingdom thus worked in effective yet unobtrusive ways, like yeast, which "a woman took and mixed in with three measures of flour until all of it was leavened" (Matt. 13:33).

The kingdom of God differed also in the sort of power exercised in it: "Among the Gentiles those whom they recognize as their rulers lord it over them, and their great ones are tyrants over them. But it is not so among you; but whoever wishes to become great among you must be your servant, and whoever wishes to be first must be slave of all" (Mark 10:42-44). Disciples of the Kingdom were not to call anyone on earth their father, for in the ancient world fatherhood was a position of power and domination. But in the kingdom of God, power was to be of a different sort. The dominating, powerful position of father was to be done away with.

The fact that Jesus' messianic kingship contrasted with the expectations of many explains why Jesus continually ordered people not to disclose anything about him, as in Mark 8:29-30. Although Jesus was indeed the promised messianic king, his kingship was part of the new thing that God was doing and therefore diverged from popular expectations. Publicly announcing that he was the messianic king could only encourage those with various agendas to use Jesus to their own ends. Consequently, he strove to keep his identity hidden so that he could define it himself through his deeds and words. In this way his ministry was a judgment upon the common conceptions of the messianic king.

▶ THE KINGDOM AND THE RULE OF GOD

The kingdom of God is God's rule in the world of sin. But in the ministry of Jesus this rule was both revealed and hidden.

Israel's hope embraced the belief that God would rule not only in heaven but also on earth. Israel looked forward to every nation coming to Jerusalem to learn from God and God's righteousness filling the earth. The kingdom of God that Jesus announced was the fulfillment of this hope. In the words and actions of Jesus, the kingdom of God was taking place—God's rule was being effected.

Jesus made the actuality and the presence of the kingdom clear when, after reading Isaiah 61, he said, "Today this scripture has been fulfilled in your hearing" (Luke 4:21). Likewise, when John's disciples asked Jesus whether he were the promised one, Jesus responded by acting in accordance with Isa. 61: "Go and tell John what you have seen and heard: the blind receive their sight, the lame walk, the lepers are cleansed, the deaf hear, the dead are raised, the poor have good news brought to them" (Luke 7:22). In other words, Jesus demonstrated the presence of the Kingdom by doing deeds of power that fulfilled the words of Isa. 61. In Jesus' preaching and deeds, the Kingdom had arrived in power.

At the same time, as the parables show us, the Kingdom was in a sense hidden. Jesus provided no incontrovertible signs attesting the Kingdom's reality, except the miracles, which some thought were rooted in demonic power, and the parables, which conveyed the truth of the Kingdom in a hidden way. The Kingdom was not a place that could be identified; it was instead found wherever God's power was manifested. In short, the kingdom of God had come with power but it remained hidden to those who did not embrace it in a spirit of obedient belief.

▶ THE KINGDOM AND THE RENEWAL OF FAITHFUL RESPONSE TO GOD

Jesus' preaching about the kingdom of God was a call for Israel to offer a faithful and obedient response to God. As a call, it forced his audience to decide. It was, accordingly, both a call and an instrument of judgment.

THE CALL FOR WISDOM

The kingdom of God called for wisdom and signaled God's judgment on foolishness.

Jesus denounced foolishness, as when he told the story of the rich person who said to himself, "Soul, you have ample goods laid up for many years; relax, eat, drink, be merry" (Luke 12:19). Jesus' exasperated response ("You fool!") was prompted by the rich person's life, which was conducted in a way that took no account of God: "So it is with those who store up treasures for themselves but are not rich toward God" (v. 21). Consequently, an appreciable portion of the gospel narrative is occupied by Jesus' denunciation of foolish and therefore wicked conduct, as when he condemned those who fail to show love and compassion (Matt. 25:41-46).

Because Jesus was the one in whose deeds the Kingdom was being actualized, he could view foolishness not only as ignorance of God but also in relation to his ministry: "Everyone then who hears these words of mine and acts on them will be like a wise man who built his house on rock. . . . And everyone who hears these words of mine and does not act on them will be like a foolish man who built his house on sand" (Matt. 7:24-27).

This passage shows us that foolishness and wisdom were no longer defined by a general notion of conformity with God's law. On the contrary, they were now defined by people's response to the proclamation of the kingdom of God. The new thing that God was doing was of such momentous importance that the fool could now be understood as the one who rejects the Kingdom, while the height of wisdom now consisted in a faithful embrace of the kingdom of God and its mercy.

THE CALL FOR RIGHTEOUSNESS

The kingdom of God called for righteousness and signaled God's judgment on unrighteousness and injustice.

Jesus' message included a strong denunciation of unrighteousness and injustice. However, the message of the gospel was that those not living faithfully according to the law of Moses could enter the kingdom by trusting

Jesus and his message. Paradoxically, then, Jesus' denunciation was direct-ed at those who were righteous according to Moses' law. Jesus charged them with being unrighteous because they did not embrace Jesus and his message and also because they failed to obey God's higher commands.

In Matthew's Gospel these seemingly righteous people are described as hypocrites, for, although punctilious in their observation of Moses' law, they lacked humility and instead sought honor. Whether in giving alms (6:2-4), prayer (vv. 5-6), or fasting (vv. 16-18), their acts of right-eousness were performed in order to gain honor and public acclaim for themselves. The kingdom of God, in contrast, called for a practice of righteousness that would not bring honor and acclaim—alms, prayer, and fasting must all be done unobtrusively. In the kingdom of God, righteousness was not to be a means of building a fine reputation.

Additionally, the righteous fell short of the righteousness of God's kingdom because they failed to observe "the weightier matters of the law: justice and mercy and faith" (Matt. 23:23). Although upholding the sanctity of the Sabbath, they failed to see that "the Sabbath was made for humankind, and not humankind for the Sabbath" (Mark 2:27). Al-though abiding by the law's prescriptions about divorce, they did not dis-cern God's intention (see Matt. 19:3-9). Although they maintained ritual purity and separation from unclean things, they could not see that "what-ever goes into a person from the outside cannot defile" and that "it is what comes out of a person that defiles" (Mark 7:18-19).

Discipleship in the kingdom of God, therefore, demands a higher sort of righteousness than that practiced by the righteous (Matt. 5:20). It requires disciples to abandon all pretensions. Accordingly, Jesus poured scorn on those who tried to make themselves righteous in God's sight. He directed the parable about the Pharisee and the tax collector "to some who trusted in themselves that they were righteous and regarded others with contempt" (Luke 18:9). Jesus condemned the Pharisee and said of the tax collector, "This man went down to his home justified rather than the other" (v. 14). Similarly, the problem with the lawyer who asked, "What must I do to inherit eternal life?" was not his failure to obey Moses' law. It was that he fell short of the righteousness of God's king-dom because he wanted to justify himself before God (Luke 10:25-29).

RIGHTEOUSNESS AND JUSTICE IN THE
NEW TESTAMENT

The English language has two words, *righteousness* and *justice*. In the New Testament, these words almost always translate one Greek word, *dikaiosune*. Translations make use of the two English words because there is a verb, *justify*, associated with justice, whereas there is no commonly used English verb associated with righteousness. Students of Christian theology should keep in mind that, in the New Testament, righteousness and justice usually have the same meaning.

The higher righteousness requires also that we bear fruit in the form of works of love. That is the point of Matt. 25:31-46: "I was hungry and you gave me food, I was thirsty and you gave me something to drink, I was a stranger and you welcomed me, I was naked and you gave me clothing, I was sick and you took care of me, I was in prison and you visited me" (vv. 35-36). Works of love are the key to the higher righteousness because on them, along with love for God, "hang all the law and the prophets" (22:40). Consequently, disciples must "hunger and thirst for righteousness" (5:6) and must seek it out (6:33).

THE CALL FOR TRUST IN GOD

The kingdom of God called for trust in God and signaled God's judgment on misplaced trust.

Jesus' teaching about foolishness and unrighteousness leads us to another aspect of sin, misplaced trust. The foolish rich person, for example, was foolish precisely because he placed his trust in wealth instead of in God. Consequently, Jesus taught, "Do not store up for yourselves treasures on earth, where moth and rust consume and where thieves break in and steal; but store up for yourselves treasures in heaven. . . . For where your treasure is, there your heart will be also" (Matt. 6:19-21). Foolishness, therefore, is closely related to misplaced trust for in both cases we locate the center of our existence in something other than God. Accordingly, John the Baptist warned his hearers about trusting in their Jewish heritage as a substitute for authentic repentance (Matt. 3:9). Like the rich fool, those who trusted in their Jewish heritage built their lives on the basis of their status instead of living for and in the presence of God. Hence the gospel warning about the impossibility of serving two masters (Luke 16:13). This passage is a warning against placing our trust in anything except God.

The alternative to misplaced trust is trust in God. In the ministry of Jesus this trust appeared in several ways. At the most basic level, it took the form of trusting God for the daily needs of life and avoiding anxiety:

> Do not worry about your life, what you will eat, or about your body, what you will wear. For life is more than food, and the body more than clothing. . . . Do not keep worrying. For it is the nations of the world that strive after all these things, and your Father knows that you need them *(Luke 12:22-23, 29-30).*

But trust meant additionally having faith in Jesus' power and willingness to work a miracle, even when that faith is as small as a mustard grain or smaller, as in the cry, "I believe; help my unbelief!" (Mark 9:24).

Within the gospel tradition, there are several outstanding examples of trust in God. One of these is Mary, whose uncomprehending submission to God's will ("Here am I, the servant of the Lord; let it be with me according to your word" [Luke 1:38]) has distinguished her among followers of Jesus. Above all, however, it is Jesus whom the Gospels present as the exemplar of trust in God. This is seen especially in the temptation stories and in the narrative of the Garden of Gethsemane. In the temptation stories (Matt. 3:1-10 and Luke 4:1-12), Jesus trusts God and God's call upon him and does not choose the easy path of notoriety. He is likewise utterly loyal to God in his refusal to worship the devil in spite of the colossal reward offered to him. In these narratives, Jesus is presented as one whose trust in God was utterly complete.

The Kingdom's call to trust in God went hand in hand with the necessity of trust in Jesus and his message. The story of Peter walking on the water is paradigmatic on this point. Peter, filled with fear because of the strong wind, cried out for Jesus to save him. Jesus' response is revealing: "You of little faith, why did you doubt?" (Matt. 14:30); it tells us that Jesus is the proper object of faith and trust. Trusting Jesus for deliverance is equivalent to trusting God.

THE CALL FOR HUMILITY

The kingdom of God called for humility and signaled God's judgment on hubris.

Hubris describes the human tendency to think of ourselves as divine—to want to usurp God's position as the Lord and Creator and to elevate ourselves. Jesus encountered *hubris* in several forms. One was the attitude of the righteous who elevated themselves above sinners: "God, I thank you that I am not like other people: thieves, rogues, adulterers, or even like this tax collector" (Luke 18:11). It is notable that it was the tax collector and not the Pharisee who was actually righteous before God. The reason is that "all who exalt themselves will be humbled, but all who humble themselves will be exalted" (v. 14). In the new thing that God was doing, humility was far more important than the Pharisee's fasting and tithing (v. 12). It was not that fasting and tithing were wrong actions; however, they were for the Pharisee a source of pride—they gave him a status that distinguished him from other human beings. His acts of righteousness were grounded in the spirit of hubris.

Jesus encountered hubris also in the attitude of the rich and powerful who used their wealth and power to gain public honor and fame, like the scribes and Pharisees who did "all their deeds to be seen by others. . . . They love to have the place of honor at banquets and the best seats in the synagogues, and to be greeted with respect in the marketplaces, and to have people call them rabbi" (Matt. 23:5-7). Jesus saw that the scribes and Pharisees were using their status as righteous and learned people to elevate themselves.

Jesus' attack on hubris explains also his harsh attitude toward the rich: "Woe to you who are rich, for you have received your consolation. Woe to you who are full now, for you will be hungry" (Luke 6:24-25). The problem with the rich is that their wealth fills them with pride and makes them arrogant. Wealth enables the wealthy, like the Pharisee, to distinguish themselves from others and to elevate themselves above others. The Book of James expands on this reproach by asking, "Is it not the rich who oppress you? Is it not they who drag you into court?" (2:6) and warns: "Come now, you rich people, weep and wail for the miseries that are coming to you. . . . The wages of the laborers who mowed your fields, which you kept back by fraud, cry out" (5:1, 4).

Finally, Jesus' attack on hubris explains his condemnation of those who judge others: "Do not judge, so that you may not be judged. . . . Why do you see the speck in your neighbor's eye, but do not notice the log in your own eye? . . . You hypocrite, first take the log out of your own eye" (Matt. 7:1, 3, 5). Those who judge and condemn others are acting out of the spirit of hubris, for what they are really doing is elevating themselves above others whom they consider to be their spiritual and moral inferiors.

It is because hubris is so opposed to the kingdom of God that Jesus commended humility: "Blessed are the poor in spirit, for theirs is the kingdom of heaven. . . . Blessed are the meek, for they will inherit the earth" (Matt. 5:3, 5). To participate in the kingdom of God is to live by the rule that "the least among all of you is the greatest" (Luke 9:48) and to take up a life characterized by denial of self (see v. 23). However, we should not think of the humility that the Kingdom demands as a matter of abject servility. On the contrary, the life of humility is the life that Jesus exemplified: "Who is greater, the one who is at the table or the one who serves? Is it not the one at the table? But I am among you as one who serves" (22:27). It is, consequently, a life in which no one is elevated above anyone: "You are not to be called rabbi, for you have one teacher, and you are all students. And call no one your father on earth, for you have one Father—the one in heaven. Nor are you to be called instructors, for you have one instructor, the Messiah" (Matt. 23:8-10). The life of humility is a life in which we patiently assume our role as human beings in God's creation and resist the temptation to elevate ourselves above others and into God's place.

THE CALL FOR A RENEWAL OF AWE

The kingdom of God called for a renewal of awe and signaled God's judgment on every attitude of false familiarity toward God.

Familiarity is the phenomenon of creating a god with which we are comfortable and which makes no difficult demands on us. Whereas in authentic worship we serve God, in familiarity, the divine serves our needs.

Jesus encountered the problem of familiarity in people's resistance to the new thing that God was doing. Jesus came upon the scene forgiving sin (Mark 2:5), eating with sinners (v. 15), neglecting fasting (v. 18), and reinterpreting the practice of the Sabbath (vv. 27-28), and other Old Testament laws (7:14-23). In all these acts, Jesus was illustrating the parable of the wineskins: "No one puts new wine into old wineskins; otherwise, the wine will burst the skins, and the wine is lost, and so are the skins; but one puts new wine into fresh wineskins" (2:22). This parable is saying that the old cannot accommodate the new. The kingdom of God—the new thing that God is doing—could not be fit into the framework of the old system of relating to God. In the Kingdom, it was permissible to eat with sinners because salvation no longer depended on strict compliance with the law of Moses. In the Kingdom, the distinction between the righteous and the sinner was replaced by the distinction between the proud and the humble. In the Kingdom, practicing the Sabbath required humanitarian acts. And in the kingdom of God, purity was measured by purity of heart and not by avoiding contact with unclean animals.

The Pharisees' fault was not that they did not follow the law of Moses well enough. Their fault was that their adherence to Moses' law did not allow them to see the new thing that God was doing. Their thinking was so adapted to the contours of Moses' law that they could not recognize the work of God in their midst. They attributed Jesus' power to Satan (Mark 3:22). Failing to recognize God's work, they had no other way of comprehending Jesus. Their problem, briefly stated, was that they were overly familiar with God. Because of their conception of God, they believed that they knew exactly what God demanded and where God's work could be found. Their theological framework could not accommodate a work of God that diverged from their expectations.

By contrast, the Gospels associate the preaching of the Kingdom with a resurgence of awe and the fear of God. At the announcement of Jesus' birth and the vision of angels and the glory of God, the shepherds "were terrified" (Luke 2:9). On seeing Jesus' power, "Amazement seized all of them, and they glorified God and were filled with awe" (5:26). In the presence of Jesus Peter felt a sense of dread: "He fell down at Jesus' knees saying, 'Go away from me, Lord, for I am a sinful man!'" (5:8). Seeing Jesus glorified and enveloped in the cloud of God's presence, the disciples "were terrified" (9:34). In contrast to the Pharisees, the shepherds, Peter, and the others who embraced the Kingdom were not in the clutches of the spirit of familiarity. Accordingly, their response to the approach of the Kingdom was not unbelief but instead awe and the fear of God.

THE CALL FOR PRAISE

The kingdom of God called for praising of God and signaled God's judgment on idolatry in all of its forms.

In its most obvious form, idolatry is the worship of idols. However, as we have seen, idolatry is rooted in a more profound spiritual problem, seeking to control divine revelation. In idolatry we attempt to secure the presence and revelation of God. In idolatry we assume an active relation to God, whereas in worship we take up a receptive relation to God. In worship, we wait upon God and receive the divine presence as God wills. In idolatry we actively try to create the presence of God at our convenience.

There was no need for Jesus to speak out against idolatry in its obvious form. Jews had long since abandoned the use of idols. But Jesus did confront the profound ground of idolatry. This confrontation is seen in the gospel narratives about seeking a sign: "The Pharisees came . . . asking him for a sign from heaven, to test him" (Mark 8:11). In response to Jesus' call for repentance and belief in the Kingdom, the Pharisees asked for confirmation. They were, in effect, asking for Jesus to prove his status as one sent from God. Instead of embracing the Kingdom "as a little child" (Luke 18:17), with simple receptiveness and trust, the Pharisees asserted themselves as authoritative judges of God's revelation. Because their question was motivated by a desire to judge God's revelation instead of receiving it, Jesus harshly stated that "an evil and adulterous generation asks for a sign" (Matt. 16:4).

Abstractly considered, asking for a sign may seem innocent. But in the context of Jesus' announcement of the Kingdom, asking for a sign was equivalent to standing in judgment over God's revelation. Many who heard Jesus failed to respond because of an unbelieving heart. They heard Jesus' words but did not accept them as God's revelation. But those who displayed a childlike trust and a receptive, believing heart did hear Jesus' words as the revelation of God. The request for a sign was precisely an attempt to control revelation by making humans the judge of revelation and of its concrete form, Jesus.

Jesus' refusal to give a sign that would prove his identity helps us understand this gospel passage: "To you has been given the secret of the kingdom of God, but for those outside, everything comes in parables; in order that 'they may indeed look, but not perceive, and may indeed listen, but not understand; so that they may not turn again and be forgiven'" (Mark 4:11-12). This passage is saying that Jesus used parables in order to conceal the presence of the Kingdom from those who refused to accept the revelation of God and instead demanded proof before they would accept it. With this attitude they signified that they lacked the trusting, obedient heart that the Kingdom demanded and instead approached God's revelation as judges. Even though they did not worship with idols, the spirit of idolatry dwelled within them. When the revelation of God approached, they sought to control it instead of receiving it.

However, some did receive the Kingdom as little children. In them dwelled the spirit of praise and worship. Take, for example, Mary: "My soul magnifies the Lord, and my spirit rejoices in God my Savior . . . for the Mighty One has done great things for me, and holy is his name" (Luke 1:46, 49).

Or take these words of Zechariah: "Blessed be the Lord God of Israel, for he has looked favorably on his people and redeemed them. He has raised up a mighty savior for us in the house of his servant David" (vv. 68-69). We see here that praise and worship resulted from embracing God's kingdom with faith and trust. The spirit of idolatry makes demands on God's revelation—it asks for proof. The attitude of faith and trust simply receives God's revelation and responds with praise. The spirit of idolatry expresses itself in unbelief; faith and trust express themselves in worship.

Jesus did more than call for a renewal of praise. Because, in his ministry, death and resurrection, he is the one who actualizes the Kingdom in history, he himself becomes the object of worship (Luke 24:51-52). Because the kingdom of God is God's coming into the world and because he is the one who brings the Kingdom into reality, worship of God now cannot be separated from worship of the resurrected, glorified Jesus.

▸ THE ESCHATOLOGICAL DIMENSION OF THE KINGDOM OF GOD

The kingdom of God is both a present and a future reality. It thus has an eschatological character.

The kingdom of God and the age of the Spirit were present in the preaching and deeds of Jesus; however, they are not completely actualized in history. The Spirit was poured out but not immediately on "all flesh." The promised era of messianic peace and blessings did not materialize. The messianic king came, but instead of ruling over a kingdom of righteousness, he was crucified.

The Gospels clearly portray this "already" but "not yet" aspect of the Kingdom. On one hand, they proclaim the presence of the Kingdom (Luke 11:20). On the other hand, they indicate that the Kingdom's fullness is still a future reality, as when Jesus advised his followers about the delay of the Kingdom (19:11). Though the Kingdom is present, it remains hidden; likewise, though it is present, it remains a future reality.

Because of its future dimension, the age of the Spirit, although a reality present in the ministry of Jesus, has not fully replaced the world of sin. On the contrary, the age of the Spirit coexists with that world. This means that the new creation—the kingdom of God and the age of the Spirit—awaits the future. From the time of Jesus onward until the final consummation of history, the new creation has both a present and a future dimension. This new reality therefore is an essentially eschatological reality because it points us toward its ultimate realization in the future that God is creating and will create.

▸ THE ETHICAL DIMENSION OF FAITH

It is not enough to believe that Jesus is the Messiah and that his deeds and his preaching brought about the kingdom of God. Authentic Christian faith demands that we enter the Kingdom by acts of repentance,

trust, and obedience and that we share in the redemption that Jesus accomplished. It demands that we take part in the restoration of wisdom,
righteousness, trust, humility, awe, and praise. And it demands that we see
the death and resurrection of Jesus not merely as historical events but as
realities in which we participate as we are joined to God by faith in Jesus.

SUMMARY STATEMENTS

1. In Jesus Christ God came into the world to create fellowship
   in a new act of creation and redemption. The kingdom of
   God is this new creation.

2. The kingdom of God in Jesus' preaching was an affirmation
   of Israel's status as the elect people of God; however, it was
   also an extension of God's grace and mercy to the entire
   world.

3. The kingdom of God in Jesus' preaching meant the renewal
   of holiness; however, Jesus' preaching about holiness emphasized the centrality of righteousness, mercy, and justice.

4. The kingdom of God in the preaching of Jesus brought with
   it the blessings that the prophets foretold.

5. The kingdom of God in the preaching of Jesus signaled the
   arrival of the age of the Spirit foretold by the prophets.

6. Jesus fulfilled Israel's hope for a messianic king; however, his
   embodiment of this hope did not conform to common expectations about the messianic king.

7. The kingdom of God is God's rule in the world of sin. But in
   the ministry of Jesus this rule was both revealed and hidden.

8. The kingdom of God called for wisdom and signaled God's
   judgment on foolishness.

9. The kingdom of God called for righteousness and signaled
   God's judgment on unrighteousness and injustice.

10. The kingdom of God called for trust in God and signaled
    God's judgment on misplaced trust.

11. The kingdom of God called for humility and signaled God's
    judgment on hubris.

12. The kingdom of God called for a renewal of awe and sig-

naled God's judgment on every attitude of familiarity toward God.

13. The kingdom of God called for praising God and signaled God's judgment on idolatry in all of its forms.

14. The kingdom of God is both a present and a future reality. It thus has an eschatological character.

QUESTIONS FOR REFLECTION

1. What are the ethical implications of the belief that the kingdom of God is a present reality and not merely a hope about the future?

2. What does it mean to live in accordance with the Kingdom and its values?

3. What is the relation of Christianity to Judaism?

4. What is the status of Judaism today in relation to the kingdom of God?

NINE

SALVATION IN JESUS CHRIST

OBJECTIVES

Your study of this chapter should help you to understand:

1. The Christian doctrine of salvation.

2. The role of Jesus Christ in salvation.

KEY WORDS TO UNDERSTAND

Atonement	Mediator
Adoption	Merit
Christus Victor	Regeneration
Enlightenment	Soteriology
Eternal life	Special revelation
General revelation	Three offices of Christ
Justification	Vicarious suffering
Logos	

QUESTIONS TO CONSIDER AS YOU READ

1. What are the various metaphors that the New Testament writers employed in presenting Jesus as the Savior?

2. What are the various ways in which the New Testament writers understood salvation and to what extent was their understanding guided by metaphors drawn from the Old Testament?

3. What is the relation between the work of Jesus Christ and the work of the Holy Spirit in salvation?

Jesus, my Lord, my God!
   The God supreme thou art,
The Lord of hosts, whose precious blood
   Is sprinkled on my heart.

Jehovah is thy name;
   And, through thy blood applied,
Convinced and certified I am
   There is no God beside.

Soon as thy Spirit shows
   That precious blood of thine,
The happy, pardoned sinner knows
   It is the blood divine.

But only he who feels
   'My Saviour died for me,'
Is sure that all the Godhead dwells
   Eternally in thee.

This hymn by the Wesleys, published in 1767, celebrates salvation and Jesus the Savior. It directs our attention to Jesus' death as a central moment in the drama of salvation (his "precious blood is sprinkled on my heart"). It affirms that it is precisely as God that Jesus suffered and died ("Through the blood applied, convinced and certified I am there is no God beside"). It asserts that God the Father has come to us in Jesus Christ and has identified with humankind to the uttermost, to the point of death, in order to create us anew.

▶ INTRODUCTION

The history of the world is the history of the holy God coming into the world, recreating fellowship. Jesus Christ is the central moment of this history. In him God came into the world as a first-century, Galilean Jew. Accordingly, Jesus' message of the kingdom was a proclamation of Israel's redemption. However, the significance of Jesus Christ goes far beyond the redemption of historical Israel. As the Church began to receive

Gentiles, it came to see the significance of Jesus for the salvation of the entire human race. Consequently, there is much more to say about the role of Jesus Christ in redemption.

Stated briefly, Jesus did more than simply proclaim salvation. On the contrary, he creates salvation as we share in his life, death and resurrection. As a result, he is the Savior. He is the Savior because of all that he was and did and all that he is and does. He is the Savior because of his death and also because of his resurrection. Consequently, when we think of Jesus as the Savior, our thoughts should dwell on his deeds, teaching, and entire life as well as his death.

SOTERIOLOGY

The theological term that designates themes associated with the doctrine of salvation is *soteriology.* This term is based on the Greek word for health and deliverance.

▶ REDEMPTION AND THE FORGIVENESS OF SIN

The life and death of Jesus Christ accomplished redemption and brought about the forgiveness of sin. The New Testament expresses its understanding of redemption in a variety of metaphors.

The death of Jesus Christ is an integral aspect of salvation. Because this death was a moment in the infinite God's coming into the world, it cannot be understood by any single idea alone. That is why the writers of the New Testament used a variety of images, drawn from familiar experiences, to expound the significance of this death.

These include the practice of animal sacrifice, the practice of buying something back ("redemption"), the phenomenon of exchange ("ransom"), and the experience of suffering for the sake of others. The fact that the New Testament's exposition of Jesus' death drew on familiar experiences reminds us of the metaphorical nature of theological language. Jesus was not literally an animal sacrifice; he was not slaughtered by the high priest in the Temple on the Day of Atonement. But New Testament writers saw that Jesus' death was *like* the death of a sacrificial animal. Similarly, Jesus was not literally a ransom; his death was not a payment made to someone. But, since the effect of Jesus' death was like the effect of a ransom paid, New Testament writers employed the concept of ransom in their attempt to grasp the significance of Jesus and his death. We see in these metaphors a variety of perspectives, each saying something of importance, each adding something to our understanding that others do not.

The New Testament abounds with references to Jesus' death. It affirms that "in him we have redemption through his blood, the forgiveness of our trespasses, according to the riches of his grace" (Eph. 1:7). We notice in this verse the connection between Jesus' blood and forgiveness. It was natural for the Church, with its Jewish heritage, to focus on the shedding of Jesus' blood and to portray Jesus as an atoning sacrifice. The basis of this portrait is the events on the Day of *Atonement*, when the high priest sacrificed a goat for the sins of the people. Entering the inmost part of the Temple, the priest would sprinkle the goat's blood on the mercy seat, where God encountered Israel. This sprinkling covered the sins of the people.

Paul understood Jesus' death to be a reenactment of this event: "God put [Jesus] forward as a sacrifice of atonement [or "place of atonement"] by his blood" (Rom. 3:25). In the shedding of Jesus' blood, Paul was arguing, God was covering sins just as the sacrifice on the Day of Atonement covered the people's sins. In this death God's judgment fell on Jesus, who became "a curse for us" and thus "redeemed us from the curse of the law" (Gal. 3:13). Jesus, in the role of a sacrificial animal, was the object of God's condemnation (see Rom. 8:3). As a result, God has freed us from the guilt of sin; we stand in a new relation to God marked by forgiveness and blamelessness.

As a sacrifice of atonement, Jesus suffered and died on behalf of others. This is often referred to as *vicarious suffering*. Jesus' vicarious suffering is saving because of the vast difference between Jesus, who suffered, and us for whom he suffered. In Paul's words, "Christ died for the ungodly" (Rom. 5:6). His death, therefore, was more than an act of heroism or humanitarian love. It was also the death of a righteous person on behalf of the unrighteous. Christ's death is saving because through it God does for us what we could not do for ourselves. Being unrighteous and ungodly, we could not make ourselves acceptable to God. But in Jesus' death, God acts for us.

JESUS' DEATH IN THE NEW TESTAMENT

The New Testament often interprets Jesus' death in terms of the Old Testament practice of animal sacrifice; however, it has other ways of interpreting his death. John's Gospel in particular is a rich source of insight, adding several important dimensions to our understanding of Jesus' death. After identifying Jesus as "the Lamb of God who takes away the sin of the world" (1:29), this Gospel sees a reflection of Jesus in the Old Testament story (Num. 21:9) of Moses placing the snake on a pole. Israelites who looked on the snake were delivered. In the same way, John's Gospel affirms, those who look upon the crucified Jesus will be saved (3:14). This gospel also portrays Jesus' death with an agricultural metaphor: "Unless a grain of wheat falls into the earth and dies, it remains just a single grain; but if it dies, it bears much fruit" (12:24). Here there is no emphasis on Jesus' blood. Instead, the significance of Jesus' death lies in the fact that by it his life bears fruit in the form of many disciples. Finally, Jesus is the good shepherd who dies while protecting his sheep (10:11). Here the emphasis falls not on his blood but instead on his care for the disciples. As these passages from John's Gospel show, Jesus' death signifies more than forgiveness of sins; it effects salvation in all of its aspects.

The idea of Jesus' suffering for us helps us understand the portrait of Jesus as a ransom (see 1 Tim. 2:6 and Rev. 5:9-10). The idea of vicarious suffering and the idea of ransom are built on the notion of exchange. Through Jesus' death we are freed as if we were hostages released from captivity. It is as though Jesus is exchanged for us, so that through the death of Jesus God wins us back. Because through this death God gains us back, this death is redemptive. Of course, the metaphor of exchange has limits, for in a real exchange something is forfeited; however, God did not forfeit or lose Jesus. Instead the emphasis falls on the benefit of Jesus' death for us. By his suffering and death we are returned to God and freed from the world of sin (Titus 2:14).

The death of Jesus covers sin but also begins the destruction of the world of sin. Paul described this destruction when he portrayed Jesus as the one "who gave himself for our sins to set us free from the present evil age" (Gal. 1:4). We see here that salvation embraces liberation from the demonic world of sin. It is not enough that God forgives our sin; such forgiveness is futile if we are left in the control and alienation of sin. That is why God "has rescued us from the power of darkness and transferred us into the kingdom of his beloved Son" (Col. 1:13). The fullness of salvation, therefore, consists in our being transferred from the domain of sin to a new domain, the kingdom of God.

THE RESURRECTION AND GLORIFICATION OF JESUS

The resurrection and glorification of Jesus should always be discussed together. It is important not only that Jesus was raised but also that he was raised as the glorified Lord. Without the glorification, Jesus' resurrection would be nothing more than the resuscitation of a dead body. The glorification was a confirmation of Jesus' status as God's anointed one and God's vindication of Jesus' message and ministry.

The creeds in our tradition join the New Testament in affirming the resurrection and glorification of Jesus: "Christ did truly rise again from the dead, and took again his body, with all things appertaining to the perfection of man's nature, wherewith he ascended into heaven, and there sitteth until he return to judge all men at the last day . . . and is there engaged in intercession for us."

Our liberation from the world of sin is grounded in Jesus Christ's victory over the demonic powers. This victory is symbolized in the image of Christ being exalted to the right hand of God, "far above all rule and authority and power and dominion" (Eph. 1:20-21). The exaltation of Jesus signifies not only his elevated status but also the submission of every cosmic power, even the demonic powers, to his rule. Colossians expresses this point even more pointedly when it proclaims that in Jesus God has "disarmed the rulers and authorities and made a public example of them, triumphing over them in it" (2:15). Because these powers have been disarmed, those who are in Christ are no longer under their dominion. The belief that the death and resurrection of Jesus constitutes a victory over demonic powers is sometimes referred to as the *Christus Victor* image.

These metaphors and symbols are all ways in which the Early Church expressed its conviction that in the death of Jesus Christ God comes into the world, unites with the world in its experience of sin's consequences and, in that death, saves the world.

▶ RECONCILIATION

In Jesus Christ God comes into the world of sin, creating and re-creating fellowship. God thus overcomes alienation and achieves reconciliation.

Reconciliation signifies deliverance from the eschatological wrath of God. The world of sin, in its alienation from God, is subject to God's judgment. However, those who are in Jesus Christ are destined to escape this wrath (1 Thess. 1:10). Because we are in Christ, we have been separated from the world of sin. Consequently we do not share in the world's alienation from God and instead have peace with God (Rom 5:1).

However, there is more to reconciliation than deliverance from eschatological wrath. It is also our **justification** and righteousness in Jesus Christ.

In the New Testament it is Paul who was most concerned with the question of righteousness. As a Jew, he began with the conviction that righteousness is a matter of obedience to God, especially as God's will is embodied in the Law of Moses. However, Paul came to see that "No one is justified before God by the law" (Gal. 3:11) because "through the law comes the knowledge of sin" (Rom. 3:20). Of course, Paul believed firmly that the Law of Moses was the law of God. He had no doubt that the law is "holy and just and good" (7:12). But, in the world of sin, the law, which "promised life," in fact has become an instrument of our spiritual death (see v. 10). Consequently, Paul argued, it was futile to seek to become righteous by obedience to Moses' law. Instead, the gospel demands that we seek "the righteousness that comes from God" (10:3).

The righteousness that we receive from God is grounded in God's grace, especially as that grace is revealed in Jesus Christ. Those who believe "are now justified [i.e., made righteous] by [God's] grace as a gift, through the redemption that is in Christ Jesus" (3:24). By sending Jesus as a sacrifice of atonement, God has made us "right," that is, has justified or made us righteous. As a result of God's grace, we are now, in the words of Colossians, "holy and blameless and irreproachable before [God]" (1:22). The law could not make us right, because (in the world of sin) it is the instrument of sin. But in Jesus Christ God has done what the law could not do (see Rom. 8:3).

Because God has made us righteous, we have been reconciled to God. In the world of sin, we were alienated from God (Eph. 2:12). The good news of the gospel, however, is that "in Christ God was reconciling the world to himself" (2 Cor. 5:19). In the life, death, and resurrection of Jesus Christ, God came into the world of sin and re-created fellowship with humankind. We, living in the world of sin, could not overcome our alienation from God. Reconciliation is accordingly an act of God's grace and love. It is God's coming into the world. As a result, "we have peace with God through our Lord Jesus Christ" (Rom. 5:1). For those who are in Christ, God's judgment against the world of sin is a thing of the past. They have already begun to enjoy the eschatological blessings of peace (*shalom*) described by the prophets.

Justification is one important metaphor for reconciliation. ***Adoption*** is another. Although, as creatures, every human being is a child of God, those who are reconciled are children of God in an elevated sense. We should think of this issue thus: every human being is a child of God by virtue of being created in God's image; however, the full actualization of being a child of God is possible only in those who have been redeemed from the world of sin and reconciled to God. The term *adoption* concretely illustrates the change of status that accompanies redemption. As Paul put it, "God has sent the Spirit of his Son into our hearts, crying, 'Abba! Father!' So you are no longer a slave but a child" (Gal. 4:6-7). While we were in the world of sin we were sin's slaves. But now we have been freed from that world and joined to God. This is what the idea of adoption points to.

ADOPTION

The creeds in our tradition define adoption as "that gracious act of God by which the justified and regenerated believer is constituted a son of God" and "becomes a partaker of all the rights, privileges and responsibilities of a child of God." They further describe it as "a filial term full of warmth, love, and acceptance . . . [which] denotes that by a new relationship in Christ believers have become His wanted children freed from the mastery of both sin and Satan." Finally, our creeds affirm that "believers have the witness of the Spirit that they are children of God."

It is important to note that reconciliation has a corporate dimension, expressed in the idea of election. As we have seen in previous chapters, election is God's act of coming into the world and creating fellowship. In the Old Testament, this fellowship is with Israel; election is God's choosing Israel to stand in a special relation to God. The New Testament applies the idea of election to a corporate body, the Church: "You are a chosen race, a royal priesthood, a holy nation, God's own people" (1 Pet. 2:9). By describing the Church in the same terms by which Exod. 19:6 describes Israel, 1 Peter wants us to see the Church as the new Israel and as the elect, holy people of God. As such, the Church is a part of God's new creation, for the "holy calling" that the Church receives from God (2 Tim. 1:9) calls the Church into being as the community of reconciled people.

Salvation, accordingly, is not only a matter of rescuing individuals from the world of sin but also includes the creation or, more accurately, the re-creation of the people of God. This is the conviction that informs Paul's understanding of Christ in 1 Cor.:

> Thus it is written, "The first man, Adam, became a living being"; the last Adam [i.e., Jesus Christ] became a life-giving spirit. . . . The first man was from the earth, man of dust; the second man is from heaven. . . . Just as we have borne the image of the man of dust, we will also bear the image of the man of heaven (*15:45, 47, 49*).

Here Paul presented Jesus as a founder of a new humanity, just as Adam is represented as the founder of the original humanity. But, whereas the original humanity became conformed to Adam's character and dwelled in the world of sin, the new humanity is being "conformed to the image of [God's] Son," with the result that Jesus Christ is "the firstborn within a large family" (Rom. 8:29), namely, the re-created people of God.

▶ REGENERATION AND NEW LIFE IN CHRIST

Salvation includes new life in Christ, comprising regeneration (or rebirth) and eternal life. We have this new life as we participate in Jesus' resurrection.

The death of Jesus is an integral part of salvation; however, it is not the only integral part; the New Testament emphasizes also Jesus' resurrection. It does so when it affirms, for instance, that God "has given us a new birth into a living hope through the resurrection of Jesus Christ" (1 Pet. 1:3) and that "baptism . . . now saves you . . . through the resurrection of Jesus Christ" (3:21). These passages show us that the resurrection of Jesus is an essential aspect of salvation. If Jesus had died but not been raised, he would indeed have suffered as a sacrificial atonement and our sins would be forgiven; however, we would not have the new life and hope that his resurrection effects. The term **regeneration** denotes the fact that salvation embraces new life through the resurrection of Jesus.

Paul expounded on this point when he asserted that while "we were reconciled to God through the death of his Son, much more surely . . . will we be saved by his life" (Rom. 5:10). As we can see, salvation is much more than having our sins wiped away by Christ's death. It includes the restoration of our created life. In the fullest sense, then, salvation is impossible without the resurrection of Jesus as the source of our new life, for our walking in "newness of life" is grounded in his resurrected life (Rom. 6:4).

Our participation in Christ's resurrection is emphasized in Ephesians, which tells us that the life of the resurrection has already begun: God "made us alive together with Christ . . . and raised us up with him and seated us with him in the heavenly places" (2:5-6). Although the resurrection of our bodies lies in the future, the resurrection of Christ means that all of us who are in Christ are already participating in the new life. It is because we participate in Jesus' resurrection that we can and should consider ourselves "dead to sin and alive to God in Christ Jesus" (Rom. 6:11).

As we have seen, the resurrection of Jesus means more than his return to life. It signifies also his exaltation to the right hand of the Father. There he plays the role of *mediator* (1 Tim. 2:5). Jesus is the mediator because, as the revelation of God, he represents God to humankind; as the ideal human, he represents humankind to God. In Jesus Christ God comes into the world and re-creates a complete and unbreakable fellowship with human beings. At the same time, in Jesus Christ the human world renders to God the perfect obedience that the righteous God demands. As a mediator, Jesus fills the role of priest, who "holds his priesthood permanently. . . . Consequently, he is able for all time to save those who approach God through him, since he always lives to make intercession for them" (Heb. 7:24-25). He is the priestly mediator because we approach God *through* Jesus Christ and because he represents us to God.

JESUS THE MEDIATOR

The creeds in our tradition affirm Jesus the mediator by stating that "He [is] the one perfect mediator between God and us" and "ascended into heaven, and there intercedes for us at the Father's right hand until He returns to judge all humanity at the last day."

One metaphor for new life is rebirth. The symbol of rebirth points to the fact that those who are in Christ have been transferred from death to life. They have been born a second time, not according to the order of nature and not into the world of sin, but instead from God into the new

REBIRTH/REGENERATION

The creeds in our tradition define rebirth or regeneration as "that gracious work of God whereby the moral nature of the repentant believer is spiritually quickened [i.e., made alive] and given a distinctively spiritual life, capable of faith, love, and obedience." They affirm that regeneration "enables the pardoned sinner to serve God with the will and affections of the heart, and by it the regenerate are delivered from the power of sin which reigns over all the unregenerate." Thereby "the believer is born again and is a new creation. The old life is past; a new life is begun."

world that God is creating. Our first birth delivers us into the power of the world of sin. The second birth is a deliverance from this world into the new world that God creates, the world of life.

Rebirth manifests itself as the life of righteous obedience and is the re-creation of our ethical and spiritual life, which formerly lay dead in the world of sin. Negatively expressed, rebirth means that we have been "ransomed from the futile ways inherited" from the past (1 Pet. 1:18) and have "escaped the defilements of the world through the knowledge of our Lord and Savior Jesus Christ" (2 Pet. 2:20). Positively stated, it means that we "live in love, as Christ loved us" (Eph. 5:2) and now exist for and in the presence of God.

Rebirth initiates us into *eternal life*. Eternal life is not simply an unending or a heavenly life. It is instead existence in the presence of God. Because our eschatological destiny is fellowship with God, human existence falls short of its fullness apart from this fellowship. To speak of eternal life is to speak of life with God, a life that fulfills our created nature and destiny. In the words of John's Gospel, "This is eternal life, that they may know you, the only true God, and Jesus Christ whom you have sent" (17:3). Eternal life, then, is the authentic knowledge of God, which consists in union with and abiding in God. Rebirth, then, is the beginning of eternal life, for in it we begin to live in the presence of God.

Paradoxically, our life before God requires our death to the world of sin: "Through the law I died to the law, so that I might live to God. I have been crucified with Christ; and it is no longer I who live, but it is Christ who lives in me" (Gal. 2:19-20). As we have seen, for Paul the law is the instrument whereby we are held captive in the world of sin. Our death to the law, then, marks our freedom from the world of sin and the possibility of a new life in and for God. But this new life is not something that we accomplish. It is instead the life of Jesus Christ formed within us, for God has "made us alive together with Christ" (Eph. 2:5). We have, in an anticipatory way, been raised with Christ and now live, through Christ, the new life of the resurrection. But our being raised presupposes our death to the world of sin.

GENERAL AND SPECIAL REVELATION

Revelation denotes God's coming into the world for the purpose of establishing fellowship. It is customary to distinguish *general revelation* from *special revelation.* General revelation is the disclosure of God in and through the features of the created world. The concept of general revelation is an attempt to account for the fact that some idea of the divine is nearly universal among humankind. This concept grounds the universal idea of the divine in God's creative power. Special revelation is the disclosure of God in and through particular events in history. Although sometimes the Bible is equated with special revelation, it is more in keeping with the Christian faith to equate special revelation with Jesus Christ and to regard the Bible as a faithful and Spirit-guided witness to Jesus Christ.

▶ ENLIGHTENMENT AND THE REVELATION OF GOD

Through Jesus Christ we come to know God. He is the Savior because he is the revelation of God.

It is not only the details of Christ's life and death that have redemptive significance. Beyond these is his status as the revelation of God.
When we say that Jesus is the revelation of God, we are saying more than
that Jesus revealed God. Standing in the line of the prophets, Jesus, like
them, disclosed God by delivering the word of God to Israel. But Jesus
was more than a prophet. Although he did indeed speak the word of
God, he was and is the Word (*logos*) of God. He, in the entirety of his
life, death, and resurrection, is the declaration of God to humankind, for
in his life God speaks to us in an ultimate and unsurpassable way. He is
that moment and event in which God comes into the world and addresses humankind.

Revelation is an act of salvation because it is only through revelation that we truly know God.

John's Gospel has a particularly strong way of presenting Jesus as
the revelation of God. It begins with the Old Testament's affirmation that
no one has ever seen God (1:18; 6:46). But it then asserts that no one
"has seen the Father except the one who is from God; he has seen the Father" (6:46). Jesus is therefore unique; he alone knows the Father. As a result, he alone is able to reveal the Father. Previous revelations of God
were only partial, for the people or things that revealed did not fully
know the Father. In Jesus, however, the Son, who knows the Father, has
appeared in the world.

However, it is not enough to say that the Son knows the Father. Jesus is the revelation of God because he is one with the Father (10:30).
Their unity is such that to behold Jesus is to behold the Father (14:9).
Even though no one ever has seen or can see God, the Father can be seen
in Jesus. That is why Jesus Christ is the revelation of God. Not only his
words but also his being in the world constitutes the revelation of the Father to the world.

In Paul's letters (2 Cor. 4:4) and in the tradition following him
(Col. 1:15), Jesus' revelatory character is expressed in the belief that he is
the image of God. Like the concept of word (*logos*), the concept of image
draws our thinking back to the opening chapter of Genesis and reminds
us of the vital connection between God's original act of creation and the
new creation that God accomplishes in Jesus Christ. In the beginning

God spoke creation into existence. As the revelation of God, Jesus Christ is the new speech of God, the speech that brings about the new creation. And just as in the beginning God created humankind in the image of God, so in Jesus Christ we see that the image in which we are created and which is our eschatological destiny is none other than Jesus Christ.

To say that Jesus is the image of God is to say that he was the visible presence of God among us. As the image, he represented God for "he is the reflection of God's glory and the exact imprint of God's very being" (Heb. 1:3). Consequently, our experience of Christ is an experience of God, for God is reflected and represented in Jesus Christ. Jesus Christ is the presence of God among us, for in him God comes into the world of sin. That is what we mean when we say that he is the revelation of God.

Because Jesus is the revelation of God, we have authentic knowledge of God (although, as Paul insisted, the critical thing is not so much our knowing God as it is our being known by God [see Gal. 4:9]). The New Testament has many ways of describing the authentic knowledge of God. Sometimes it uses the language of *enlightenment,* as in the prayer for "the God of our Lord Jesus Christ . . . [to] give you a spirit of wisdom and revelation as you come to know him, so that, with the eyes of your heart enlightened, you may know what is the hope to which he has called you" (Eph. 1:17-18). The term *enlightenment* points us to the fact that our knowledge of God is the result of God's grace, not of human inquiry.

In speaking about this knowledge, however, the New Testament more often uses the idea of truth: "If you continue in my word . . . you will know the truth, and the truth will make you free" (John 8:31-32). But the truth that Jesus speaks about here is not a collection of true statements. It is in fact none other than God's revelation, for Jesus is the truth (John 14:6) and the Spirit as well is the truth (1 John 5:6). To know the truth is to know Jesus Christ and the Holy Spirit. It is to receive the revelation of God and thus to know God.

Sometimes the New Testament uses the language of sharing to help us understand the knowledge of God, as when 2 Pet. 1:4 speaks of our becoming "participants of the divine nature," when 1 John 1:3 affirms that "our fellowship is with the Father and with his Son Jesus Christ," and when Heb. 6:4 asserts that we have "shared in the Holy Spirit." The language of sharing, fellowship, and participation is another way of saying that our knowledge of God is really a form of union with God. The knowledge of God, in other words, is not a form of scientific or objective knowledge. It is, on the contrary, a sharing in the divine life of fellowship. That is why the Johannine tradition places great emphasis on the notion of our abiding in God as the branch abides in the vine (see John 15:1-6). This metaphor tells us that our relation to God is not that of subjects seeking to know an object in an objective way. Our relation to God is instead a union with God. To know God is to dwell in God—to participate in the divine nature, to have fellowship with the Father and the Son, and to share in the Holy Spirit.

Like the other aspects of salvation, the new life in Christ also has a corporate dimension. It is important that we keep this dimension in mind, for it is all too easy to imagine rebirth and eternal life only in individualistic terms. However, the New Testament presents us with a powerful corrective to this temptation by reminding us that our new life in Christ is a part of the world's eschatological destiny. This eschatological destiny provides us with the fullest context for understanding the new life available in Jesus Christ.

The corporate aspect of salvation is hinted at by Ephesians, which speaks of God's plan "to gather up all things in [Christ], things in heaven and things on earth" (1:10) and by Colossians, which states that through Christ "God was pleased to reconcile to himself all things, whether on earth or in heaven" (1:20). These passages point us to the cosmic dimension of new life in Christ. They suggest that the eschatological destiny of the world is to be united to God in Christ. Rebirth and eternal life, accordingly, do not pertain only to human beings. On the contrary, Jesus Christ effects the renewal of the entire created world (Rom. 8:19-21). This comprehensive vision of a new creation completes the Christian faith's belief in rebirth and eternal life by enlarging their scope to include the entirety of the new world that God is bringing into being.

The corporate aspect of salvation is expressed in the Johannine tradition with the distinction between the world of darkness and God's domain of light: "The darkness is passing away and the true light is already shining" (1 John 2:8). The "darkness" is not simply the world's ignorance of God. It is also the Johannine symbol for the world of sin that resists God. The world of sin consists of those who persist in walking in the darkness. To assert that the darkness is already passing away is to affirm with Ephesians and Colossians that Jesus has already triumphed over the demonic powers and that the fallen world of darkness has come to its end. Salvation, then, means that we have been transferred from the darkness to the light—we can walk in the light just as Jesus Christ is in the light (1 John 1:7). By walking in the light we conquer the world (1 John 5:4) and take part in the new world that God creates.

▶ THE ESCHATOLOGICAL DIMENSION OF SALVATION

As an eschatological reality, salvation is both present and future.

Salvation is an eschatological reality. This means that it has both a present and a future dimension. Because we know God and live in the presence of God, we have already entered into eternal life. As 1 John expresses it, "We know that we have passed from death to life because we love one another" (3:14). But the full actualization of this knowledge and presence remains a reality for which we hope (Titus 3:7).

Until the eschatological consummation of the new world that God is creating, our new life "is hidden with Christ in God" (Col. 3:3). Although we participate already in Christ's resurrection, the fullness of salvation is not yet. For that reason, it is necessary that we continually "put away [the] former way of life, [the] old self, corrupt and deluded by its lusts" and that we "clothe [ourselves] with the new self, created according to the likeness of God in true righteousness and holiness" (Eph. 4:22-24). The eschatological nature of salvation means that we are saved in the midst of the world and that the world that God creates subsists alongside the persisting world of sin. As a result, we have to exercise diligence and resist sin's world lest we lose the object of our hope.

The future dimension of eternal life is signified by the hope of resurrection. As with eternal life, it is important to note what this idea does not mean. It does not mean the simple continuation of our existence after death. The mere continuation of existence would not in itself represent a victory over the world of sin. Instead, resurrection signifies the consummation of our union with Christ. In our current state, we are in

Christ. Yet, as Paul knew, "While we are at home in the body we are away from the Lord" (2 Cor. 5:6). In this life, even in Christ, there is an element of separation. The hope of resurrection points us toward the overcoming of this separation at the end, when "we will certainly be united with him in a resurrection like his" (Rom. 6:5). The hope of resurrection accordingly is the New Testament's way of affirming that our eschatological destiny is to be united with Jesus Christ in the fullest possible way in every dimension of our being.

There is an important sense, therefore, in which salvation is a future event, as when Paul affirmed that "we *will be* saved" (Rom. 5:9, emphasis added) and when salvation is said to be "ready to be revealed in the last time" (1 Pet. 1:5). Although, with the coming of Jesus, salvation is an accomplished fact, it is nonetheless an eschatological reality, for salvation is not complete until the final consummation of God's creation. Salvation has already begun and its effects are already being experienced; however, its fulfillment lies in the future. This points us toward the soteriological importance of the return of Jesus. If salvation were only a matter of having our sins forgiven, then Jesus' death would suffice for salvation. But salvation is larger than forgiveness. It means the complete renewal of God's created world. The return of Jesus points us to this future of renewal. The fullest extent of salvation, then, is thrust into the future. As a result, hope is an essential aspect of the Christian life: "Set your hope on the grace that Jesus Christ will bring you when he is revealed" (1 Pet. 1:13). The New Testament, consequently, regards the return of Christ as a vital moment in the history of human salvation, for with that return will come the fulfillment of the new creation.

▶ POSTBIBLICAL DEVELOPMENTS IN THE
   DOCTRINE OF SALVATION

In later Christian thinking, the doctrine of salvation underwent further development as the Church sought to understand the implications of the New Testament's teaching.

In previous chapters we have recorded the development of Christian thinking by taking brief note, in sidebars, of creedal statements. However, Christian thinking about Jesus Christ has been so voluminous that occasional sidebars are not sufficient. As a result, we will have a look at postbiblical Christian thinking in an extended review.

DEVELOPMENTS IN THINKING ABOUT THE SAVING WORK OF CHRIST

Writers in the early centuries of Christianity did not attempt a systematic understanding of Jesus' work in salvation. They were content to repeat the variety of metaphors employed in the New Testament such as ransom and defeating the fallen, demonic powers. Additionally, they often thought of God working a deal with Satan. In this view, humankind had come under the dominion of Satan because of our sin. In the deal with Satan, God the Father won us back in exchange for Jesus. Then, by resurrecting Jesus, the Father reclaimed Jesus and left Satan with nothing.

The first sustained attempt to present an understanding of Jesus' work on the basis of one leading idea was offered in the 11th century by Anselm of Canterbury (1033—1109). Anselm argued that the main issue at stake in Christ's work as Savior was not a deal between God and Satan but instead the need for sinful humankind to restore God's honor. Humankind had, he argued, dishonored God by withholding the obedience that we owed to God. Since we were obliged to restore God's honor but, being sinful and weak, could not restore it, God became human. By rendering perfect obedience, the incarnated Son restored God's honor and earned an incalculable reward from God. This reward he made available as a store of *merit* available to cancel out the guilt of human sin.

A bit later than Anselm, Peter Abelard (1079—1142) offered an alternative understanding. He argued that the critical point in salvation was God's desire that humankind come to love God. To this end, the Son entered the human world and, in every aspect of his life, including his death, revealed God's love for us. In doing so, Christ inspires our love for God. As, through Christ, we come to love God, God's will for humankind is fulfilled and reconciliation takes place.

The next phase in the development of Christian thinking came in the era of the Reformation. In that context, Protestant theologians adopted Anselm's view as the best exposition of scriptural teaching; however, they tended to represent Jesus as satisfying God's *justice*, whereas Anselm had put more emphasis on the satisfaction of God's *honor*. Moreover, they have, with Anselm, placed most soteriological emphasis on the death of Jesus, in contrast to Abelard, who also emphasized Jesus' life. Their emphasis is reflected in the creeds in our tradition. When those creeds describe Jesus' saving work, they speak of "the offering of Christ," of "His sufferings and meritorious death on the cross," of "the shedding of His own blood." They affirm that Jesus was "the one perfect sacrifice" and that "He poured out His life as a blameless sacrifice." As these phrases reveal, the emphasis falls not only on the death of Jesus but also on the biblical language of vicarious suffering and sacrificial atonement.

However, the Wesleyan-Arminian tradition has differed from other Protestant theologies on the subject of our righteousness in relation to Christ's righteousness. Theologians have drawn attention to the fact that Christ obeyed God not only by dying on the cross (which they call Christ's passive righteousness, so called because it involves his passion or suffering) but also by carrying out God's will in every other respect (which they call Christ's active righteousness). The Protestant tradition has generally affirmed that the righteousness that we receive by grace is in fact Christ's active righteousness. In other words, Jesus, by his active righteousness and as humankind's representative, fulfilled God's commands on our behalf. In turn God credits (the traditional term is *imputes*) Christ's righteousness to those who have faith, even though our obedience to God's command is not perfect. Those with faith are therefore righteous enough to stand in God's presence not because of their own faulty obedience but because of Christ's perfect obedience.

Wesleyan-Arminian theologians have been uneasy with this notion of imputation, at least to the extent that it suggests that God is satisfied with something less than our complete obedience and that Christ's perfect obedience somehow takes the place of our obedience. Accordingly, John Wesley reinterpreted the idea of imputation to mean that God saves us strictly by grace and for the sake of Christ and not at all because of any merit on our part. The creeds in our tradition follow suit by affirming that "We are accounted righteous before God only for the merit of our Lord and Saviour Jesus Christ, by faith, and not for our own works;" that God "grants . . . acceptance as righteous, to all who believe on Jesus Christ;" and that "by a new relationship in Jesus Christ people are in fact accounted righteous." They thus ground our righteousness in Christ's work and our faith in Christ's work without introducing the idea of imputation.

The theologians in our tradition have differed from some other Protestants also with respect to the question of the extent of Christ's saving work. Churches in the Reformed (or Calvinist) tradition have held that the benefit of Christ's work is limited to those who are predestined for salvation. The creeds in our tradition affirm on the contrary that Jesus "made a full atonement for all human sin" and that "this atonement is sufficient for every individual of Adam's race." Of course, only those who have faith in Jesus receive the full benefit of Christ's saving work; however, every human being without restriction is a potential recipient of salvation and everyone receives some benefit, for God has, because of Christ's work, removed from every human being the guilt and penalty of original sin.

Theologians have also developed a more comprehensive scheme for understanding Jesus' work of salvation. In this scheme, Christ filled three roles or offices: prophet, priest, and king. Hence discussions of Christ's work often refer to the *three offices of Christ*. The prophetic office designates Jesus as the one who reveals God. The priestly office describes Jesus as both the atoning sacrifice for sin and the priestly mediator who offers a sacrifice to God on behalf of human sin. The kingly office denotes the resurrected Jesus as sitting at the right hand of God, subduing the world of sin until all of God's enemies are overcome.

DEVELOPMENTS IN THINKING ABOUT THE NATURE OF SALVATION

When it comes to the question about the nature of salvation, Protestant theology has typically placed special emphasis on righteousness (or *justification*) because this issue was a matter of great debate between the reformers and the late medieval Church and because of its prominence in Paul's theology. For Protestants, it was especially important to assert that justification (or righteousness) precedes sanctification (or holiness) and that the former in no way depends on the latter. In other words, they argued that our righteous standing before God was due strictly to God's act of declaring us righteous, on the basis of Christ's work and our faith in Christ's work. They regarded sanctification as dependent on our justification, for, they argued, only those who were in a right relation to God (i.e., justified or righteous) could then become holy.

From the previous quotations we can see that the creeds in our tradition have followed Protestant theology on this issue.

The Protestant view was developed in controversy with medieval theology, which generally represented justification as depending on sanctification. In other words, the medieval Church taught that our righteous standing depends on our progress in the Christian way as we cooperate with God in the task of developing the virtues infused in the soul by baptism. Those who, through faithful participation in the Church's sacraments and discipline, became virtuous Christian disciples were accordingly judged by God to be righteous and thus justified.

In recent years, there has been considerable dialogue between some Protestant churches and the Roman Catholic Church. The result has been a mutual understanding that the sharp disagreements on these issues were products of controversy and that, on fundamental matters, there is broad agreement on the relation of justification and sanctification. Further dialogue is required for other issues, but it is important to note that, on the issue of salvation, Protestant and Roman Catholic views are no longer so polarized as they were in the 16th century.

▶ THE ETHICAL DIMENSION OF FAITH

As with all doctrines, the doctrine of salvation and the Savior are as much to be lived as to be believed. For instance, the New Testament's teaching about Jesus places great emphasis on the crucifixion. But we misunderstand this teaching if we think of the cross merely as an instrument by which God saves us. On the contrary, the cross is given to us as a pattern by which we are to live. In the words of Mark's Gospel, "If any want to become my followers, let them deny themselves and take up their cross and follow me" (8:34). Or, as Paul expressed it, "I have been crucified with Christ" (Gal. 2:19). The New Testament writers saw the cross not only as an event for Jesus but also as a paradigm for the Christian life. To believe the doctrine of salvation is therefore not only to believe that Jesus is the Savior but also to conform our lives to the crucified Jesus and to take up the cross.

SUMMARY STATEMENTS

1. The life and death of Jesus Christ accomplished redemption

and brought about the forgiveness of sin. The New Testament expresses its understanding of redemption in a variety of metaphors.

2. In Jesus Christ God comes into the world of sin, creating and re-creating fellowship. God thus overcomes alienation and achieves reconciliation.

3. Salvation includes new life in Christ, comprising regeneration (or rebirth) and eternal life. We have this new life as we participate in Jesus' resurrection.

4. Through Jesus Christ we come to know God. He is the Savior because he is the revelation of God.

5. As an eschatological reality, salvation is both present and future.

6. In later Christian thinking, belief in Jesus the Savior underwent further development as the Church sought to understand the implications of the New Testament's teaching.

QUESTIONS FOR REFLECTION

1. Why is it important to consider the metaphorical character of the New Testament's understanding of salvation and to recognize the use of diverse metaphors?

2. Why are the doctrines pertaining to Jesus Christ the most crucial for the Christian faith?

TEN

LIFE IN THE SPIRIT
FAITH

OBJECTIVES

Your study of this chapter should help you to understand:

1. The nature of conscience and spiritual awakening.
2. The relation of faith to good works in the Christian life.
3. The characteristics of life in the Spirit.
4. The nature of the Christian ethical life.

KEY WORDS TO UNDERSTAND

Antinomianism	Faith
Assurance	Good works
Awakening	Illumination
Conscience	Prevenient grace
Consecration	Repentance
Ethical participation in the world	Sealing
Ethical transcendence over the world	

QUESTIONS TO CONSIDER AS YOU READ

1. What is the role of the Holy Spirit in the new creation?
2. What is faith?
3. What does it mean to say that life in the Spirit is an eschatological existence?

Spirit of faith, come down,
    Reveal the things of God,
And make to us the Godhead known,
    And witness with the blood:
'Tis thine the blood to apply,
    And give us eyes to see,
Who did for every sinner die
    Hath surely died for me.

No man can truly say
    That Jesus is the Lord
Unless thou take the veil away,
    And breathe the living word;
Then, only then we feel
    Our interest in his blood,
And cry with joy unspeakable,
    Thou are my Lord, my God!

O that the world might know
    The all-atoning Lamb!
Spirit of faith, descend, and show
    The virtue of his name;
The grace which all may find,
    The saving power impart,
And testify to all mankind,
    And speak in every heart!

Inspire the living faith
    (Which whosoe'er receives,
The witness in himself he hath,
    And consciously believes),
The faith that conquers all,
    And doth the mountain move,
And saves whoe'er on Jesus call,
    And perfects them in love.

This hymn, composed by the Wesleys in 1746, celebrates faith and the Holy Spirit, who evokes our faith. It reminds us that faith is the way in which we truly know God and the means by which we share in Jesus' atonement. It tells us that the object of faith is Jesus Christ. Finally, it affirms that the goal of faith is perfect love.

▶ THE ACTUALIZATION OF THE NEW CREATION IN THE HOLY SPIRIT

The Holy Spirit actualizes within us the new creation accomplished by Jesus. The Christian life accordingly takes place in the power of the Spirit.

THE ACTIVITY OF THE HOLY SPIRIT

The creeds in our tradition affirm the activity of the Spirit in the salient moments of the Christian life: "He is ever present and efficiently active in and with the Church of Christ, convincing the world of sin, regenerating those who repent and believe, sanctifying believers, and guiding into all truth as it is in Jesus." "He is ever present, assuring, preserving, guiding, and enabling the believer." In particular, "regeneration, or the new birth, is [a] work of the Holy Spirit," "repentance is prompted by the convicting ministry of the Holy Spirit," and "believers have the witness of the Spirit that they are children of God."

The new creation, accomplished by the life, death, and resurrection of Jesus, remains a promise until it is actualized in human hearts and human community. It is by the power of the Holy Spirit that this actualization occurs. In the Spirit we are restored to fellowship with God, find new life in Christ, and obtain freedom from sin.

What is the work of the Spirit by which we are created anew? It is to draw us out of the world of sin and to implant us in the new world that God creates. The work of the Holy Spirit, therefore, is to realize the eschatological goal of creation, which is fellowship between God and the world. In Jesus Christ this goal is actualized in one person and made available to all. In the Holy Spirit, this goal is actualized in all those who are incorporated into the Body of Christ.

As the one in whom the goal of creation is realized, the Holy Spirit is the movement of God into the world. This divine movement proceeds from the Father, definitively comes into the world through Jesus Christ, and finds its conclusion as, in the Spirit, we are drawn into the fellowship between the Father and the Son. That is why the New Testament affirms that the Christian life is conducted in the power of the Spirit. To be in the Spirit is to dwell in God's new creation and to share in the divine Trinitarian life.

▶ THE PRELUDE TO LIFE IN THE SPIRIT

God's grace comes to every human being. The universal, prevenient grace of God is the source of conscience and spiritual awakening.

In grace the triune God comes to every human being. No one is untouched by God's coming into the world. Although many do not respond to God's approach with the faithfulness that is due, God's grace approaches all, seeking, enabling and evoking a faithful response.

We see the universality of God's grace in the fact that it elicits a response even among those who have not heard the gospel. The classic illustration of this faithful, pre-Christian response is Cornelius in Acts 10. Although neither Jewish nor Christian—indeed, he was a Roman centurion—he was "a devout man who feared God with all his household; he gave alms generously to the people and prayed constantly to God" (10:2). How could he be devout and God-fearing, being outside the covenant people of God? It was possible only because God's grace is not limited to the covenant people. On the contrary, God comes to everyone, seeking a faithful response. Cornelius exemplifies those who respond faithfully to God's grace but who know nothing about Jesus Christ.

The theological term that designates God's coming to every person and seeking a response is ***prevenient grace.*** In grace God approaches us and draws us into the triune life. We thus come to be characterized by our relation to God. Because of grace, we are no longer determined by the world of sin; we are instead theological beings, for we exist in relation to God. For those who reject God's grace, this is a relation of alienation and forgetfulness; for those who receive grace, it is a relation of faithful obedience. But every human being stands in some relation to God by virtue of God's Trinitarian creation of and entrance into the world. The term *prevenient grace* signifies humankind's existence in relation to God and the fact that this relation is grounded in God's movement into the world.

In those who do not yet have faith in Jesus, God's prevenient grace takes two principal forms: conscience and awakening.

Conscience refers to the phenomenon described by Paul: "When Gentiles, who do not possess the law, do instinctively what the law requires. . . . they show that what the law requires is written on their hearts, to which their own consciences also bear witness; and their conflicting thoughts will accuse or perhaps excuse them" on the day of judgment (Rom. 2:14-16). Although the Gentile world had no knowledge of Moses' law, it had a sense of God's righteous demands and some capacity to fulfill those demands. In conscience, then, those outside the covenant people of God have a limited knowledge of God or at least of God's ethical demands. Because of this knowledge, every human being stands in a relation of ethical responsibility to God. God calls everyone to respond obediently according to their knowledge of God's righteous commands.

Like conscience, *awakening* is a way in which we know God. However, being awakened is a step beyond conscience. Whereas conscience is the knowledge of God's law, awakening is the knowledge of our sin, for it results from hearing the good news of the Kingdom. To be awakened means to know ourselves not only as people who fall short of the moral law but also as people who are ignorant of God and alienated from God. In other words, it is to know ourselves to be sinners who are captives in the world of sin.

At the same time, awakening is a state in which we know ourselves to be called by God to enter the new world that God creates. Awakening thus marks an advance upon conscience, for awakening is knowing ourselves in relation to God's revelation in Jesus Christ. Additionally, being awakened is a step beyond conscience because our conformity to God's law, if even flawless, would not be full participation in God's Trinitarian life. Moral perfection, even if it were possible, would still be a state of alienation from God, for it is the knowledge of God's law, not knowledge of God the Father, in the Son and through the Spirit. Awakening signifies the dawning of this knowledge. Paradoxically, then, although awakening is the knowledge of our alienation from God, it is at the same time the beginning of our knowledge of God as Father, Son, and Holy Spirit. In being awakened we are thus drawn into God's Trinitarian life. The result is a heightened awareness of the distance that separates us from the holy God.

It is important to keep in mind that, in the movement from conscience to awakening, the triune God normally comes to us through the ordinary means of grace in the Church's ministries. Of course, God can and does come to us by other means; any created thing can be a means of grace. Nonetheless, the Church's ministries and practices, from preaching to worship to evangelism to education, constitute the ordinary means that God uses to lead people into an awakened state and from there to repentance and then to faith in Jesus Christ.

▶ FAITH

Faith is a multidimensional reality, embracing repentance, decision, response, trust, and knowledge. As the new creation, faith is the result of God's grace.

Life in the Spirit is a life of *faith*. Faith is our obedient response to God's grace and comprises several aspects.

One of these is *repentance,* which is the intensification of the awakened state. In it we progress from awareness to decision as we turn away from the world of sin and enter the new world that God is creating. That is why the New Testament associates repentance with the kingdom of God (Mark 1:15)—it is the doorway to life in that Kingdom. Repentance calls attention to the fact that faith is a decision—it is a decisive act of turning toward God. In this decision, the life that we have made in the world of sin is undone and our created life in God is remade.

As the event of entering God's new creation, repentance is an act of *consecration,* for in it we give ourselves to God and resolve to abide in God. Because consecration is the act of making something holy, it may seem unusual to think of repentance as an act of consecration. However, it is such an act; for in turning away from the world of sin and toward God, we become part of the holy people of God.

REPENTANCE

The creeds in our tradition describe repentance as "a sincere and thorough change of the mind in regard to sin, involving a sense of personal guilt and a voluntary turning away from sin" and "a willful change of mind that renounces sin and longs for righteousness, a godly sorrow for and a confession of past sins, proper restitution for wrong doings, and a resolution to reform."

However, we must not think of faith only as a decision. Like awakening and repentance, it is a result of God's prevenient grace. It is both our response to God's grace and a reality prompted by that grace, for "it is God who is at work in you, enabling you both to will and to work for his good pleasure" (Phil. 2:13). Faith is God's new creation in us and is at the same time our obedient reception of that new creation. Although it may seem paradoxical that faith can be the gracious work of God within us and also our response to that grace, the paradox is resolved once we see that faith is our participation in God's Trinitarian life and movement into the world. By faith we live in the Spirit, with the result that God lives through us. Authentic prayer, for instance, is God's Spirit praying through us. Our confession that Jesus is Lord is likewise spoken in the power of the Spirit. In the Spirit, then, God lives through us and brings about the faithful response that is faith.

Faith is a decision and a response to God's grace. But it is also our knowledge of God. Conscience and awakening are steps on the path toward the knowledge of God; however, it is only in faith that we fully, in the Spirit, know the Father through the Son. Faith is the consummate knowledge of God and the fulfillment of the movement that begins in conscience and passes through awakening and repentance. As an act of knowledge, faith is enlightenment or *illumination*, as Hebrews indicates in speaking about those "who have once been enlightened, and have tasted the heavenly gift, and have shared in the Holy Spirit" (6:4). *Illumination* preserves the sense that faith is a work of God, for it is God "who has shone in our hearts to give the light of the knowledge of the glory of God in the face of Jesus Christ" (2 Cor. 4:6).

To see that faith includes illumination helps us remember that faith is far more than belief. We form beliefs based on our experience. Faith, however, is the knowledge of God that we have through our life in God's Spirit. Moreover, faith is also an act of trust. To have faith in God is to put our trust in God, whereas the objects of belief do not necessarily inspire our trust.

As an aspect of life in the Spirit, faith brings with it an *assurance* of our salvation. As Paul taught, our certainty of being children of God is grounded in the presence of the Spirit: "When we cry 'Abba! Father!' it is that very Spirit bearing witness with our spirit that we are children of God" (Rom. 8:15-16). In the Spirit we know ourselves to be restored to fellowship with God. We are able to call upon God as our Father (and thus to see ourselves as children of God) by virtue of the power of the Spirit. To have faith, then, is to know ourselves to be children of God in the fullest sense of the word.

▸ GOOD WORKS

Good works are a consequence of our participation in God's Trinitarian life; however, they do not make us righteous and do not in themselves effect our movement from the world of sin into the kingdom of God.

The Christian life is a life of **good works**. However, it is easy to be confused about the role of good works. The potential confusion arises because of Paul's critique of some of his fellow Jews: "They did not strive for [righteousness] on the basis of faith, but as if it were based on works" (Rom. 9:32). In contrast, we are to be like Abraham "who without works trust[ed] him who justifies the ungodly" (Rom. 4:5). Paul's assessment of works, that is, of obedience to the law of Moses, is based on his insight that such obedience cannot make us righteous (Rom. 3:20) and that the law instead brings upon us God's wrath (Rom. 4:15). So, it is important to insist that no human deed, even obedience to the Old Testament law, can make us righteous or bring us into a right relation to God. On the contrary, we become righteous and qualified to stand in the presence of the holy God as a gift of God's grace. Faith is this reception of and response to this grace.

It is possible to misunderstand Paul, as though he were denying the importance of good works altogether. Such a misunderstanding is called *antinomianism*. This is the view of those who are so anxious about human attempts to achieve righteousness by good works that they deny that works have any bearing on our relation to God. The truth is that good works are an essential component of the Christian life as responses to God's grace. They do not prompt or cause God's grace; however, it is essential that we do good works in order to remain in God's grace. This is because good works are a return to God of the divine life in which we participate. As we have noted, God comes into the world to establish fellowship. In faith we participate in that Trinitarian movement into the world. However, this movement does not end in us. On the contrary, the purpose of our participation in the divine life is to return that life to God. Good works are one way in which we return the divine life. In performing good works, God lives through us. In them the life of God and our participation in that life are manifest. In them we give back to God the divine life that we have received.

The absence of good works signifies that we have interrupted our participation in God's Trinitarian life and have returned, if only momentarily, to the world of sin. The absence of works, accordingly, signals the absence of faith, while their presence is the result of a living faith. Good works, therefore, are not so much something commanded as something that indicates our participation in God. The presence of good works is a testimony to our participation in the divine life. Their absence signals the disruption of that life and our return to the world of sin.

GOOD WORKS

The creeds in our tradition affirm that "although good works, which are the fruits of faith, and follow after justification, cannot put away our sins, and endure the severity of God's judgment; yet are they pleasing and acceptable to God in Christ, and spring out of a true and lively faith, insomuch that by them a lively faith may be as evidently known as a tree is discerned by its fruit."

▶ FAITHFUL OBEDIENCE

Life in the Spirit is the restoration of humankind's obedient response to God. As such, it is characterized by wisdom, righteousness, hope, humility, fear, and praise. These characteristics are more than simply virtues. They are acts of transcendence by which we participate in God's Trinitarian life.

God calls upon us to respond to grace with faithful obedience: with wisdom, righteousness and justice, hope, humility, fear, and praise. We are now in a position to get a better grasp of this response, for each of these aspects of faithful obedience is a way in which we participate in God's Trinitarian life and are united to God the Father through Jesus Christ in the Spirit. Each of these modes of obedience is a way of abiding in God and consequently describes life in the Spirit.

Seen from the perspective of God's Trinitarian life, wisdom is more than simply cleverness or insight. True wisdom is instead the result of our participation in and union with God. This is because, according to the New Testament, wisdom has a thoroughly Trinitarian character. It comes to us from God the Father and is possessed in Christ as we live in the Spirit. As Paul indicated,

> We speak God's wisdom. . . . And we speak of these things in words not taught by human wisdom but taught by the Spirit. . . . Those who are unspiritual do not receive the gifts of God's Spirit, for they are foolishness to them, and they are unable to understand them because they are spiritually discerned. Those who are spiritual discern all things. . . . We have the mind of Christ *(1 Cor. 2:7, 13-16).*

This passage teaches us that God's wisdom—the capacity to comprehend the ways of God—is attained only through the Spirit of God. And if we ask about the content of that wisdom, we learn that it is Jesus Christ and his cross (1:18-25). To be wise, then, is to see that in Jesus Christ God has come into the world and has identified with the world to the point of death. It is to embrace this coming into the world and by faith and love to participate in it. But such embracing and participation is possible only in the power of the Spirit. Only as the Spirit draws us out of the world of sin and into God's Trinitarian life can we truly embody God's wisdom. True wisdom, then, is an act of transcendence toward

God, in which we leave behind the wisdom that is "earthly, unspiritual, devilish" (James 3:15) and it is an act of union, by which we come to be in Jesus Christ, who is the wisdom of God (1 Cor. 1:24).

Like wisdom, righteousness has a Trinitarian sense. It is more than merely obeying God's law. It is, in fact, the result of our walking in the Spirit and, consequently, is an act of transcendence toward God. In Paul's words,

> The law of the Spirit of life in Christ Jesus has set you free from the law of sin and of death. . . . Those who live according to the flesh set their minds on the things of the flesh, but those who live according to the Spirit set their minds on the things of the Spirit. . . . The mind that is set on the flesh is hostile to God; it does not submit to God's law—indeed it cannot" *(Rom. 8:2, 5, 7).*

This passage presents human existence as being ruled either by the flesh (the power of the world of sin) or by the Spirit of God. Those who dwell in the flesh, "being ignorant of the righteousness that comes from God, and seeking to establish their own . . . have not submitted to God's righteousness" (Rom. 10:3). Those who walk in the Spirit share in the true righteousness, which is God's righteousness, because they alone have experienced the transformation of life that results from being in Christ and living by the power of the Spirit. To be righteous, then, is an act of transcendence because it is to turn away from our own self-made righteousness and to embrace God's righteousness in Jesus Christ. And it is an act of union with God, for we attain God's righteousness as we are in Christ and walk in the Spirit.

Hope likewise has a Trinitarian character. It is not merely a confidence in the future based on our assessment of the past or of history's direction. It is instead a reflection of our participation in God. This is seen in its Trinitarian structure. On one hand, hope is grounded in the new life in Jesus Christ (1 Cor. 15:17-19). Because Jesus has been raised from the dead, we can walk in newness of life by sharing in his resurrection. On the other hand, hope is grounded in the Holy Spirit (Eph. 1:13-14). Life in the Spirit, as an eschatological reality, is God's pledge on our ultimate redemption. Because we live in the Spirit, we already share in the new world that God is creating, in spite of our living alongside the world of sin. Christian hope, then, is not a wish about the future. It is instead a way of saying that we now, in the present, live in the Spirit and share in the resurrection of Jesus Christ and that the future God promises is the continuation of this present reality.

The same is true of humility and thanksgiving. It is possible to feel a sense of humility and thankfulness in the presence of many sorts of things—great people, great events, and so on. But in the highest sense, we are humbled and filled with thankfulness only in the presence of God. But for this we need the authentic knowledge of God. Only when we truly know God do we realize true humility. Only when we have received God's revelation in Jesus Christ can we reach the heights of thanksgiving.

It would seem that fear is not part of the Christian life. After all, 1 John declares that "there is no fear in love, but perfect love casts our fear" (4:18). However, this verse is speaking, not of awe, but of anxiety about punishment: "For fear has to do with punishment; and whoever fears has not reached perfection" (v. 18). The New Testament, then, does not negate the Old Testament's teaching about the fear of God, that is, our sense of awe in the face of God's holiness and transcendence. On the contrary, as Hebrews indicates, having reverence and awe is a vital aspect of the Christian life (12:28). Still, reverence and awe are more than attitudes that we adopt in the presence of the holy God. This is because authentic reverence and awe presuppose the authentic knowledge of God. Toward a false god of our own making we may feel something that we mistakenly identify with awe; however, true reverence can be felt only in the presence of the living God, the holy God who has come into the world.

Finally, praise is a response to God's holiness and transcendence. But in revelation, that is, in Jesus Christ, the holy, transcendent God has come into the world. Praise, accordingly, is a response to God's holiness among us in revelation. However, praise is more than verbal behavior. First of all, the entirety of our lives is to be an act of praise: "You were bought with a price; therefore glorify God in your body" (1 Cor. 6:20). But our lives can glorify God only in so far as we share in the divine life of holiness and righteousness. In the world of sin, our bodies and our lives are anything but God's praise. They become an act of praising God only as we are drawn into God's life through acts of consecration.

▶ Power

Life in the Spirit is a life of faithful obedience; however, faith and obedience are the result of the Holy Spirit working within us. The Spirit, therefore, is the divine power by which the Christian life is conducted.

In the Old Testament, the Spirit was experienced as the divine power that gives human beings extraordinary gifts for the purpose of serving God. The work of the Spirit in the Christian life is similar, for it is by the Spirit's power that we are drawn into the presence of God. Every aspect of the Christian life is therefore a way in which God in the Holy Spirit draws us out of the world of sin and places us in the world of the new creation.

Take, for instance, the fruit of the Spirit—love, joy, peace, and so on. We miss an important point if we think of these merely as characteristics of the ideal Christian life and especially if we think of them simply as the products of human striving after a moral ideal. Because they are fruit of the Spirit, they are manifestations of God's power within us. They are the result of the Spirit's drawing us out of the world of sin and placing us in the new world that God creates. To speak of love, joy, peace, and the other fruit is to speak of the sort of existence that is found in this newly created world. Those who possess these fruit are those who participate in the new creation.

The same is true of the gifts of the Spirit enumerated in 1 Cor. 12: healing, leadership, power, and so on. It is possible to regard at least some of these simply as human capacities, for some people surely do have the ability to lead or teach. But to speak of these as gifts of the Spirit means that we see them, not as human talents that are useful for an organization such as the Church, but instead as functions by which the eschatological people of God exist socially. This people—the Church—have been called out of the world of sin and has been incorporated into the resurrected Jesus Christ. They are his body. The gifts, therefore, are not simply organizational skills. They are instead the Spirit's use of human capacities and skills in and for the eschatological people of God. They are in one sense ordinary functions such as speaking and leading. But they are also extraordinary because in the Spirit they become God's tools and are consecrated to God's service in the Church.

It is because the Holy Spirit is the movement of God that accomplishes something extraordinary in us that the Holy Spirit is associated with power. As Paul testified, "My speech and my proclamation were not with plausible words of wisdom, but with a demonstration of the Spirit and of power" (1 Cor. 2:4). He was saying that his preaching was delivered and received in the power of the Spirit. Of course, his preaching consisted of ordinary human words. But they were in fact the Word of God, for both the speaking and the hearing were consecrated by the Holy Spirit and placed in God's service. Similarly, he noted that the Thessalonians had "received the word with joy inspired by the Holy Spirit" (1 Thess. 1:6). Paul's point was that his words could not have had their divine effect if the Spirit had not been drawing his hearers out of the world of sin and into God's world. Preaching—both the speaking and the hearing—is possible only by the power of the Spirit. Although the preacher uses ordinary human words, these words become God's word when the Spirit elevates both speaker and hearer out of the world of sin and places them in the presence of God.

This is why blasphemy against the Holy Spirit is the unforgivable sin. We blaspheme the Spirit when we attribute the work of the Spirit to demonic or worldly powers. It is not that God is unable or unwilling to forgive this sin. But because the Spirit is that by which we enter into the new creation of God, sin against the Spirit is a rejection of that power by which the new creation is possible. Our sin against the Spirit cannot be forgiven, not because of any unwillingness on God's part, but because if we reject the power of the new creation, we reject the possibility of our participating in that new creation. To sin against the Spirit is to reject God's grace and to exist perpetually in the world of sin.

▶ ESCHATOLOGICAL EXISTENCE

Life in the Spirit is an eschatological existence. It is a life in God's new creation alongside the world of sin.

The Christian life is a journey, in the power of the Spirit, from the world of sin into the new world of God's presence. However, the world of sin is not yet subdued. As the Old Testament reminds us, chaos returns with its destructive power. The world of sin thus remains a power that can draw us away from God and away from love.

As a result, although a continuous and perpetual life in the Spirit is a possibility, it is not attained by all. That is the problem that Paul addressed in the early chapters of 1 Cor. The Corinthians, whom Paul regarded as sanctified and as saints (1:2), were nonetheless caught in the power of sin:

> I could not speak to you as spiritual people, but rather as people of the flesh, as infants in Christ. . . . For as long as there is jealousy and quarreling among you, are you not of the flesh, and behaving according to human inclinations? For when one says, "I belong to Paul," and another, "I belong to Apollos," are you not merely human? (3:1, 3-4).

We can see here that the Corinthians were acting in a merely human fashion. They were existing on the flat moral plane of human existence in its separation from God (the "flesh"). They were not dwelling in the new world of God's creation.

The situation represented by the Corinthians is possible because of the eschatological nature of life in the Spirit. While a continuous living in the Spirit is possible, it is also possible to continue to live according to the flesh, as the Corinthians were doing. This is because, in this eschatological state, the world of sin coexists with the new world of God's creation. The life of the flesh coexists alongside life in the Spirit. That is why the New Testament writers so frequently engaged in exhortation—they sought in their writings to stir their readers to live continuously in the Spirit and to turn their backs once and for all on the flesh and the world of sin.

In this tensed situation, where the kingdom of God coexists with the world of sin and in which the victory of the Kingdom may seem doubtful, Paul portrayed the Holy Spirit as a pledge or guarantee of the world's eschatological future. God, he affirmed, "has anointed us by putting his seal on us and giving us his Spirit in our hearts as a first installment" (2 Cor. 1:21-22). In this and similar passages, Paul was presenting the Spirit as a reality that God has given to us in anticipation of the world's eschatological fulfillment. The Spirit is thus the "first fruits" (Rom. 8:23) of God's final subduing of the world of sin. The Spirit is also our being sealed for salvation. *Sealing* is a metaphor that indicates an official marking by which something is identified with the one doing the sealing. Hence to say that we "were marked with the seal of the promised Holy Spirit" (Eph. 1:13) is to say that we have been identified as the people of God.

This metaphor of the seal has eschatological significance, for in the Spirit we have been "marked with a seal for the day of redemption" (Eph. 4:30). The gift of the Holy Spirit signals the fact that we have received God's mark, characterizing us as the people who are under God's rule and members of God's kingdom. It signifies that we are no longer part of the world of sin and that we are instead "aliens and exiles" (1 Pet. 2:11).

Finally, the eschatological tension between God's kingdom and the world of sin requires the Church to exercise discernment in things of the Spirit. Because the kingdom of God coexists with the world of sin, it is sometimes easy to confuse the Spirit of God with the spirit of this world. Consequently, Paul had to warn the Corinthians to pass judgment on the words of prophets (1 Cor. 14:29). This need arose because not everything that a prophet might say would come from the inspiration of the Spirit. Similarly, while counseling us not to "despise the words of prophets," he urged us to "test everything" (1 Thess. 5:20-21). Even prophets could be confused about the source of their words. In response to this problem, 1 John provides a criterion for distinguishing the divine Spirit from the spirit of the world: "By this you know the Spirit of God: every spirit that confesses that Jesus Christ has come in the flesh is from God" (4:2). We see here a point of great importance, namely that Jesus Christ constitutes the standard by which we are to judge whether a teaching is truly from the Spirit.

The Christian life, therefore, as an eschatological life in the Spirit is an anticipation of the future age of God's unrestrained rule. Life in the Spirit is the presence of the future—God's future—in the midst of the present age of the world of sin. In the Spirit, God has brought the future into our present and allowed the future to be a reality in which we may dwell. In so doing, God has declared the world of sin to be a thing of the past. It is something that is being superseded by God's future. The Holy Spirit, accordingly, is the power of God's future experienced in our present.

▶ CHRISTIAN ETHICAL LIFE

INTRODUCTION

Life in the Spirit is a life of love as well as of faith. It issues forth in an ethical life in the world. It is necessarily an ethical life *in the world* because of the eschatological nature of Christian existence. Although we are citizens of the kingdom of God, this Kingdom is not an otherworldly phenomenon. It is not the negation of or an alternative to God's created world. On the contrary, it is God's re-creation of the world. It is true that it exists alongside the world of sin and is God's alternative to that world. But it is also true that the world of sin is our distortion of God's created world. The world of sin is the created world in the state of alienation and sin. The kingdom of God is, accordingly, not the destruction of the world of sin but instead its redemption and transformation. As a result, the kingdom of God is not an escape from the world; it is the life of freedom from sin in the world of sin.

Life in the Spirit is necessarily an *ethical life* in the world because human existence is inescapably ethical. This is Paul's point in Romans, where he asserted that Gentiles have an intuitive knowledge of God's law and a capacity to fulfill that law. Human existence is determined by our knowledge of God's righteous demands, whether or not we fulfill those demands. It is, therefore, essentially ethical, for we are the beings whose existence is defined by our capacity to act on the basis of ideals and to develop mature, fulfilled character in response to God. Sometimes our ideals are destructive. Often we fail to act consistently according to our ideals. Always we fall short of achieving a mature and fulfilled character. Nonetheless, the ethical character of our nature is inescapable, even when we contradict our nature by our actions.

In summary, life in the Spirit is a life conducted in God's world, a life that is ethical because it is an authentically human life.

WORLD-PARTICIPATION AND WORLD-TRANSCENDENCE

The Christian ethical life is the call simultaneously to ethically transcend the world of sin and to participate in the world of God's creation.

The worldly character of the kingdom of God and the eschatological nature of life in the Spirit present us with the central ethical challenge of the Christian life. That challenge is to live and act as citizens of the kingdom of God while dwelling alongside the world of sin. Because we dwell in God's kingdom, our conduct must differ from those who dwell in the world of sin. But because we continue to exist alongside that world, we remain susceptible to sin's influence. As a result, we must struggle to ensure that our conduct differs from the world of sin.

Life in the Spirit is, therefore, simultaneously our *ethical transcendence over the world* and our *ethical participation in the world.* It cannot be otherwise, for *world* has a two-fold significance for the Christian life: the world of sin, which we must ethically transcend, and the created world, in which, as creatures, we participate.

To speak of an ethical transcendence over the world is to affirm the words of 1 John: "Whatever is born of God conquers the world. And this is the victory that conquers the world, our faith" (5:4). Faith is our transcendence over the world because faith is that decision by which we come to participate in God's Trinitarian life and leave behind the world of sin. Transcendence means that we decisively turn away from the world of sin and that we repudiate that world, even though it is a world that we have made. It means that our values and practices must be those of God's kingdom and not those of the world of sin.

However, ethical transcendence does *not* mean a flight from the world. We cannot escape the world of sin and its effects by physically removing ourselves from that world, for the world of sin is the world that we make in our alienation from God. Physical relocation does not remove us from the world of sin, for it dwells in us. The world of sin is found wherever human beings are found. That is why our transcendence over the world is of an ethical and spiritual nature. We must conquer the world that we make and dwell in the new world that God is making.

But because we are creatures who dwell in God's created world, we participate in that world. And because the kingdom of God is the redemption and transformation of the created world that has been distorted into the world of sin, life in the Spirit is a life conducted in full participation in this world and with thankful enjoyment of the good things that God has given us. In the words of 1 Timothy, "Everything created by God is good, and nothing is to be rejected, provided it is received with thanksgiving; for it is sanctified by God's word and prayer" (4:4-5). Hence the harsh words for those who insist on regulations about food and other practices which have only "an appearance of wisdom" (see Col.

2:20-23). Consequently, life in the Spirit is a life devoted to bringing the world into conformity with the kingdom of God. This devotion takes many forms, from loving the neighbor in concrete acts of mercy to efforts to achieve justice and peace among the nations. Regardless of the form it takes, this devotion to the world is a necessary consequence of our participation in the world.

ETHICAL LIFE IN THE WORLD

The Christian ethical life is a life of virtues. Some of these the Christian shares with those who are outside the Church. But the coming of God into the world radically transforms ethical life and brings it under the rule of love.

The life of the Christian disciple in the world is the life of a very specific sort of character. It is possible to state, with great specificity, the attitudes and practices that characterize the Christian life. In Luke's Gospel, for instance, we find, among others, the following characteristics: humility (14:7-11; 18:9-17), generosity (14:12-14), obedience (6:46-49; 11:27-28), faith (8:22-25; 17:5-6), dedication to the kingdom of God (9:57-62; 10:38-42; 14:25-33), being alert (12:35-40; 21:34-36), and freedom from greed (12:13-34; 16:13-15; 18:18-25).

Some features of the Christian ethical life are not distinctively Christian. The letter to Titus, for example, urges us to embody temperance (or self-control), seriousness, and prudence (2:2). It declares that "the grace of God has appeared . . . training us to renounce impiety and worldly passions, and in the present age to live lives that are self-controlled, upright, and godly" (2:11-12). Although these are laudable qualities, they are by no means unique to Christians. On the contrary, they are the sorts of virtues that every culture has enjoined on people. So, there is no reason to pretend that Christian ethics is unique, for nearly every community has recognized the importance of characteristics such as truth-telling and self-control. It is important that we affirm these points of agreement and help other communities to see that their ethical systems point toward God.

At the same time, it is important to see that God's coming into the world results in the transformation of ethics. In God's kingdom, the first will be last and the last first; those who would lead must be servants of all. God's will is therefore not simply identical with fulfilling the requirements of conventional ethics. It is not enough to be self-controlled, serious, and prudent. We must also participate in God's Trinitarian coming into the world, with the transformation of ethics that it brings. We see this transformation, for instance, in the New Testament's household codes. Passages such as Eph. 5:22—6:9 instruct disciples about relationships in the household (husband-wife, parent-child, master-slave). At one level, these instructions are quite conventional and reflect the norms of ancient society. They do not, for example, urge Christians to free their slaves. On the contrary, they retain the forms of ancient social organization. However, within these societal forms the grace of God should bring about a remarkable transformation. Although wives are counseled to be subject to husbands (5:22), in fact every disciple is to be subject to every other disciple, regardless of gender (5:21). And although slaves are instructed to obey their masters, Christian slave-owners are ordered to treat their slaves in the same way in which their slaves are to act toward them (6:9). We can see then that the gospel introduces a radical element into human ethics. Although respecting the basic forms of social organization of the Roman world, the gospel has brought those forms under the rule of love.

In some respects, then, the Christian ethical life will resemble the ethics of other communities. But in other respects, the Christian's life in the world will differ as we seek to be faithful to the radical demands of the kingdom of God.

▶ THE ETHICAL DIMENSION OF FAITH

The doctrine of the Holy Spirit and the Spirit's work is a doctrine that we should affirm and also live. In fact, we affirm it by living it, for the Spirit is not a concept to think about but is instead the divine reality in which we are to dwell. We affirm the doctrine of the Spirit when we live in the Spirit and experience the Spirit's transformation of our existence. We believe the doctrine of the Spirit when we allow ourselves to be moved from the world of sin to God's new creation.

SUMMARY STATEMENTS

1. The Holy Spirit actualizes within us the new creation accomplished by Jesus. The Christian life accordingly takes place in the power of the Spirit.

2. God's grace comes to every human being. The universal, pre-venient grace of God is the source of conscience and spiritual awakening.

3. Faith is a multidimensional reality, embracing repentance, decision, response, trust, and knowledge. As the new creation, faith is the result of God's grace.

4. Good works are a consequence of our participation in God's Trinitarian life; however, they do not make us righteous and do not in themselves effect our movement from the world of sin into the kingdom of God.

5. Life in the Spirit is the restoration of humankind's obedient response to God. As such, it is characterized by wisdom, righteousness, hope, humility, fear, and praise. These characteristics are more than simply virtues. They are acts of transcendence by which we participate in God's Trinitarian life.

6. Life in the Spirit is a life of faithful obedience; however, faith and obedience are the result of the Holy Spirit working within us. The Spirit, therefore, is the divine power by which the Christian life is conducted.

7. Life in the Spirit is an eschatological existence. It is a life in God's new creation alongside the world of sin.

8. The Christian ethical life is the call simultaneously to ethically transcend the world of sin and to participate in the world of God's creation.

9. The Christian ethical life is a life of virtues. Some of these the Christian shares with those who are outside the Church. But the coming of God into the world radically transforms ethical life and brings it under the rule of love.

QUESTIONS FOR REFLECTION

1. What does the work of the Spirit tell us about the Spirit's divinity?

2. What is the relation between the Spirit's work and Jesus Christ's work in the new creation?

ELEVEN

LIFE IN THE SPIRIT
THE PERFECTION OF LOVE

OBJECTIVES

Your study of this chapter should help you to understand:

1. The relation of the Christian life to sin.

2. The meaning of entire sanctification and perfect love.

3. The characteristics of the holy life.

KEY WORDS TO UNDERSTAND

Deification

Entire sanctification

Holiness

Initial sanctification

Love

Mortification

Perfect love

Purgation

Sanctification

Union

QUESTIONS TO CONSIDER AS YOU READ

1. What is the relation of grace to self-discipline in the Christian life?

2. How is it that we are, according to Paul, dead to sin and yet we continue to be susceptible to the power of sin?

3. Why is love a central aspect of the Christian life?

Jesu, my life, thyself apply,
   Thy Holy Spirit breathe,
My vile affections crucify,
   Conform me to thy death.

Conqu'ror of hell, and earth, and sin,
   Still with thy rebel strive;
Enter my soul, and work within,
   and kill, and make alive!

More of thy life and more I have
   As the old Adam dies;
Bury me, Saviour, in thy grave,
   That I with thee may rise.

Reign in me, Lord, thy foes control
   Who would not own thy sway;
Diffuse thine image through my soul,
   Shine to the perfect day.

Scatter the last remains of sin,
   And seal me thine abode;
O make me glorious all within,
   A temple built by God!

This hymn by the Wesleys, published in 1740, speaks forcefully about the subject of this chapter, the Christian life. It portrays that life in a trinitarian frame by its appeal to Jesus to conform our lives to him and in its prayer for the Holy Spirit's breathing. It depicts the Christian life as a yielding to Christ's lordship as we die and rise with Christ to new life. It sets forth the result of Christ's work as his image shining forth in our lives and our becoming temples of God. Each verse presents the Christian life as a life of growing conformity to Jesus Christ, a life in which sin is overcome and we increasingly reflect the image of Jesus and the glory of God. Each verse, in short, presents the Christian life as a life of holiness.

▶ THE DEATH OF SIN

Life in the Spirit means the death of sin and freedom from its power and corruption.

In the new creation we journey from the world of sin into the new world that God creates. As we walk in the Spirit we turn our backs on the world of sin and thus become free from its grip. Justification describes our freedom from the guilt and condemnation associated with sin. **Sanctification** (or **holiness**) describes our freedom from the corrupting effects of sin.

Paul's letters give us an especially powerful picture of life in the Spirit as a victory over sin. In baptism "our old self was crucified with [Jesus], so that . . . we might no longer be enslaved to sin" (Rom. 6:6). And "those who belong to Christ Jesus have crucified the flesh with its passions and desires" (Gal. 5:24). As a result, we are able to "walk in newness of life" (Rom. 6:4). Moreover, sin no longer rules over us (see v. 14), for we "have been freed from sin" (v. 22).

Our freedom from sin is a result of living in the Spirit. Those who live in the flesh (the world of sin) dwell in a state of alienation and hostility toward God's law (Rom. 8:7-8). Those who live in the Spirit put to death sinful deeds (v. 13) and "do not gratify the desires of the flesh" (Gal. 5:16).

For Paul, then, life in the Spirit is a life of sanctification (Rom. 8:1-12). It is a life in which sin is dead and godly fruit, above all love, abounds.

▶ THE LIFE OF LOVE

Life in the Spirit is a life of union with God. It is, accordingly, a life of love and holiness.

In the Old Testament, physical things became holy when they were consecrated for use in the Temple or dedicated exclusively to God. Their holiness consisted in their being related to God. Before consecration, an altar is just a pile of rocks. After consecration, these rocks stand in a special relation to God and thus are holy. Holiness, therefore, occurs when something is drawn into relation to God.

Human beings become holy when they too are drawn into relation to God. But because we are beings who can respond to God's grace, our relation to God consists in our participation in God's Trinitarian life, which is a life of communion or fellowship. It is the fellowship between the Father and the Son, a fellowship that transpires in the communion of the Spirit. God is this life of fellowship in communion. As we are drawn into this life, we share in the fellowship between the Father and the Son through the power of the Spirit.

To say that God's life is a life of fellowship and communion is to say that it is a life of love, for *love* is **union**. It is the way in which we share in the life and being of others. We love others when we share their lives—when their lives become integral parts of our life in such a way that to desire their good and to desire our own good is one and the same. The death of loved ones is so painful because it rips an essential part of our life from us. God's life is inherently a life of love because it is a life of union, for the Father exists in the Son and the Son exists in the Father (see John 17:21). The Father and Son dwell in mutual love because each abides in union with the other. The Holy Spirit, being the Spirit of the Father and of the Son, is the principle of their union. Consequently, the ultimate statement about God is that "God is love" (1 John 4:8). God not only loves but is love itself—the act of union. This union is eternal in the Trinitarian fellowship and then passes over into God's act of coming into the world, creating fellowship with creatures.

The life of holiness, therefore, which consists in participating in the divine life, is also the life of love, for our participation in God is our union with God. To love God is to be united with God in such a way that the divine life becomes an integral and defining part of our life. It is a life in which there is no distinction between God's good and our good. It is to find our being in God's being. In love we share, through the power of the Spirit, in the movement from the Father to the Son and back to the Father. In love we participate in the unity of the Father and the Son. We abide in them; they abide in us. This is exactly what holiness, that is, our participation in God, is. Love—our union with God—is accordingly the definition and measure of holiness for human beings.

We can now see that love is the alternative to sin. In love, we are drawn out of the small, selfish world we have created for ourselves and are elevated into the God who is love. In love we transcend (without negating or abandoning) all merely human reality and participate in the eternal life of God. In the Spirit we transcend the limitations of the human world we have created and fulfill our destiny as the creation of God. This is why for Jesus the greatest commandment was to love God (Mark 12:29-30) and why "the only thing that counts is faith working through love" (Gal. 5:6). Without this love, we remain plunged hopelessly into the world of sin. Without this love we fall short of our essential being as God's creatures and God's image.

We can also now see that holiness (or sanctification) can be defined in two ways. Negatively, it is freedom from sin. Affirmatively, it is the life of love, a participation in God's Trinitarian life.

▶ THE STRUGGLE WITH SIN

Life in the Spirit is an eschatological existence, in which sin is dead and yet can live again.

Freedom from sin, although authentic, is far from being a simple reality. This is because life in the Spirit is an eschatological existence; the world of sin continues to exist alongside the new world that God creates. Although in the power of the Spirit we dwell in the new creation, we remain susceptible to the power of the world of sin. As the Old Testament reminds us, the power of chaos is not fully overcome until the eschatological consummation of all things.

So, although we have, in baptism, "died to sin" (Rom. 6:2), we "must consider [ourselves] dead to sin and alive to God in Christ Jesus" (v. 11). Our death to sin, in other words, is not a permanent, static state that requires nothing more from us. Having died to sin, we must now, Paul wrote, take steps to ensure that sin remains dead: "Do not let sin exercise dominion in your mortal bodies." We must accordingly "present [ourselves] to God as those who have been brought from death to life" (vv. 12-13).

What does it means to present ourselves to God in this fashion? It means offering ourselves to God as living sacrifices (Rom. 12:1). It means, in other words, to consecrate ourselves to God. Just as, in the Old

Testament, animals were devoted to God for use in sacrifice, so we are to give ourselves over to God in an act of worship. However, this act of consecration is something that must be consciously and intentionally performed. Further, it is distinct from and subsequent to repentance and baptism, which are initial acts of consecration.

As we consecrate ourselves to God, sin no longer has dominion over us, because we have passed out of the domain of sin and into the world of God's grace (Rom. 6:14). In consecration we have, as Paul explained, become slaves of a new lord: "If you present yourselves to anyone as obedient slaves, you are slaves of the one whom you obey, either of sin, which leads to death, or of obedience, which leads to righteousness" (v. 16). According to Paul, we are thus controlled either by our devotion to the world of sin or by our devotion to God. Those who, through consecration, have become devoted to God are now righteous and, being "slaves of righteousness," have been "set free from sin" (v. 18). And yet, their continued freedom from sin depends on their actually and continually presenting themselves "as slaves to righteousness for sanctification" (v. 19). The Christian life is thus a life tensed between the world of sin and the kingdom of God, a life in which sin has died but is quite capable of resurrection.

Under what circumstances is sin's power resurrected within us? Here the example of the Corinthians is instructive. These believers, Paul affirmed, had been justified and sanctified (1 Cor. 6:11); however, they were nonetheless not "spiritual people" but "people of the flesh . . . infants in Christ" (3:1). Although they were not falling away from God through overt apostasy, they had not turned decisively away from the world of sin: "You are still of the flesh. For as long as there is jealousy and quarreling among you, are you not of the flesh, and behaving according to human inclinations?" (v. 3). Instead of walking in the Spirit, they were driven by human inclinations, that is, by the impulses of the world of sin.

The Corinthians dramatically illustrate the nature of eschatological existence. To live eschatologically is to have left the world of sin and to live in God's new creation. However, although the new creation is a present reality, it is not present in its fullness. In history it exists alongside the world of sin and those who walk in the Spirit remain susceptible to sin's power. The Corinthians are an example of disciples on whom the residue of sin clung with unusual stubbornness. They had died to sin, but their journey into God's new creation was, we might say, interrupted; as a result, sin was powerful among them.

The eschatological nature of Christian existence tells us that sanctification is not achieved all at once in the first moments of repentance and faith. Faith, repentance, and baptism initiate us into life in the Spirit and are signposts on the journey from the world of sin into God's creation. This enables us to speak of *initial sanctification*, which describes our turning from sin to God and the first glimmers of love and holiness. However, as the Corinthians show us, this initial turning to God does not suffice in itself to destroy the power of sin and to deliver us with utter decisiveness from the world of sin. As we have seen, it is necessary to present ourselves to God as "instruments of righteousness" and as a "living sacrifice." This is not accomplished at the beginning of our journey to God.

▶ THE PERFECTION OF LOVE

Initial sanctification is not the totality of sanctification. The churches in our tradition affirm that there is a state of sanctification characterized by the freedom from sin that Paul spoke of and by the perfection of love. They affirm as well that this freedom is not only an ideal but also a reality that we can attain. The name that our tradition gives to such freedom is *entire sanctification*.

ENTIRE SANCTIFICATION AND PERFECT LOVE

Entire sanctification is the perfection of our love for God.

Perhaps the best way to understand the doctrine of entire sanctification is to return to the idea of love. Love is our union with and participation in another's being. Our love for God is our union with God and participation in God's Trinitarian life. To love God completely is to have our being so thoroughly immersed in God's life that our identity is changed. Instead of being people characterized by sin, we become people whose being and identity are defined by their participation in God. To love God is to have God as such an integral part of life that a return to the world of sin would mean the disruption and fragmentation of the new self that God creates.

ENTIRE SANCTIFICATION

The churches in our tradition make several affirmations about entire sanctification. They assert that it is an "act of God," a "work of the Holy Spirit," and that it is "effected by the baptism with the Holy Spirit." They assert as well that it is "subsequent to regeneration" and that it is "wrought instantaneously when believers present themselves as living sacrifices, holy and acceptable to God, through faith in Jesus Christ." They believe that in entire sanctification we are "cleansed in that moment from all inward sin and empowered for service" and that it "enables believers to love God with all their hearts, souls, strength, and minds, and their neighbor as themselves." They affirm that "The resulting relationship [to God] is attested by the witness of the Holy Spirit." Finally, they declare that "the grace of entire sanctification includes the impulse to grow in grace. However, this impulse must be consciously nurtured, and careful attention given to the requisites and processes of spiritual development and improvement in Christlikeness of character and personality. Without such purposeful endeavor one's witness may be impaired and the grace itself frustrated and ultimately lost."

To be entirely sanctified, then, is to love God with a perfect love. *Perfect love* is a love that is unmixed. The Corinthians provide us with an illustration of mixed love. No doubt they loved God in some degree; however, they loved themselves and their own good more. They were envious and proud, contentious and profligate. They had not grasped Paul's teaching that participation in God means the imitation of Jesus, who exemplified humility and obedience to God. Perfect love is characterized by a pure devotion to God that is unmixed by devotion to ourselves or to any other created thing.

At the same time, perfect love for God must be matched by perfect love for our neighbors (1 John 4:12). In this context, perfect love means a sincere concern for others' well-being that manifests itself in concrete acts of goodness. The parable of the good Samaritan is our guide here. Ignoring the fact that the person in need was a Jew, the Samaritan was moved by compassion and engaged in acts of kindness. That is the meaning of Matt. 5:48, which urges us to be perfect as the "Father is perfect." Such perfection seems impossible, until we see that the Father causes rain to fall on the righteous and the unrighteous (v. 45). Our love is likewise to be offered to all, without discrimination. Only in this way is our love for others perfect.

It is no exaggeration to say that the churches in our tradition exist largely for the purpose of bearing witness to the doctrine of entire sanctification and of urging Christians to love God perfectly. Our reason for being is to testify to the importance of this doctrine and to insist that the perfection of love is eminently obtainable and the disciple's highest priority.

THE PATH TO PERFECT LOVE

We attain perfect love through God's grace, through using the means of grace, through spiritual disciplines, and through consecration.

How do we arrive at this love? First, we must note that it is the result of God's grace; it is not something that we accomplish by our efforts alone. On the contrary, such love is possible only in the power of the Spirit as we participate in God's triune life. It is this abiding in God that enables us to love perfectly.

Having noted the importance of grace, we turn to the means of grace and spiritual disciplines as significant markers on the path to perfect love. The means of grace include baptism and the Lord's Supper as well as the Bible, preaching and many other things that mediate God's grace to us. Through them we enter into the realm of grace, that is, of God's Trinitarian life. Participating in the Lord's Supper, for instance, draws us into the fellowship between the Father and the Son through the power of the Holy Spirit. In the supper, we continue and strengthen our journey into the new world that God creates. The same is true of reading the Bible in faith, love, and hope. This reading is a means of grace, for it draws us into the life of the triune God by mediating to us the good news of the kingdom of God. In using the means of grace, then, we strengthen our Godward journey.

Closely related to the ordinary means of grace is the practice of spiritual disciplines. These are a vital aspect of the holy life. As Paul noted, "Athletes exercise self-control in all things. . . . [Therefore] I punish my body and enslave it" (1 Cor. 9:25, 27). More broadly, we can say that perfect love is obtained in part through the careful performance of the practices that God's people have found useful and fruitful. These include prayer and various forms of self-denial. Through these means, the power of sin's world is diminished and our love for God is enlivened. The traditional terms for the process of overcoming sin's power through spiritual disciplines are **mortification** and **purgation**. *Mortification* suggests the killing off of sin through the practice of spiritual disciplines. As we discipline ourselves and bring our thoughts and desires into the obedience of faith, the power of sin dies away. *Purgation*, at home in the language of Christian mysticism, signifies our purification from the power and effects of sin.

Beyond the means of grace and the hard work of spiritual disciplines, we attain perfect love through consecration. We are to present ourselves to God as living sacrifices (Rom. 12:1). This entails a transformation from being people who are identified with and conform to the world of sin to being people whose identity is found in God. To consecrate ourselves is to give ourselves to God. It is to place ourselves decisively into God's new creation and to abandon the world of sin. In consecration we devote ourselves to God and thus come to participate in the divine life.

CRISIS AND DEVELOPMENT IN SANCTIFICATION

The path to perfect love is for some characterized by a momentous event of faith and consecration, while for others is it characterized by a development that culminates in the perfection of love.

An aspect of the holy life that writers in our tradition have discussed is whether holiness is received all at once in an experiential crisis or whether there is a development of holiness that culminates in a moment of entire sanctification. John Wesley taught the latter view; the former is typical of some subsequent writers, especially in America.

In coming to an understanding of this issue, however, it is important to keep in mind that we are not debating whether Christian perfection is obtainable in this life. The churches in our tradition uniformly affirm that it is. The question at hand is whether there is, within our tradition, a place for us to understand entire sanctification as the development of love from the first moments of the Christian life until this development comes to a culmination and love is perfected. If this concept is vacuous, then we must conclude that believers are not holy and do not love God until, in an instant, through God's grace they love God perfectly. Some in our tradition think that we do develop in holiness before we attain the perfection of love, while others have denied such development.

As in most theological matters, it is best not to present these two views as an absolute either-or choice. Although it is possible to interpret these positions as utterly opposed to one another, some reflection will help us see that this is not the case. We can see this by attending to what each view emphasizes and presupposes.

The view that holiness (and hence love) begins with the new birth, increases, and finally comes to perfection in entire sanctification rests upon the insight that holiness is measured by faith, love, and the other fruit of the Spirit. As these increase, holiness increases, until they are perfected. There is great merit in this view, for holiness certainly is measured by these virtues and experience shows that believers show patterns of development in these virtues.

The view that sanctification is received all at once in a moment of experiential crisis has historically been a way of emphasizing the completeness of entire sanctification. The concern has been that presenting sanctification strictly as a progressive development leaves no room for speaking of *entire* sanctification, for a progressive development might well have no end. Writers in our tradition have, therefore, insisted on the instantaneous character of entire sanctification.

A bit of reflection will help us see that these two views are not mutually contradictory on the essential affirmation of our tradition, that the perfection of love in this life is possible. The developmental view does not at all exclude the reality of perfect love. It insists only that love is perfected as the culminating moment of a prior development.

How are we to reconcile these two views, which portray quite different experiential paths to perfect love? The wisest course is to honor both experiences as valid and to find a way of understanding that will justify that honor. The way forward here is to acknowledge that, due to differences of personality, some of us experience God's grace in terms of momentous, decisive events that steer life in a radically different direction, while others experience God's grace as a process of more or less continuous growth. In the former experience, entire sanctification is a dramatic and sudden elevation into a qualitatively higher spiritual plane. In the latter experience, it is similar to becoming an adult: there is a moment when one becomes an adult, but it is preceded by significant growth and development. For some, the path to holiness is characterized by a sudden movement from a Corinthian-like state into the state of perfect love, through a momentous act of faith and consecration. For others the journey is marked less by dramatic moments and more by gradual realization that culminates in perfection.

THE LIMITATIONS OF PERFECT LOVE

Although perfect love signifies the death of sin, it does not solve every human problem.

The churches in our tradition hold that there is a tremendous difference between a believer in the first days of faith and a believer who has attained the perfection of love. At the same time, our churches have frankly recognized that entire sanctification does not in itself immediately solve every human problem. That is why the term *perfection* should be used with great care and with suitable qualifications. In fact it helps to remember that our tradition, in its teaching about entire sanctification, places special emphasis on one aspect of life in the world of sin, namely the way in which it creates in us an inclination toward wicked deeds and desires. It is this inclination that is overcome in the perfection of love; however, many other effects of life in sin are not removed until the resurrection of the body. Perfect love, accordingly, is not the end of the new creation.

The perfection of love does not signify that we cannot sin. A return to sin is possible for every Christian believer regardless of spiritual maturity, even if the devotion and spiritual discipline associated with perfect love will make a full-scale return into the world of sin less likely. Perfect love also does not signify that we are free of temptation. If Jesus was tempted, then we will also be tempted. But again, the maturity and discipline that characterizes those perfected in love should make them less susceptible to temptation.

Additionally, the perfection of love does not mean the end of our finitude. Even in the resurrection state human beings will be finite and therefore limited. Similarly, it does not mean the end of our humanity. Human beings have needs and desires that are natural. In the world of sin these needs and desires can get out of control and be instruments of sin. Nonetheless, they are natural and the perfection of love does not destroy or diminish them. It only ensures that they are integrated into our devotion to God.

Perfect love also does not mean the end of the various problems our tradition refers to as infirmities. We may think of infirmities as nonsinful results of our dwelling in the world of sin. Although in sanctification we overcome the power of sin, we do not entirely escape all the corruption of sin. Some of sin's effects remain with us until the resurrection of the body.

Writers in our tradition have devoted considerable attention to understanding these infirmities and their relation to the holy life. They have learned from psychology and other social sciences that there are many features of human life that, although contrary to God's ideal, are the result not of sin but of other factors. They have noted, for example, that an episode of anger may not be an expression of sin but instead may be due to physical and mental strain. Or, anger toward a friend may arise from psychological trauma that one experienced early in life. Although the Church does not encourage anger in any form, it is important, from a pastoral perspective, to note that not all anger is rooted in sin. The appropriate pastoral approach is not to condemn this anger as a sin but instead to guide us into the full maturity of the Christian life and to help us find ways of dealing effectively with anger and its causes.

Similarly, there is a host of objectionable behaviors and attitudes human beings exhibit that are derived from psychological and sociological forces and not from overt acts of sin. As a result, the perfection of love does not instantaneously eliminate them. Someone who, for example, was raised in a racist culture, will find that the perfection of love does not immediately remove that racist attitude. On the contrary, it can be overcome only by a long maturity in the Christian life of love.

Finally, it is important to note that entire sanctification is not inevitably a permanent state; those who have reached entire sanctification are still susceptible to the power of sin. The life of holiness is maintained only by continual acts of consecration and discipline. If, through careless inattention or willful choice, those acts of consecration and discipline falter, our progress on the path of holiness and love will slow or stop and, if our devotion is not resumed, our direction on the path will reverse and we will find ourselves plunging back into the world of sin. The state of entire sanctification, in other words, is a dynamic state. It describes us only to the extent that we maintain ourselves on the path through continual acts of consecration and discipline.

▶ THE MATURING OF LOVE

A LIFE OF REPENTANCE

The life of holiness is a life in which we are always aware that, despite the perfection of love, we are not perfect in all respects. This awareness constitutes the mature believer's repentance.

Entire sanctification is not the end of life in the Spirit; it is not the end of God's transforming new creation. Even for those far advanced on the path of holiness and love, there is still much to learn and extensive aspects of our character that God must repair. The New Testament, for instance, counsels us to speak only what is edifying (Eph. 4:29) and to be content with what we have (Phil. 4:11-12). No one can imagine that these characteristics of the holy life can be attained easily or so securely that no further attention would be necessary. No one, even those most advanced on the path of holiness, are such masters of humility, gentleness, kindness, and love that no further progress is possible. On the contrary, an entire lifetime of walking in the Spirit is necessary to train ourselves to speak only what is edifying. An entire lifetime may not suffice to learn how to be content with what we have. The same is true of the other characteristics, such as humility, gentleness, and sound judgment, that we are called to embody. Even those who are entirely sanctified have much to learn in the attaining and exercising of these characteristics.

As a result, the life of holiness and love must be a life of repentance and renewed consecration, for "all of us make many mistakes" (James 3:2). Repentance is the state of mind of disciples who so thoroughly walk in the light that they intimately know their shortcomings and who feel the discrepancy between actual practice and the spiritual greatness to which we are called, which is nothing less than *deification*, to be "imitators of God" (Eph. 5:1). This is a daunting task that inspires within us both a sorrow at our failing to imitate God well and a confidence that "the one who began a good work [in us] will bring it completion by the day of Jesus Christ" (Phil. 1:6). To live a life of repentance, then, is to hunger and thirst for God's righteousness. This hunger and this repentance are our awareness that we do not yet fully imitate God as we ought.

It may seem odd to think of someone who is *entirely* sanctified needing to repent; however this oddity points us toward a great truth of the life of holiness, namely that, the closer we draw to the light that is God, the more evident our shortcomings become. The closer we come to God, the greater the distance between us and God seems. It is those who do not walk in the light who most easily deceive themselves about their freedom from sin, for, being in darkness, nothing reveals the power of sin in their lives. Movement into God's light is therefore inevitably painful, for we then begin to see the great gulf that separates us from God and we see how poorly we imitate God. Nonetheless, this pain, the pain of repentance, is a great good and a blessing, for it is a signal that we are drawing close to God. The greater the pain of repentance, the closer to God we are.

THE IMITATION OF CHRIST

We practice love by imitating Jesus Christ, especially in his cross and his suffering.

In the New Testament, the most overt way of describing holiness as a life of love and of participation in God is to portray it as having a life conformed to Jesus Christ. Paul, for instance, urging the importance of humility, wrote, "Let each of you look not to your own interests, but to the interests of others. Let the same mind be in you that was in Christ Jesus" (Phil. 2:4). He then recited the story of Christ's self-emptying and obedience to God (see vv. 5-11). Similarly, attempting to help the Corinthians to become more generous, he used an expressly Christological argument: "You know the generous act of our Lord Jesus Christ, that though he was rich, yet for your sakes he became poor, so that by his poverty you might become rich" (2 Cor. 8:9).

The New Testament rather consistently depicts our imitation of Jesus as a participation in his suffering and as a life shaped by his cross. Notable in this respect is Mark's Gospel: "If any want to become my followers, let them deny themselves and take up their cross and follow me. For those who want to save their life will lose it, and those who lose their life for my sake . . . will save it" (8:34-35). The holy life, in short, is a life that, like Jesus', is given up to and for God as an offering. It is a life that does not insist on its own good or rights: "Whoever wishes to be first among you must be slave of all. For the Son of Man came not to be served but to serve" (Mark 10:44-45). And it is a life that embraces suffering, for God "has graciously granted you the privilege not only of believing in Christ, but of suffering for him as well" (Phil. 1:29).

Of course, suffering does not always mean physical or emotional pain. Paul, for instance, had "suffered the loss of all things" by turning to Christ and responding to God's call (Phil. 3:8). As the context makes clear, the "all things" whose loss he had suffered was the identity and world of meaning that he had constructed for himself—his being "a Hebrew born of Hebrews" and a Pharisee (v. 5)—before his encounter with the risen Jesus.

Suffering, in other words, denotes everything that we endure as a result of being faithful to God's call. For some, suffering means death and physical pain. For others, it means loss of material goods and social status. For every disciple it means a life of being radically directed to the good of others, even at cost of our own good. It means turning our back on the self-serving world that we have or might have made in the world of sin. It means allowing God's grace and judgment to destroy and transform the identity that we have or might have constructed for ourselves in utter forgetfulness of God. All this explains Paul's assertion that "we are children of God . . . if, in fact, we suffer with him so that we may also be glorified with him" (Rom. 8:16-17). Our suffering with Jesus is a corollary of our participation in the divine life, which is itself a life of self-giving love, a life that in radical abandonment gave itself over to death and in that death established the victory of love over death. This is the life to which we are called.

The participatory character of the life of holiness shows us why the imitation of Jesus is more than a mere imitation. It is more than simply trying to live as Jesus lived as though Jesus were only an example of moral courage or probity. It is, on the contrary, a participation in the Trinitarian life of the God who is love, a life lived in the power of the Spirit. This understanding explains Paul's insistent language about the power of Christ within us: "It is no longer I who live, but it is Christ who lives in me" (Gal. 2:20). These powerful words tell us that the life of holiness is more than pursuing a moral ideal. It is having Christ formed in us and having Christ live in us as an operative power.

The Christological character of the life of holiness reveals to us the meaning of the statement, "You were taught . . . to be renewed in the spirit of your minds, and to clothe yourselves with the new self, created according to the likeness of God in true righteousness and holiness" (Eph. 4:22-24). The term *likeness* here is carefully chosen. It brings us back to the first chapter of Genesis and the affirmation that human beings have been created in the image of God. Ephesians tells us that the new creation is the restoration of humankind in its created image and that the restoration occurs as we become righteous and holy.

To this passage we must add Paul's affirmation that Jesus is the image of God (Rom. 8:29 and 2 Cor. 4:4). Paul thus insisted that our restoration in the image of God is in fact our being conformed to Jesus Christ. Our creation in the image of God, then, has from the beginning a Christological focus. From the beginning God intends that our existence will conform to Jesus Christ and the way of the cross and of suffering. To speak of life in the Spirit is therefore to speak of a life that is shaped by the power of Jesus Christ in the Spirit and of a life that embraces his suffering.

▶ THE ETHICAL DIMENSION OF FAITH

Like every doctrine, those pertaining to the Christian life have an ethical dimension. This dimension consists in the practices that are a part of the Christian life. To take an example, we cannot truly say that we believe that love is central to the Christian life unless we actually practice love to God and neighbor. And we do not truly believe the doctrine of the sacraments unless we have been baptized and celebrate the Lord's Supper. Authentic faith, in other words, is inseparable from faithful practice.

SUMMARY STATEMENTS

1. Life in the Spirit means the death of sin and freedom from its power and corruption.

2. The life of holiness is a life of union with God. It is, accordingly, a life of love.

3. Life in the Spirit is an eschatological existence, in which sin is dead and yet can live again.

4. Entire sanctification is the perfection of our love for God.

5. We attain perfect love through God's grace, through using the means of grace, through spiritual disciplines, and through consecration.

6. The path to perfect love is for some characterized by a momentous event of faith and consecration, while for others is it characterized by a development that culminates in the perfection of love.

7. Although perfect love signifies the death of sin, it does not solve every human problem.

8. The life of holiness is a life in which we are always aware that, despite the perfection of love, we are not perfect in all respects. This awareness constitutes the mature believer's repentance.

9. We practice love by imitating Jesus Christ, especially in his cross and his suffering.

QUESTIONS FOR REFLECTION

1. How does the Christian life differ from the lives of people in other religious communities? What are the differences in practices?

2. How does the Trinitarian character of the Christian life distinguish it from other varieties of ethical life?

3. Why is the affirmation that God is love the most central of biblical affirmations?

TWELVE

THE CHURCH IN THE POWER OF THE SPIRIT

OBJECTIVES

Your study of this chapter should help you to understand:

1. The Church's holiness.
2. The Church's apostolic character and authority.
3. The means of grace.
4. The Church's unity.
5. The Church's mission.

KEY WORDS TO UNDERSTAND:

Apochrypha	Council	Rule of faith
Apostolic	Creed	Sacraments
Authority	Dogma	Schism
Canon of Scripture	Eucharist	*Sola scriptura*
Catholic	Heresy	Spiritual priesthood
Church militant	Inspiration	of believers
Church triumphant	Mission	Tradition
Communion	Orthodoxy	

QUESTIONS TO CONSIDER AS YOU READ

1. How can we best understand the contrast between the Church's holiness and unity as the Body of Christ and the empirical holiness and unity of the Church in history?

2. How is the mission of the Church related to the movement of God into the world?

3. Why is it important that God's grace is given to us by the mediation of physical means of grace?

Father, Son, and Spirit, hear
Faith's effectual, fervent prayer!
Hear, and our petitions seal;
Let us now the answer feel.

Still our fellowship increase,
Knit us in the bond of peace,
Join our new-born spirit, join
Each to each, and all to thine!

Build us in one body up,
Called in one high calling's hope:
One the Spirit whom we claim,
One pure, baptismal flame;

One the faith and common Lord,
One the Father lives adored,
Over, through, and in us all,
God incomprehensible.

One with God, the source of bliss,
Ground of our communion this;
Life of all that live below,
Let thine emanations flow!

Rise eternal in our heart!
Thou our long sought Eden art:
Father, Son, and Holy Ghost,
Be to us what Adam lost!

This hymn, written in 1740, expresses John Wesley's view of the Church. It begins and ends with an invocation of the Trinity because the Church is an extension of the Trinitarian movement of God into the world. The second stanza presents the Church as a fellowship of newly born spirits, joined to each other and to God, because the Church is a communion—a unity composed of members who are united together and who collectively dwell in God. The third stanza calls on God to build up the Church, pictured as Christ's Body and as a reality that God has called. Finally, this hymn tells us that the Church exists in unity with the Father, Son, and Spirit, from whom life, communion, and bliss emanate.

▶ INTRODUCTION

The movement of God into the world takes place in the life, death, and resurrection of Jesus Christ and continues in the work of the Holy Spirit. The Church, as the Body of Christ and the creation of the Holy Spirit, is the extension of God's Trinitarian movement into the world and is the concrete and social form that God's fellowship with the world takes. For that reason, the Church has the task of being faithful to its calling to be an extension of God's coming into the world. The Church's *mission* and ministry is nothing other than its striving to be faithful to this calling.

▶ THE HOLY GOD AND THE HOLY CHURCH

METAPHORS OF THE CHURCH'S HOLINESS

The Church, separated from the world of sin and consecrated to God, is holy because it participates in the Trinitarian movement of God into the world.

God's holiness is God's transcendence and infinity—God's difference from the world. As the embodiment and extension of the holy God's movement into the world, the Church participates in God's holiness. Its holiness thus does not rest on its organizational structure or its beliefs or its members. It is holy only because and as it embodies God's movement into the world and thus is drawn, by the power of the Spirit, into God's Trinitarian life. Apart from the power of the Spirit, the Church is as much a part of the world of sin as is any other worldly phenomenon.

To say that the Church is holy is to say that it is separated from the world and consecrated to God. The New Testament depicts this separation and consecration with several metaphors. One metaphor is the priesthood. 1 Peter, echoing Exod. 19, describes the Church as "a holy priesthood" that is called "to offer spiritual sacrifices" (2:5) and "a royal priesthood, a holy nation" (v. 9). This language presents the Church as the continuation of the elect people Israel. Like Israel, the Church is to be a priestly people who are holy by virtue of their calling to be ministers of God.

There are other metaphors describing the Church's separation from the world of sin and consecration to God. These include the Church as a community of aliens and exiles (1 Pet. 2:11), as members of God's household (Eph. 2:19, 1 Pet. 4:17, 1 Tim. 3:15), and as God's people (Eph. 1:14, 1 Pet. 2:9). These metaphors tell us that the Church is to be the people who no longer identify with the world of sin and who instead find their identity in God. These are the people who belong to God and who therefore live in the midst of the world of sin as aliens.

The Church's consecration to God can be seen as well when the New Testament calls the Church a temple (Eph. 2:21-22; 1 Pet. 2:5; 1 Cor. 3:16-17). This metaphor tells us that the Church, as the dwelling of God, is consecrated for divine use. Like Israel's temple, the Church is holy because it stands in an exclusive relation to God and God's service. The same point is made with the metaphor of the Church as the spouse of Christ (Eph. 5:25-27). In this metaphor, the Church is presented as holy by virtue of its having been purified in preparation for its marriage to Jesus Christ. As with the temple metaphor, the marriage metaphor tells us that the Church is holy because of its relationship of consecration to God.

THE HOLINESS OF THE CHURCH AND DIVINE ELECTION

The Church is the elect and therefore holy people of God. In Christ, God has elected, or chosen, the Church to be a separated and consecrated people.

As we have seen in previous chapters, Israel was the holy people of God because it was the elect people of God. Their status as God's own people, the people whom God had chosen, constituted their holiness, for it distinguished them from the other nations and consecrated them to God. What was true of Israel in the Old Testament is true of the Church in the New Testament. The Church is the holy people of God because it is the elect people of God. God has chosen the Church by separating out from the world of sin a people who are consecrated to God.

God "chose us in Christ before the foundation of the world to be holy and blameless before him in love. He destined us for adoption as his children through Jesus Christ" (Eph. 1:4-5). This passage tells us that the Church's election is an aspect of God's creation and is an integral part of the world's eschatological destiny. It tells us also that the purpose and effect of election is the Church's holiness and blamelessness. Election, therefore, is a call to be the holy people of God, "chosen and destined by God the Father and sanctified by the Spirit [in order] to be obedient to Jesus Christ" (1 Pet. 1:2).

THE ESCHATOLOGICAL DIMENSION OF THE CHURCH'S HOLINESS

The Church's holiness is an eschatological reality as the Church lives between its calling as the elect, holy people of God and its struggle to be faithful to that calling.

The Church of Jesus Christ is the holy, elect people of God. However, its holiness is an eschatological reality; it lives in the tension between the present world of sin and the future of God's new creation. Even though the new creation is a present reality, its full presence lies in our future. In the present time, it grows alongside the world of sin. Although the Church participates in the new creation, it remains susceptible to the power of sin's world. As a result, the holiness of individual disciples may fall short of the Church's ideal holiness as the elect people of God. Like the Corinthians, individual disciples may continue to live under the influence of sin.

The eschatological nature of the Church's holiness explains why it is a mistake to identify the Church and the kingdom of God. Although the Church is the spouse of Christ and the household of God, it is also a human, earthly reality that is composed of human beings who remain affected by the world of sin. Until the eschatological consummation—until God is all in all—the Church's holiness is both a fact, grounded in its relation to God and its participation in the Trinitarian movement of God into the world, and a calling to be holy in conduct. While the Church anticipates the kingdom of God and is, so to speak, the human reflection of the Kingdom, the Church remains a human reality. As a result, its holiness is imperfect. That is why the Church's holiness is a calling. It is a summons to the Church to be as holy in its practice as it is in its relation to Jesus Christ.

CHURCH MILITANT VS. CHURCH TRIUMPHANT

It is common to distinguish the **Church militant** from the **Church triumphant** as a way of articulating the Church's eschatological character. The Church militant is the Church in history, caught in the eschatological tension between the world of sin and the kingdom of God. The Church triumphant consists of believers who have died and have thus triumphed over the world of sin.

▶ THE CHURCH AND THE REVELATION OF GOD

THE APOSTOLIC CHARACTER OF THE CHURCH

The Church is called to be faithful to the traditions handed on by the apostles.

The holy, triune God comes into the world; this movement is the revelation of God. The Church is the body of people who have heard and responded, in faith and obedience, to the triune God's revelation. The Church receives and witnesses to God's revelation and thereby participates in God's revelatory coming into the world. This participation in revelation gives the Church the basis of its mission into the world, which is to preserve the faith and to proclaim it. The Church's faithful response to revelation constitutes its *apostolic* character. As Ephesians reminds us, the Church is "built upon the foundation of the apostles and prophets, with Christ Jesus himself as the cornerstone" (Eph. 2:20). So, to say with the ancient creeds that the Church is apostolic is to say that it is faithful to the teaching of Jesus and the apostles.

The Church is called to be faithful to the apostolic foundation because it is an authoritative witness to the revelation of the triune God. The basis of this *authority* is Jesus Christ, who is the revelation of God and to whom "all authority in heaven and on earth has been given" (Matt. 28:18). However, the apostles and through them the Church share in the authority of Jesus—hence Paul's insistence that "whoever rejects this [teaching] rejects not human authority but God" (1 Thess. 4:8). The apostolic preaching, then, is divinely authorized and a faithful and true witness to God's revelation.

The Church, therefore, has the task of preserving and passing on the apostolic preaching. This is one vital dimension of the Church's mission. It is because the early disciples "devoted themselves to the apostles' teaching" (Acts 2:42) that they are a paradigm for the Church. The Church, then, is to "guard what has been entrusted" to it (1 Tim. 6:20) and "entrust [that teaching] to faithful people who will be able to teach others as well" (2 Tim. 2:2). The task of preserving and passing on the apostles' teaching means that the idea of *tradition* is of pivotal importance for the Church. Tradition is the transmission of the apostles' teaching from one generation to another or from one congregation to another, as when Paul handed on the tradition to the Corinthians (1 Cor. 15:3).

The New Testament writers knew the danger of not preserving this tradition: "Everyone who does not abide in the teaching of Christ, but goes beyond it, does not have God; whoever abides in the teaching has both the Father and the Son" (2 John 9). In other words, no one can fully know God without receiving the apostolic testimony to God's revelation. Consequently, there is great danger in departing from this tradition. The Church calls such departure *heresy*.

HERESY

The idea of heresy was developed in the early centuries of Christianity. It ultimately came to signify the act of consciously departing from the Christian faith and at the same time separating from the Church. Heresy is, therefore, more than holding beliefs contrary to the Christian faith. Some disciples believe things that are contrary to the Christian faith because of ignorance or lack of understanding. They are not heretics. Heresy implies knowingly contradicting the Christian faith and also separating oneself from the Church that preserves that faith.

REVELATION AND THE CHURCH'S TASK

The Church is a servant of God's revelation in the world and therefore must remain receptive to the Holy Spirit's prophetic ministry.

Revelation is the Trinitarian movement of God into the world. The Church's teaching is part of its faithful response to that revelation. The Church is the body of those who have received this revelation and responded to it in faith. Its calling is to always be the people in whom revelation is received in faith.

If the Church is to fulfill its calling, then it must forever be the house of the Spirit, for it is only as we abide in the power of God's Spirit that we can receive God's revelation. Consider, for instance, Paul's words to the Thessalonians: "Our message of the gospel came to you not in word only, but also in power and in the Holy Spirit" (1 Thess. 1:5). Or, his words to the Corinthians: "These things God has revealed to us through the Spirit" (1 Cor. 2:10). Unless we are in the Spirit, the apostolic message remains mere words. In the Spirit, we hear those words as the Word of God and in that moment God's revelation in Jesus Christ is actualized in us.

The imperative that the Church be the house of the Spirit, the place in which revelation is received in faith, helps us understand the office of the prophet. Prophecy is the declaration of God's message to the Church and is a means by which the Spirit speaks to the Church (1 Tim. 4:1; Rev. 2:7). By nurturing prophecy the Church participates in the revelation of God by hearing that revelation and responding to it in faith. The Church, then, must always take care to be the people in whom the Spirit dwells and who hear what the Spirit says to the Church. It is not enough to preserve the apostolic teaching and transmit it to others, for it is possible for such preservation and transmission to occur without the Church participating in revelation. If this teaching were thought of merely as a fixed body of words to be handed over intact to others, the character of those words as a witness to revelation would be lost. If the Church forgot to be the house of the Spirit, then those words would lose their power as testimony and would instead become relics. It is only as the Church lives in the Spirit that the apostles' teaching and the words of Jesus become bearers of God's revelation and means by which the divine movement into the world takes root in the human heart.

THE ESCHATOLOGICAL DIMENSION OF THE CHURCH'S APOSTOLIC CHARACTER

The Church fulfills its calling to be faithful to the apostolic tradition and to be the servant of God's revelation under the conditions of its eschatological existence. As a result, it sometimes fails to live up to its calling.

The Church is an eschatological reality, living between the world of sin and future of the new creation. Consequently, it must constantly examine itself to make sure that it is being faithful to its apostolic character.

As history shows, sometimes the Church fails in its custodial task. This happens when the Church forgets that it is the principal means by which God's revelation is now embodied in the world. It happens in particular when the Church forgets "to contend for the faith that was once for all entrusted to the saints" (Jude 3). It happens whenever the Church departs from the apostle's teaching by adopting beliefs from the world of sin and confusing them with the Christian faith. But the fact that the Church is an eschatological reality—the fact that the Church dwells alongside the world of sin and remains affected by sin—means that the Church will always have to struggle to maintain the purity of its teaching. Sometimes it is only in retrospect, with the wisdom of later experience, that the Church can see that its teaching wrongly incorporated ideas from the world of sin. This is why the Church, in its eschatological condition, exists in a state of perpetual repentance.

The Church also fails in its task when it ceases to be a house of the Spirit, that is, when it is no longer a place in which revelation is received in faith. This happens when the Church is incapable of hearing what the Spirit is saying and instead is capable only of hearing what the apostles said. Although, as John's Gospel reminds us, the Spirit continues the ministry of Jesus Christ, the Spirit can also lead the Church into a deeper insight into the implications of revelation. For example, it took many centuries for the Church to see that the practice of slavery contradicts God's revelation. Likewise, the Church (and only parts of the Church) has only recently acknowledged the validity and wisdom of ordaining women to the Church's ministry. The Church, in other words, often fails to hear the Spirit and thus falls short of God's wisdom. Of course, not every new idea represents the voice of the Spirit. Some ideas presented to the Church are drawn from the world of sin. Therefore the Church must test the spirits to determine whether or not they are from the Spirit of God.

POSTBIBLICAL DEVELOPMENTS

In the early centuries of Christianity the need arose to distinguish authentic forms of the Christian faith from the beliefs of heretical groups, especially the various Gnostic communities. Some of these communities were in some respects Christian, for they regarded Jesus Christ as the revelation of God and had a conception of the apostolic tradition about Jesus. However, their version of that tradition differed dramatically from that of the mainstream Church. In response, theologians within the Church developed the idea of the *rule (i.e., standard) of faith*. They proposed that the standard by which beliefs should be judged is the apostolic tradition: that the Father of Jesus Christ was also the Creator; that Jesus was truly and in every sense human; that he had truly died; and so on. Each of these affirmations was denied by some Gnostic communities.

In time the rule of faith came to be more formally stated in *creeds*. Many creeds were the products of *councils*, which were assemblies of bishops charged with defining the Christian faith verbally. Examples of early creeds include the creed of Constantinople (381), which helped define the doctrine of the Trinity, and the creed of Chalcedon (451), which helped define the doctrine about Jesus Christ. The idea of a creed gives rise to the idea of *dogma*, which is a teaching that is both central to the Christian faith and formally defined by the Church. *Orthodox* (from the Greek word for "right belief") denotes those who affirm the Church's dogmas.

The formal definition of Christian dogmas and the statement of these dogmas in creeds served to distinguish the Christian Church from heretical groups. The result of this distinction was the idea of the *catholic* (from the Greek word for "universal") Church. *Catholic* denotes the mainstream, authentic Church in contrast to heretical offshoots. Because these offshoots were usually small and local, *catholic* described the Church as a universal body, one found in the whole world. But *catholic* means as well the Church that is orthodox because it preserves the apostles' teaching.

At the same time that these conceptions were developing, the Church faced the need to distinguish reliable from unreliable early writings. The Church from its beginning had used the Jewish scriptures as its Bible, with Greek-speaking Christians using the Septuagint translation of those scriptures. But, as is well known, there were many Christian writings in the early centuries. Some writings were by early Christian leaders (e.g., 1 Clement and the Shepherd of Hermas) offering advice to churches. Other were historical novels (e.g., the Acts of Paul and Thecla) designed for edification. Additionally, some Gnostic communities had their own writings about Jesus and the apostles. By the second century, leaders of the Church were aware that the teaching in some of these writings was inconsistent with the rule of faith. As a result, churches began compiling lists of writings considered reliable, authoritative, and in agreement with the rule of faith. The four Gospels, Acts, 1 Peter, 1 John, and most of Paul's letters were thus recognized as authoritative by the end of the second century. In time, all 27 books now forming the New Testament came to be regarded as reliable and authoritative. This process is the origin of the idea of the *canon* (from the Greek word for "rule") of scripture. The canon was the collection of accepted writings. Other writings, including many that the Church regarded as valuable, were categorized as *apocryphal.*

In the Reformation era, the Church's apostolic character and the nature of doctrinal authority once again became controversial. The critical issue was whether the Church's long tradition of authoritative teaching, en-

THE AUTHORITY OF THE BIBLE

The churches in our tradition follow the general contours of Protestant theology on the matter of the authority of the Church's tradition and that of the Bible. They assert that the Bible is the Church's only standard of doctrine and affirm the Bible's inspiration and reliability.

shrined in creeds, customs, and theological writings, was an infallible guide to the meaning of revelation. In the preceding centuries, the medieval Church had advanced the view that not only the Bible but also the entire body of the Church's teaching was authoritative, inspired, and infallible.

WESLEY'S VIEW ON THE AUTHORITY OF THE BIBLE

John Wesley's view of the Bible's authority is instructive. He was convinced that any valid interpretation of Scripture will be experientially confirmed in the Christian life. Such confirmation, he believed, guides us toward a correct understanding of the Bible. He also recognized that the Bible must be interpreted in light of its soteriological purpose. He was convinced that, within the multitude of biblical passages, there is a central and vital core of doctrine relating to sin, faith, grace, repentance, justification, regeneration, and sanctification. In other words, it consists of those teachings that describe the way of salvation. Wesley believed that all true Christians should agree and in fact do agree on this vital center. At the same time, he acknowledged that Christians can and do disagree about doctrines (such as eschatology and predestination) lying outside the vital center. He felt that such disagreement poses no threat to the Christian life or to the unity of the Church and happily allowed that Christians are free to understand these doctrines in various ways. He called this attitude toward biblical teaching the "catholic spirit." By this he meant the attitude that insists on unity in the essential matters of the Christian faith and that allows diversity of opinion on nonessential matters.

Protestants, however, were convinced that some of the Church's teachings and practices were contrary to God's revelation. In an attempt to purify the Church's teaching and its practices, Protestants proposed that the Bible be regarded as the sole norm of doctrine and practice, a position sometimes referred to as the principle of *sola scriptura*. Of course,

Protestants did not propose that the Church cast away the historic creeds of the early centuries. On the contrary, they embraced them as reliable interpretations of the Bible. Nonetheless, Protestants differed from the medieval Church in seeing only the Bible as the product of the Spirit's *inspiration*. Creeds, customs, and theologians, they argued, were human and therefore, unlike the Bible, liable to error. The Bible, being inspired, fully, accurately, and without error reveals the will of God.

▶ The Church and the Grace of God

The Church is the custodian of the means of grace, including the sacraments. Moreover, as an embodiment and extension of God's Trinitarian, gracious movement into the world, the Church is itself a means of grace and has a sacramental character. This means that the Church is an embodiment and therefore an extension of God's Trinitarian, gracious movement into the world.

THE IDEA OF THE MEANS OF GRACE

God's grace is mediated to us through physical realities, which thus have a sacramental character.

We have previously seen the importance of the idea of mediation in our knowledge of God. This idea expresses the fact that we do not have direct knowledge or experience of God. On the contrary, our knowledge and experience of God are always mediated by some worldly reality. The idea of the means of grace is an extension of the idea of mediation. To speak of means of grace is to assert that God's grace comes to us, not directly, but always through the mediation of worldly realities.

In the New Testament, it is John's Gospel that most clearly explicates the mediating function of physical things. Take, for example, the way in which the woman who comes to draw water from the well encounters in Jesus the water of eternal life (chapter 4) or the way in which the miraculous feeding of the multitude is simultaneously their encounter with the true bread from heaven (chapter 6). In each case something ordinary—water, bread—has become an instrument of grace and revelation.

There are many means of grace. Anything, in fact, can be a means of grace because God can use anything in the created world to approach us. However, the Church is the custodian of the ordinary means of grace, including preaching, Bible, prayer, music, art, and works of love toward our neighbors. In each of these some physical reality—the human voice, gestures, written texts, and so on—mediate God's revelatory, creative power.

Of all the means of grace, two have special importance for the churches in our tradition. They are the two *sacraments,* baptism and the Lord's Supper. Every means of grace, as a physical reality that conveys God's grace to us, has a sacramental character. But baptism and the Lord's Supper not only have a sacramental character but are sacraments because they were specially ordained by Jesus.

BAPTISM

Baptism is an eschatological event in which life in the Spirit begins and which constitutes the Church as a unity of believers.

Baptism is a means of grace because in it God comes to us with the power of the new creation and draws us into the divine life.

Baptism is therefore an eschatological event, for in it we receive the Holy Spirit, the power of the new creation. In it we leave behind the world of sin and enter into the new world that God is creating. That is why the New Testament associates baptism with repentance and forgiveness (Acts 2:38) and washing sins away (Acts 22:16; Titus 3:5). Forgiveness and washing signify the annulment of our life in the world of sin and the beginning of our life in God's Spirit. In turning away from the world of sin through repentance and baptism, that world is nullified. That is the meaning of the forgiveness of sins. In entering the new world of God's creation through baptism, we become new creatures and begin to live in God's Spirit. Baptism thus signals our movement out of the world of sin and into the age of the Spirit and the kingdom of God.

Paul's letter to the Romans gives us a rich insight into baptism as an eschatological event: "Do you not know that all of us who have been baptized into Christ Jesus were baptized into his death? Therefore we have been buried with him by baptism into death, so that, just as Christ was raised from the dead by the glory of the Father, so we too might walk in newness of life" (6:3-4). This important passage succinctly summarizes the eschatological nature of baptism, signifying our death to sin and the beginning of our new life in God.

Baptism also had a corporate significance for Paul, for it is baptism (along with the Lord's Supper) that constitutes the Church as the Body of Christ: "In the one Spirit we were all baptized into one body—Jews or Greeks, slaves or free" (1 Cor. 12:13). Baptism, then, signifies more than just the individual's dying and rising with Christ. By uniting us with Christ, baptism unites us with one another as the Body of Christ and thus creates the Church. The things that separate people, such as ethnic, social, and gender-based distinctions, are dissolved in baptism: "As many of you as were baptized into Christ have clothed yourselves with Christ. There is no longer Jew or Greek, . . . slave or free, . . . male or female; for all of you are one in Christ Jesus" (Gal. 3:27-28). The unity of the Church, created in baptism, means that these sorts of distinctions, which are of critical importance in the world of sin, are null and void in the new world that God is creating.

BAPTISM

The creeds in our tradition affirm that baptism is "commanded by our Lord," that it is "to be administered to believers," that it is a "declaration of their faith in Jesus Christ as Savior," that it signifies "acceptance of the benefits of the atonement of Jesus Christ," and that it is "a sign of the new birth" and "a symbol of the new covenant of grace."

THE LORD'S SUPPER

The Lord's Supper is an eschatological event of remembrance, thanksgiving, and incorporation into the Body of Christ.

The importance of the Lord's Supper in the life of the Church is indicated by its place in the apostolic tradition (1 Cor. 11:23).

Like baptism, the Lord's Supper is an eschatological event, for it too marks the passage from the old world of sin to the new world that God is creating. We see the eschatological dimension in the words of Jesus, "From now on I will not drink of the fruit of the vine until the kingdom of God comes" (Luke 22:18). These words show us that the supper is celebrated in the tension between the present and the future when the kingdom of God will be present in its fullness. Participating in this meal signifies both the physical absence of Christ and our reunion with him in the fullness of the Kingdom. It signifies as well and anticipates the eschatological banquet that Jesus preached. The Lord's Supper, then, is the kingdom of God in its eschatological form, that is, it is the Kingdom in its existence alongside the world of sin, present and yet not in its fullness. The supper thus reminds us of the world from which we have been delivered and points us to the world's eschatological destiny.

The Lord's Supper reminds us also of Jesus Christ: "Do this in remembrance of me" (Luke 22:19). But this meal is not a reminder, like a post-it note that we might use to avoid forgetting. Instead the meal is itself an act of remembrance. In the Lord's Supper we ritually reenact the events of Jesus' death. We thereby place ourselves as participants in those events and identify with Jesus and his death. Just as in baptism we die with Christ, so in this meal we participate in the events surrounding Jesus' death. In this way we gather the past into the present and celebrate that past in the light of God's future.

The Lord's Supper is also our act of thanksgiving to God. Just as Jesus "took a cup, and after giving thanks, he gave it to them" (Mark 14:23), so the Church, in its celebration of the Lord's Supper, gives thanks for God's grace. This is the origin of the term *Eucharist*, which is a Greek word for thanksgiving. In this meal the Church responds to God's grace (*charis* in Greek) with an act of thanks and blessing *(eucharistia)*. In this way it shares in the divine life that God gives to it in Jesus Christ.

Finally, the Lord's Supper is a means by which we are incorporated into Jesus Christ and Christ's Body, the Church. In the Gospel of John, this truth is portrayed in the language of abiding: "I am the bread of life. . . . Whoever eats of this bread will live forever; and the bread that I will give for the life of the world is my flesh. . . . Those who eat my flesh and drink my blood have eternal life. . . . Those who eat my flesh and drink my blood abide in me, and I in them" (6:48, 51, 54, 56). Consuming

Christ is thus the means by which we dwell in Christ and Christ dwells in us. First Corinthians makes the same point when it states, "The cup of blessing that we bless, is it not a sharing in the blood of Christ? The bread that we break is it not a sharing in the body of Christ? Because there is one bread, we who are many are one body, for we all partake of one bread" (10:16-17). Participation in the meal, then, is a sharing or fellowship in the body and blood of Christ. This is why another word for the Lord's Supper is *communion*, which points to the participatory nature of the Lord's Supper. In this meal we are united with Christ's death and with his eternal life.

THE LORD'S SUPPER

The creeds in our tradition define the Lord's Supper as "a sign of the love that Christians have for each other" and as "a sacrament of our redemption by Christ's death." They draw attention to its eschatological dimension by noting that those who participate in the meal "show forth the Lord's death till He come again" and by describing it as "a sacrament of our hope in [Christ's] victorious return." They also use Paul's language of participation ("the bread which we break is a partaking of the body of Christ; and likewise the cup of blessing is a partaking of the blood of Christ") to explicate the meaning of this meal.

THE CHURCH AS A COMMUNITY OF GRACE

The Church is called to be a community in which God's grace is effective.

The Church is called to be a community of grace. Although, as the Body of Christ, it is in fact a means of grace, it is also called to be a community in which God's grace is powerfully effective and brings about the new creation.

In order for the Church to be a community of grace, it is not enough that it preach and administer the sacraments. Doctrine and sacraments are critical for the Church's existence but they are not the full extent of the Church's ministry. Besides the ordained ministry it is necessary for every believer to exercise his or her spiritual gifts, which are given "for the common good" (1 Cor. 12:7). The exercise of these gifts for the common good is what Martin Luther (1483—1546) called the *spiritual priesthood of believers*, the exercise of ministry by each believer on behalf of others. As the Body of Christ, disciples are means of grace toward each other, for "God has so arranged the body . . . [that] the members may have the same care for one another. If one member suffers, all suffer together with it; if one member is honored, all rejoice together with it" (1 Cor. 12:24-26). The basis of this care is the fact that we are "one body in Christ, and individually we are members of one another" (Rom. 12:5). As members of the Body of Christ, we exist not only in Jesus Christ but also in one another.

This spiritual priesthood is exercised in various ways. One is the practice of forgiveness. The Church is a community of grace when it practices forgiveness because it thereby embodies God's grace. In forgiveness the Church allows itself to be God's instrument for the creation and restoration of fellowship.

The Church becomes a community of grace also in the practice of corrective discipline. Such discipline is necessary whenever sin becomes such a public and serious matter that the Church's well-being is threatened. We can see this illustrated in 1 Cor. 5, in which Paul confronted a case of open sexual immorality and delivered the offender "to Satan for the destruction of the flesh, so that his spirit may be saved in the day of the Lord" (5:5). In an act of corrective discipline, Paul had excommunicated this person and caused him to be excluded from the Church's fellowship. The purpose of this act was to safeguard the Church's well-being and witness but also to bring about the offender's deliverance. The Church acts as a community of grace in the practice of excommunication because it thereby preserves its integrity as a custodian of God's grace and because this act is intended to bring about salvation.

However, excommunication is an extraordinary and official case of corrective discipline. The ordinary means of such discipline is teaching and admonishing one another in wisdom (Col. 3:16). Through such admonition, which each Christian is obliged to offer and model, the

Church fulfills its character as a community in which discipline is a means of grace.

The Church becomes a community of grace also by anticipating the ethos of God's kingdom, especially in regards to power. The critical passage here is Jesus' saying,

> You know that among the Gentiles those whom they recognize as their rulers lord it over them, and their great ones are tyrants over them. But it is not so among you; but whoever wishes to become great among you must be your servant, and whoever wishes to be first among you must be slave of all. For the Son of Man came not to be served but to serve, and to give his life a ransom for many (Mark 10:42-45).

The Church is a community of grace when it conforms itself to Jesus Christ by exercising power as Jesus indicated and when its members seek to serve instead of seeking to be served.

Finally, the Church becomes a community of grace by honoring the gifts of the Spirit. It is because of these gifts that the Church is a means of grace, for they are simply God's grace extended to us (Rom. 12:6; Eph. 4:7). To say that the gifts are grace is to say that "it is the same God who activates all of them in everyone" and that they are "the manifestation of the Spirit" (1 Cor. 12:6-7). The gifts, in other words, are the creative power of God at work within us, creating a community of grace that embodies God's coming into the world. Because they are gifts of and for the Body of Christ, their purpose is to contribute to the well-being of the Body. They must, in other words, be used only for the good of the entire Body with the purpose of enabling that Body to be a community of grace (1 Cor. 12:7; 14:12).

THE ESCHATOLOGICAL DIMENSION OF THE CHURCH AS THE CUSTODIAN OF THE MEANS OF GRACE

As an eschatological community, the Church sometimes fails in its calling to be a community of grace.

The Church, as the Body of Christ and in the power of the Spirit, has a sacramental character and is the custodian of the means of grace. However, the Church labors alongside the world of sin and is affected by that world. As a result, sometimes the Church falls short of its calling. Sometimes the Church is not a community of grace but instead a community of strife and death. Instead of living by the ethos of the kingdom, sometimes the Church adopts modes of leadership from the world of sin. Instead of exercising corrective discipline as a means of grace, sometimes the Church either fails to exercise discipline or exercises it without a redemptive purpose. Sometimes the gifts of the Spirit are exercised not for the good of the Body but for the good of the individual. Sometimes the Church fails to forgive and instead is an agent of unjust condemnation.

However, God is faithful and extends grace to the Church even when the Church does not function well as the community of grace. The gifts of the Spirit endure, even if they are put to bad use. The Church continues to be the Body of Christ even when it fails to conform itself to Jesus Christ. All this is true because God's grace is given to the undeserving and to the needy. The Church is called to be the community of grace, not because it always acts graciously, but because it has received God's grace and has been chosen to be an instrument of that grace as it is extended into the world of sin.

POSTBIBLICAL DEVELOPMENTS

As with other doctrines associated with the Church, the doctrine of the sacraments has been a subject of contention.

One issue concerns the number of sacraments. The Greek and other Orthodox churches have not and, throughout the middle ages, the Latin Church did not clearly enumerate a list of sacraments. However, by approximately 1500 it was common in the Latin Church to speak of seven sacraments (baptism, confirmation, the Eucharist, penance, extreme unction, ordination, and marriage). Protestants, however, accepted as sacraments only those practices that were directly instituted by Jesus Christ, baptism and the Lord's Supper.

Another contentious issue has been the validity of infant baptism. It is impossible to know when this practice began but there is evidence from the early third century that it was an accepted practice in at least some churches. At any rate, infant baptism became a common practice in the middle ages. In the Protestant era, John Calvin (1509-1564) affirmed the practice of infant baptism as the sign of the new covenant and on that basis argued that children of Christian disciples are participants in this covenant. However, other Protestants, eventually known as the Anabaptists (i.e., "re-baptizers") rejected the validity of infant baptism; asserted that only adults could be baptized (since only adults could make the required affirmation of faith); and insisted that those baptized as infants be rebaptized as adults. The churches in our tradition generally side with Calvin on this issue. They affirm the validity of infant baptism as long as it is accompanied by suitable Christian training, asserting that "baptism [is] a symbol of the new covenant" and that "infants are recognized as being included in the atonement."

The Lord's Supper has likewise generated considerable debate over the proper interpretation of the phrases, "This is my body" and "This is my blood." The medieval Latin Church had developed a rather clear understanding according to which the body and blood of the resurrected Christ are truly received in eating the bread and drinking from the cup. In this account, the substance of the bread and wine are transformed into the body and blood of Christ. The term *transubstantiation* describes this view. The Protestant Reformation brought about a reconsideration of this issue. The Lutheran Churches agreed with the medieval view that Christ is physically present in the bread and wine; however, they did not affirm the idea of transubstantiation, asserting only that Christ is present in the bread and wine and not that the bread and wine are transformed. The Reformed churches (e.g., the Presbyterian churches) denied that Christ is physically present in the bread and wine, affirming instead that in the eating of the Lord's Supper we feast on Christ and are nourished spiritually. Other Protestant churches preferred to think of the Lord's Supper as strictly a memorial or act of remembering the death of Jesus Christ.

The creeds in our tradition generally follow the Reformed tradition's understanding of the Lord's Supper. They affirm that "the body of Christ is given, taken, and eaten in the Supper, only after a heavenly and spiritual manner. And the means whereby the body of Christ is received and eaten in the Supper is faith" and that "Christ, according to His promise, is really present in the sacrament. But His body is given, taken, and eaten only after a heavenly and spiritual manner. The body of Christ is received and eaten in faith."

Additionally, denominations differ on the question of who may participate in the Lord's Supper. The Roman Catholic Church, regarding the Supper as an act of communion, restricts participation to those who are in communion with it. In other words, it restricts participation to those baptized in the Roman Catholic Church. In our tradition as in most Protestant churches, everyone may participate who "rightly, worthily, and with faith receive" the Lord's Supper or "who are prepared for reverent appreciation of its significance" and "receive it humbly, with a proper spirit and by faith."

▶ THE CHURCH AND RECONCILIATION

THE NEW CREATION AND RECONCILIATION

The Church is called to be a community of reconciliation in which God's fellowship with the world is actualized.

The Trinitarian movement of God into the world creates fellowship with the world. This fellowship is the new creation. The Church is the principal form that this fellowship takes; it is the outpost of God's fellowship with the world—the first fruits of God's revelatory grace. The Church is accordingly an eschatological reality that anticipates the world's destiny. As the Body of Christ and in the power of the Spirit, it is the realization of God's fellowship with the world and is therefore God's new creation.

The creation of fellowship means that God becomes reconciled to the world. This reconciliation extends to every dimension of our existence. We become reconciled to one another, to ourselves, and to the world. Paul, for instance, wrote forcefully about the way in which the new creation means reconciliation in the human community. He lived in a time when hostility between Jews and Gentiles was common and extreme. But in Christ, Paul was convinced, the historic hatred between these communities was overcome:

> In his flesh he has made both groups into one and has broken down the dividing wall, that is, the hostility between us. He has abolished the law with its commandments and ordinances, that he might create in himself one new humanity in place of the two, thus making

peace, and might reconcile both groups to God in one body *(Eph. 2:14-16).*

The Church is the community that God has created by reconciling Jews and Gentiles.

But God's creative, reconciling activity goes far beyond the reconciliation of Jews and Gentiles. It extends to every sort of alienation that we experience. Paul reminds us that in Christ there is "no longer Jew or Greek . . . [or] slave or free . . . [or] male and female" (Gal. 3:28). In Christ the distinctions that divide human beings from each other in the world of sin are nullified. Eventually, Paul taught, reconciliation would be extended to the entire cosmos: "The creation itself will be set free from its bondage to decay and will obtain the freedom of the glory of the children of God" (Rom. 8:21). The world's destiny is therefore the complete reconciliation of all things and the demise of all alienation, for "through [Christ] God was pleased to reconcile to himself all things, whether on earth or in heaven, by making peace through the blood of his cross" (Col. 1:20).

The Church, as God's new creation, is called to be both an agent of reconciliation and a community in which reconciliation is realized. In this way it anticipates the eschatological consummation of all things.

RECONCILIATION AND THE UNITY OF THE CHURCH

As the community of reconciliation, the Church is called to be one.

As the Body of Christ, the Church is one. As the community of reconciliation, the Church is called to be a unity; for as the community by which God seeks to reconcile all things, division is foreign to the Church. The Church accordingly faces the daunting task of realizing in practice its oneness as the Body of Christ.

Paul's first letter to the Corinthians is a sustained argument about the Church's unity and its capacity to maintain this unity. Having (in chapters 1-3) castigated the Corinthians for their divisive attitude, he introduced the metaphor of the body in order to reveal the nature of the Church's unity. Just as a body, despite the variety of its parts, is a unity, "so it is with Christ," that is, with Christ's Body, the Church. "For in the one Spirit we were all baptized into one body . . . and we were all made to drink of one Spirit" (12:12-13).

Paul was deeply disturbed by the Corinthians' divisive behavior when he asked: "Has Christ been divided?" (1:13). By this question Paul was arguing that the Corinthians' penchant for factions threatened to divide not only the Church but also, because the Church is the Body of Christ, Jesus Christ himself. Similarly, the Church's status as the holy temple of the Spirit means that God would "destroy" those who were dividing the Church (3:16-17). In response, Paul urged his readers to overcome the divisions so that the Church would have an empirical unity agreeing with its unity in Christ.

The unity of the Church, then, is a matter of the utmost importance. At the same time, this unity is compatible with diverse modes of worship and custom and even with diverse ways of understanding the Christian faith. For example, as noted previously, Christians have various ways of understanding the significance of the Lord's Supper. Some see it as a real communion with and sharing in the body and blood of the risen Jesus. Others see it as an event of remembrance. Similarly, Paul recognized the legitimacy of diverse practices in such matters as food (Rom. 14:2-3) and worship (14:5-6). This sort of diversity does not compromise the Church's unity.

SCHISM

Paul's first letter to the Corinthians helps us distinguish heresy from *schism*. As noted previously, heresy involves rejecting the Christian faith and separating from the Church because of that rejection. Schism, as illustrated by the Corinthians, involves dividing the Church or separating from the Church for reasons other than doctrinal disagreement. As we see from Paul's letter, schism is a serious matter, because it tears apart the empirical unity of the Church.

THE CHURCH AS THE COMMUNITY OF RECONCILIATION

As the community of reconciliation, the Church's mission is to invite people into God's Trinitarian fellowship and to offer praise.

To say that the Church is the community of reconciliation is to say that the Church embodies God's Trinitarian movement into the world, a movement whose purpose is to create fellowship with the world.

It is John's Gospel that most clearly describes the Church's participation in the Trinitarian life of God. "As you, Father, are in me and I am in you, may they also be in us" (17:21). These simple words state succinctly the Church's fellowship with God. In the power of the Spirit, the Church participates in the fellowship between the Father and the Son (1 John 1:3). In the Spirit we are drawn into the unity of the Father and the Son. Just as the Trinitarian persons dwell in and through each other, so the Church comes to dwell in them. In this way, the Church becomes a part of God's Trinitarian movement into the world. It becomes an embodiment of this Trinitarian movement.

The Church embodies this movement by inviting those who dwell in the world of sin to enter into this Trinitarian life. Consequently, the Church's mission in the world is identical to and is an extension of God's movement into the world. God comes into the world to create fellowship. The Church is that fellowship. The Church's task is to invite those who are in the world of sin to abandon that world and instead to dwell in God by being incorporated into the Body of Christ. Its mission is to be an instrument by which God incorporates the world into the unity of and fellowship between the Father and the Son.

However, the Church's mission is broader than the work of inviting and incorporating. Reconciliation means not only the restoration of fellowship but also the return of divine life to God in the form of praise. Praise is the sacrifice that the priestly people of God render to the Father through the Son and in the power of the Spirit (Heb. 13:15; 1 Pet. 2:5). Praise is more than a verbalization of our feelings. It is, in fact, the entirety of our lives consecrated to God and given back to God. In praise the Church shows itself to be the first fruits of grace, the outpost of the world's redemption. In this act the Church anticipates the universal praise that will be given to God in the eschatological consummation when the world's destiny has been fulfilled. Praise, then, is a vital component of the Church's mission in the world for it is the act by which the Church completes the Trinitarian movement of God into the world and offers the reconciling fruits of that movement back to God.

THE ESCHATOLOGICAL DIMENSION OF RECONCILIATION

Because of its eschatological status, the Church must struggle to realize its status as the community of reconciliation and the one Body of Christ.

The Church, as the Body of Christ and in the power of the Spirit, is the community of reconciliation. However, it is this community eschatologically, for it lives alongside the world of sin. As a result, the Church sometimes resembles the old world of sin more than it resembles the new world that God is creating. Sometimes it is an instrument not of reconciliation but instead of alienation. Moreover, its empirical unity has been, from the beginning of its existence, little more than an ideal. Although the Church is the new creation and the community of reconciliation through its participation in the Trinitarian life of God, its behavior and outward form frequently do not correspond to its reality in God.

All this is why New Testament writers had to urge the Church to be in empirical reality what it is in God: "Maintain the unity of the Spirit in the bond of peace" (Eph. 4:3). This exhortation is necessary because the Church's unity is constantly threatened. The Church's task is to actualize its reality as the new creation, as the community of reconciliation, and as a unity. Although the full actualization of this reality awaits the eschatological consummation, the Church is obliged to struggle, in the power of the Spirit, toward that actuality, knowing that as the Body of Christ it is an anticipation of the world's destiny.

▶ THE ETHICAL DIMENSION OF FAITH

Authentic Christian faith requires that we believe *in* the Church. This means that we enter into the reality of the Church as the new creation and as the Body of Christ. We thus share in the Church's holiness and election and its character as the one, holy, catholic, and apostolic people of God. But it means as well that we allow God, through the ministries of the Church, to shape us into new creatures. To believe in the Church is to practice the Christian life in and with the Church, allowing its teaching and examples to guide us.

SUMMARY STATEMENTS

1. The Church, separated from the world and consecrated to

God, is holy because it participates in the Trinitarian movement of God into the world.

2. The Church is the elect and therefore holy people of God. In Christ, God has elected, or chosen, the Church to be a separated and consecrated people.

3. The Church's holiness is an eschatological reality as the Church lives between its calling as the elect, holy people of God and its struggle to be faithful to that calling.

4. The Church is called to be faithful to the traditions handed on by the apostles.

5. The Church is a servant of God's revelation in the world and therefore must remain receptive to the Holy Spirit's prophetic ministry.

6. The Church fulfills its calling to be faithful to the apostolic tradition and to be the servant of God's revelation under the conditions of its eschatological existence. As a result, it sometimes fails to live up to its calling.

7. God's grace is mediated to us through physical realities, which thus have a sacramental character.

8. Baptism is an eschatological event in which life in the Spirit begins and which constitutes the Church as a unity of believers.

9. The Lord's Supper is an eschatological event of remembrance, thanksgiving, and incorporation into the Body of Christ.

10. The Church is called to be a community in which God's grace is effective.

11. As an eschatological community, the Church sometimes fails in its calling to be a community of grace.

12. The Church is called to be a community of reconciliation in which God's fellowship with the world is actualized.

13. As the community of reconciliation, the Church is called to be one.

14. As the community of reconciliation, the Church's mission is to invite people into God's Trinitarian fellowship and to offer praise.

15. Because of its eschatological status, the Church must struggle to realize its status as the community of reconciliation and the one Body of Christ.

QUESTIONS FOR REFLECTION

1. Why do Christians state, in the Apostles' Creed, "I believe *in* . . . the holy, catholic Church"? Why is the Church an object of faith?

2. What is the individual disciple's role in helping the Church fulfill its status as the Body of Christ?

3. What is the best way to understand the relation between the division of Christianity into denominations and the unity of the Church?

THIRTEEN

THE END OF GOD'S NEW CREATION

OBJECTIVES

Your study of this chapter should help you to understand:

1. The principal themes of Christian eschatology.

2. The purpose of the Bible's eschatological teaching.

3. Important hermeneutical issues in the study of eschatology.

4. The relation of eschatology to other doctrines, such as creation, redemption, and the doctrine of God.

KEY WORDS TO UNDERSTAND

Advent	Hermeneutics
Eschaton	Millennium

QUESTIONS TO CONSIDER AS YOU READ

1. What is the central message of eschatology?

2. What is the role of hope in the Christian life?

3. How does eschatology shape the doctrine of God?

Thou judge of quick and dead,
Before whose bar severe,
With holy joy, or guilty dread,
We all shall soon appear;
Our cautioned souls prepare
For that tremendous day,
And fill us now with watchful care,
And stir us up to pray.

To pray, and wait the hour,
That awful hour unknown,
When robed in majesty and power
Thou shalt from heaven come down,
Th'immortal Son of Man,
To judge the human race,
With all thy Father's dazzling train,
With all thy glorious grace.

To damp our earthly joys,
T'increase our gracious fears,
Forever let th'archangel's voice
Be sounding in our ears
The solemn midnight cry,
'Ye dead, the Judge is come;
Arise and meet him in the sky,
And meet your instant doom!'

O may we thus be found
Obedient to his word,
Attentive to the trumpet's sound,
And looking for our Lord!
O may we thus ensure
A lot among the blest,
And watch a moment, to secure
An everlasting rest!

This hymn, written by the Wesleys in 1749, expresses some of the central themes of eschatology: judgment, the return of Jesus Christ, and eternal reward. It also shows us how eschatology is to shape the Christian life when it asks that God would prepare us "for that tremendous day," fill us "with watchful care," and stir us to pray. It urges us to allow "th'archangel's voice" to "damp our earthly joys" and increase "our gracious fears." Finally, it encourages us to be "obedient to his word" and "attentive to the trumpet's sound." It thus reinforces the central message of eschatology, namely the importance of living as we should and of remaining alert and hopeful.

▶ INTRODUCTION

God comes into the world in order to create fellowship and unite all things in the Trinitarian life of God. Eschatology is about the consummation of this movement, the full actualization of fellowship, and the union of the world with God.

▶ THE MESSAGE OF NEW TESTAMENT ESCHATOLOGY

The New Testament presents the eschatological end of the world as the completion of God's redemptive new creation. This completion embraces the return of Jesus Christ, judgment, resurrection, and the restoration of the created world. These events constitute the *eschaton.*

THE CONSUMMATION OF THE NEW CREATION

The eschaton is the realization of the new world that God is creating. The Christian life is accordingly oriented toward the future.

Christian existence is an eschatological existence. It is the presence of God's future, the eschaton, alongside the world of sin. In this existence the new creation is a powerful reality, but one whose full actuality lies in the future. That is why we still contend with the effects of sin.

Because the new creation has a future dimension, life in the Spirit has a temporal structure; it is a life subsisting between the past and the future. For those in the Spirit, the past is determined by two contrary facts: our membership in the world of sin and God's Trinitarian movement into the world. The future is the world's eschatological destiny, the new world that God is creating. In this future, the world of sin will be a thing of the past and God will be all in all. Our present life in the Spirit is that mode of existence in which the future is a reality, a present but not fully present reality, which coexists alongside the world of sin. Life in the Spirit, as an eschatological existence, is therefore a tensed existence, stretched out between the kingdom of God and the world of sin. To live eschatologically is to exist with an eye cast back to the past—the world of sin—but also with an eye straining toward the future—God's future.

Hope is, accordingly, a critical component of that life. It is the triumph of the present future over the past and sin. Eschatological existence is therefore essentially a life of hope and promise. The basis of that hope is the gift of the Spirit, who is God's down payment on the future. It is because we live in the Spirit and feel the power of this life that we have confidence in the promised reality of the new creation (Rom. 5:5). Life in the Spirit is thus oriented toward the future, for it is a life that has turned away from the past, the world of sin, and has staked its salvation on the future of God's kingdom. To live in hope is to have this orientation to the future as the defining fact of one's existence. It is to believe in a God who is "the God of hope" (15:13), the one "who gives life to the dead and calls into existence the things that do not exist" (4:17) and the one who makes all things new (Rev. 21:5). Hope, accordingly, is the decision to live on the belief that God's Trinitarian movement into the world will bring to completion the work of redemptive new creation that God has already begun.

THE RETURN OF JESUS CHRIST

The return of Jesus Christ is the consummation of his revelation in the world.

The New Testament affirms that Jesus Christ will return, an event sometimes referred to as the second **advent** (from the Latin word for come or arrive). But his return is more than an arrival. It is also the revelation of Jesus Christ (1 Pet. 1:13; 1 John 2:28 and 3:2). As such, his return is the completion of his revelation in history 2000 years ago.

As the revelation of Jesus Christ, the Second Coming signifies that event in which Jesus will be fully disclosed and known, when the truth and reality of Jesus will stand forth with utter clarity. His revelation in history was, like all historical revelation, a combination of disclosure and concealment, revelation and hiddenness, and in a word, ambiguity. That is why many of Jesus' contemporaries could behold him and fail to see him as the Savior. The idea of the eschaton, however, is the idea of a revelation that transcends the ambiguity of historical revelation. It is the idea of a revelation of Jesus Christ in which the reality of Jesus stands forth with unchallengeable power and authority.

The Second Coming is also the consummation of what Jesus revealed—God's Trinitarian coming into the world. The revelation of Jesus Christ in history was the revelation of the Trinitarian life of God, the movement of salvation from the Father, revealed in Jesus, and actualized through the Spirit. The return of Jesus, accordingly, is the final and ultimate revelation of God's Trinitarian life, the event in which the triune God completes the divine movement into the world.

SECOND COMING

The creeds in our tradition affirm that "the Lord Jesus Christ will come again," that "the return of Christ is certain and may occur at any moment, although it is not given us to know the hour," and that "at His return He will fulfill all prophecies concerning His final triumph over all evil."

JUDGMENT, REWARD AND PUNISHMENT

The eschaton is the completion of God's judgment on the world. Judgment results in reward, which is the perfection of life in God, and punishment, which is life without God.

God comes into the world to create fellowship. This helps us understand the nature of the final judgment. Judgment separates those who share in the fellowship between the Father and the Son from those who do not. The reward of the final judgment is life everlasting in God's presence. The punishment of judgment is exclusion from God's presence.

We can see this by examining some New Testament passages. Second Thessalonians, for instance, states that the wicked "will suffer the punishment of eternal destruction, separated from the presence of the Lord and from the glory of his might" (1:9). The parables of the wicked slave (Matt. 24:51), the foolish bridesmaids (25:10-12), and the worthless slave (25:30) all make the same point, that punishment is exclusion from the divine presence. Reward is consistently portrayed as everlasting fellowship with God, as when John's Gospel depicts eternal life as the knowledge of God (John 17:3) and when Paul portrayed the resurrection state as an existence with Jesus (1 Thess. 4:17). The concrete images (such as heavenly dwelling places, victors' crowns, fire, eternal destruction, outer darkness) with which the New Testament portrays judgment are various ways in which it affirms that just as salvation is our participation in God's Trinitarian life, damnation is our being excluded from such participation.

The final judgment is a continuation of the divine judgment already transpiring in history. Jesus' presence in history was itself an event of judgment, for he compelled decision. His words and deeds forced people to come a decision about God's coming into the world and about the new world that God was creating. Some responded with faithful obedience and others did not. This separation, this distinction between faithful obedience and rejection, is judgment. The final judgment is simply the completion of this separation. For as, in the eschaton, Jesus comes to be fully revealed and known, so in the eschaton the decision about Jesus and about God's coming into the world is forced upon humankind with great clarity and urgency.

FINAL JUDGMENT

The creeds in our tradition affirm the New Testament's teaching that "God has appointed a day in which He will judge the world in righteousness in accordance with the gospel and our deeds in this life" and that "for those who trust Him and obediently follow Jesus as Savior and Lord, there is a heaven of eternal glory and the blessedness of Christ's presence. But for the finally impenitent there is a hell of eternal suffering and of separation from God."

RESURRECTION

Resurrection is the perfection of the new creation and our transformation in the image of Christ.

The doctrine of the resurrection is the affirmation that, for human beings, the new creation is not completed until the body is transformed. To speak of resurrection is to speak of the body's participation in the new creation. As we have seen, the new creation is a present reality. But God's new creation subsists alongside the world of sin. That means that there are scars and effects of sin from which we are not yet freed. The doctrine of the resurrection is about our ultimate and complete freedom from sin's effects.

As final freedom from sin's effects, resurrection is a victory over death, the final enemy (1 Cor. 15:26) and principal New Testament symbol of alienation and the effects of sin. Our resurrection follows the pattern of Christ's: "We know that Christ, being raised from the dead, will never die again; death no longer has dominion over him. The death he died, he died to sin" (Rom. 6:9-10). The resurrection of Jesus was his liberation from the effects of his contact with the world of sin and his freedom from bondage to death. Our resurrection has the same significance. We "groan inwardly while we wait for adoption, the redemption of our bodies" (8:23). We groan and have to wait for this redemption because "the body is dead because of sin" (v. 10). To be resurrected is to have the last vestige of sin's effects overcome. Resurrection thus completes God's work of sanctification and brings to perfection the process of deification and union with God.

The New Testament's teaching about the resurrection state is summarized in 1 Corinthians: "It is sown a physical body, it is raised a spiritual body. . . . The first man was from the earth, a man of dust; the second man is from heaven. . . . Just as we have borne the image of the man of dust, we will also bear the image of the man of heaven" (15:44, 47, 49).

This passage tells us that resurrection is more than the revivification of the body. On the contrary, it is a transformation from being a physical body to a spiritual body. It is impossible to imagine the effects of this transformation; we have no concept of a spiritual body. However, we can affirm that to be a "spiritual body" is to attain our eschatological destiny, for *body* and *spiritual* are symbols. For Paul, to be in the body is to experience the corrupting effects of sin and to be absent from the Lord (2 Cor. 5:6). To be a spiritual being is to be part of the new creation and to live in the Spirit. The spiritual body, then, is a mode of existence in which we have escaped the corruption of sin and are no longer absent from the Lord and in which the body participates in the new creation.

RESURRECTION

The creeds in our tradition assert that "there will be a bodily resurrection from the dead of both the just and the unjust, they that have done good unto the resurrection of life; they that have done evil unto the resurrection of damnation. The resurrection of Christ is the guarantee of the resurrection of those who are in Christ. The resurrected body will be a spiritual body, but the person will be whole and identifiable."

THE NEW HEAVENS AND THE NEW EARTH

The new creation culminates with the redemption and transformation of the world.

The Christian faith affirms the salvation of the created world. Of course, the world is not sinful or evil, and so it does not need salvation in the sense in which human beings need salvation. To speak of the world's salvation is to speak of its participation in the new creation and its union with God. The world's salvation restores its status as the unimpeded field of God's grace and revelation.

Paul expressly linked the salvation of the created world to human redemption: "The creation itself will be set free from its bondage to decay and will obtain the freedom of the glory of the children of God" (Rom. 8:21). Here Paul saw that salvation is liberation from sin and its effects and also that the entire created world participates in this salvation. Humankind's salvation is accordingly incomplete without the salvation of the rest of the created world. This is true not only because the created world is God's world but also because humankind is an integral part of the created world. Human beings cannot be fully saved without the salvation of the created context of human existence.

One way of thinking about the new heavens and earth is to see them as analogies of spiritual rebirth and resurrection. Those who are born again are in one sense new persons; however, this new creation does not mean that God first destroyed them and then re-created them from nothing. Similarly, those who will be resurrected are not first destroyed by God and then re-created. On the contrary, in the resurrection God restores to us and transforms the body that has been damaged by the effects of sin. It is the same with the renovation of the created world. It is God's created world that is redeemed and becomes the new heavens and new earth. Like the resurrected body, the new heavens and earth are the transformed original world of creation, not a replacement for that original world.

The doctrine of the new heavens and new earth reminds us that eschatology is the consummation of God's originating creation. The end of creation is thus the restoration of its beginning. This connection between creation and eschatology further reminds us that the originating creation is the act of the triune God. Like the new creation, originating creation proceeds from the Father, through the Son, and in the Spirit. This means that the created world from its beginning has been drawn into the fellowship of the Father and the Son through the power of the Spirit. As such, it is the object of God's love and the recipient of God's grace. The eschaton is the culmination of God's grace and love manifested in originating creation.

▶ DISPUTED TOPICS IN ESCHATOLOGY

Eschatology has generated a considerable number of competing understandings and conjectures and lends itself to imaginative interpretation far more than do other doctrines. As a result, the history of Christian eschatology shows us an unusually rich variety of interpretations and also the distressingly speculative character of many of these interpretations.

There are two theological issues that are of special relevance to the doctrine of eschatology. The first issue is one of *hermeneutics*. This pertains to the question of how we should understand the biblical passages upon which the various interpretations are built. The second issue is related to the fact that a Christian doctrine such as eschatology has a practical or ethical dimension.

HERMENEUTICAL ISSUES IN CHRISTIAN ESCHATOLOGY

The Bible's prophetic texts are messages of warning and encouragement.

People sometimes regard biblical prophecy, especially books such as Revelation, as concrete and specific predictions of future events. Such an understanding of prophetic texts, however, fails to grasp the true nature of these texts, which are far more about warning than about prediction. Jeremiah 18:7-8 makes this point with great clarity: "At one moment I may declare concerning a nation or a kingdom, that I will pluck up and break down and destroy it, but if that nation . . . turns from its evil, I will change my mind about the disaster that I intended to bring on it." This passage states quite clearly that a prophetic utterance is not an iron-clad prediction about future events. It is instead a warning about what may happen in the absence of a suitable response to the prophetic word. The Book of Jonah is a concrete illustration of this principle. At God's behest, Jonah preaches that "forty days more, and Nineveh shall be overthrown!" (3:4). In response, the people of Nineveh repent and the king hopes that "God may relent and change his mind." As a result, "God changed his mind about the calamity that he had said he would bring upon them; and he did not do it" (vv. 9-10).

These texts tell us that God does not concretely determine the course of human history; what happens in the future depends on the actions that we take today. They tell us also that events in history do not proceed on the basis of a cosmic timetable. Historical events do not transpire according to a rigid, predetermined sequence. Prophecy, therefore, cannot be a declaration of any such predetermined sequence of events. On the contrary, prophecy is the Word of God delivered in a very concrete setting to a people who need to hear that word. It sometimes refers to the future, but when it does, it does not provide a fixed narrative of future events. Instead it offers a warning of what may happen.

Consequently, whenever we read books such as Revelation, we

should not think of them as portraying, with great specificity, future events that are already fixed and determined. To do so is to ignore express indications in the Bible itself that prophecy is more about warning than about prediction.

This characteristic of prophecy goes hand in hand with the fact that prophetic texts were written primarily to the prophets' contemporaries and about events in their near future. The Book of Revelation illustrates this, for its main message is one of encouragement to Christians who were facing the prospect of persecution (2:3, 10, 25). These words of encouragement and exhortation tell us that Revelation describes events of immediate concern to its original readers, not events lying thousands of years in their future. The exhortations would fail to encourage unless they pertained to events that the original readers were experiencing or expected soon. That is why the book frequently (1:1; 6:11; 22:6-7, 10) says that the end is near. It is written with the expectation that the eschatological events (judgment, resurrection, and so on) were about to take place. The purpose of Revelation and other prophetic writings is, therefore, not so much to predict a predetermined, far-off future as to encourage the people of God in the face of suffering and threatened persecution.

At the same time, the meaning of prophetic texts transcends their original setting. Although, for John and his original readers, the Beast of Revelation was a symbol of the Roman Empire and its emperors, the meaning of these texts is not exhausted by events in the first century. The Beast is more than the Roman Empire. It is instead an archetype of demonic power manifesting itself in the political and nationalistic domain. In almost every century Christians in one location or another have believed that the Beast had arisen in their generation, for in almost every century some Christians have suffered under demonic political oppression and have identified the source of that oppression with the Beast of Revelation. They were not mistaken, for the message of biblical eschatology speaks powerfully to God's people in every historical and cultural situation. In every era, Christians who suffer from the demonic powers of the world of sin look to Revelation and other eschatological texts and find in them the Word of God for them in their situation.

ETHICAL ISSUES IN CHRISTIAN ESCHATOLOGY

It is important to focus on the ethical and practical significance of eschatology and to avoid speculative issues.

As noted, the purpose of prophecy and eschatological literature is to warn about what may happen and to encourage the people of God in the face of suffering and persecution. This twofold purpose helps us to see the importance of grasping the ethical aspect of eschatology, that is, the way in which eschatology relates to Christian conduct.

Unfortunately, much teaching about eschatology has little to do with promoting "love that comes from a pure heart, a good conscience, and sincere faith" (1 Tim. 1:5). On the contrary, much teaching on this subject gives the appearance of being an intellectual exercise in predicting the future. The popular exponents of this brand of eschatology have not heeded scriptural warnings to "avoid wrangling over words, which does no good but only ruins those who are listening" (2 Tim. 2:14); to "have nothing to do with stupid and senseless controversies; you know that they breed quarrels" (v. 23); and to avoid teachings "that promote speculations rather than the divine training that is known by faith" (1 Tim. 1:4). The problem is not an interest in eschatology but is instead a misunderstanding of the purpose of biblical eschatology. This misunderstanding results in a preoccupation with sensational and imaginative predictions of the future, frequently for commercial purposes.

The centrality of the ethical dimension of doctrine helps us see the futility of debates about the many speculative issues that surround eschatology. One such issue is the state of the human person after death. Does the soul fall into a sleeplike state after death until the resurrection? Does it exist in a purgatorial state? What about the Old Testament's idea of *sheol?* What is paradise? Questions like these are not asked or answered by God's revelation because it is not the purpose of revelation to respond to speculative questions about the soul. On the contrary, the Bible's teaching about the afterlife is focused on the resurrection of the body. Christian doctrine, accordingly, directs our hopes to this future manifestation of God's creative power. Although throughout history people have offered various theories about the afterlife, the focus of the Christian faith is the Bible's teaching about the resurrection.

Similarly, take Revelation's vision of the thousand-year reign of Jesus Christ (20:4-6). There has been endless conjecture about this reign, which is often referred to as the millennial reign or *millennium*. Is it a literal reign of Jesus on the earth or a figurative way of speaking about his rule in history? Is it a literal thousand years or is this a symbolic number? Does the return of Christ precede it (premillennial view) or follow it (postmillennial view)? It should be clear to any serious student of the Bible that Revelation's brief mention of an event that is nowhere else noted in the Bible cannot be the basis of a doctrine. For the purpose of being a Christian, it is utterly irrelevant whether the millennium is to be understood in a literal or figurative way and whether it precedes or follows the Second Coming. These issues are entirely idle, useless, and devoid of importance for the practice of the Christian life. What is important is the conviction that God's movement into the world is the ultimate reality that confronts us, that our destiny lies in participating in this divine movement, and that judgment overtakes those who do not faithfully respond to God's call.

In summary: we do justice to the Bible's eschatological teaching when we hear in it a warning to abandon the world of sin and an encouragement to abide in God and to trust in the victory of God's movement into the world, a movement that transforms the world of sin and redeems it. Using the Bible to answer speculative questions, however, serves only the interest of curiosity. It does not serve God's interest, and it does not produce the "love that comes from a pure heart, a good conscience, and sincere faith" (1 Tim. 1:5).

▶ ESCHATOLOGY AND THE DOCTRINE OF GOD

God's union with the created world means that God takes the world's alienation into the divine being. The eschaton signifies the final overcoming of alienation.

So far, we have discussed eschatology mainly in connection with the destiny of humankind and the rest of the created world. But eschatology also has a bearing on the doctrine of God.

We see this by considering that God's history with the world is the history of God's progressive identification with the world. In the act of creation, God not only brings forth the world but at the same time be-comes its Lord. Creation thereby establishes an everlasting relation be-tween God and the created world. Subsequently, God elects Israel and thus identifies further with the world by becoming the Lord of this par-ticular people. At length, God comes to the world in the incarnate Son. Here God's identification with the world is such that the divine and the human are united in a single person. The incarnation is followed by the giving of the Spirit, in whom God is united with the Christian commu-nity. World history, then, is the story of God's increasing identification with and union with the world, first generally with the whole creation, then more concretely with Israel, then with human nature, and finally with the Christian community.

The eschaton, accordingly, is the culmination of this history and consists in the consummation of God's union with the world. It is that state in which God is all in all and is the final determination of who God is in relation to the world. In acts of creation, election, redemption, and in the incarnation, God unites with the world and is declared to be the Lord of creation. The eschaton is the event in which God's identity as the Lord of creation is established for all to see.

God's identification with and union with the world tells us that God covenantally chooses to be God in relationship with the created world and that, as the Creator, God does not will to be God apart from the world. In the eternal being of God, God is independent of the world. Creation, therefore, is an act of God's freedom, for nothing constrains God to create. However, in creating, God determines to be the Lord of the created world. In this way, God connects the divine being to the world with a covenant that is everlasting. The creation of the world thus establishes a bond of fellowship between God and the world that is undy-ing. In this way, God's identity as the Lord of the world is bound to the world. God would be God without the world, but God's identity as the world's Lord happens in and through the world.

We can see this point by attending to God's relation to Israel. On one hand, God freely chose Israel to be the holy people of God. God was under no compulsion to choose Israel; God would remain the Lord of creation without that choice. On the other hand, by electing Israel to be the people of God, God bound God's self to Israel in an everlasting covenant. That act of election united God with Israel so that God was no longer just the Creator but was now the God of Israel. God's identity, in other words, was from that time on bound with Israel, for God is now the God of Israel. In election God chooses to side with Israel and be identified as Israel's God. As a result, God's status as the God of Israel depended on Israel's obedience.

Similarly, in the act of creation God's identity comes to be tied to the created world in such a way that God chooses to be God in relation to the world and not without the world. This helps us understand why the new creation is the corollary of creation, for God's identification with the created world means that it is unthinkable that God could abandon this world to sin and perpetual alienation. An everlasting alienation, a world delivered over to sin, would negate God's identification with the world and would mean a repudiation of God's identity as Lord of the world. It is important to note, however, that God's identity with and union with the created world does not imply union with every human being considered individually. Just as chaos remained in original creation, so even in the eschaton there may be individuals who continue to stand outside the new world that God creates.

Because God unites with the created world in acts of election and redemption and especially in the incarnation, God experiences the world's alienation. In Jesus Christ, the Trinitarian being of God extends itself into human life and unites itself with the world to such an extent that the triune God takes the world's sin and alienation onto itself. The incarnation, the life of Jesus, and his death are thus all phases of God's identification with the world and steps by which God comes to share in the alienation of sin. That is the meaning of Paul's assertion that Jesus came "in the likeness of sinful flesh" (Rom. 8:3) and bore God's curse (Gal. 3:13). In Jesus, God internalized the world's alienation and thus does not remain untouched by sin and its corrupting effects. On the contrary, in the death of Jesus, the triune God identifies with the world to the furthest extent of alienation and, in Christ's resurrection, emerges victorious over the world of sin and its alienation. The resurrection, then, was not simply a matter of bringing

Jesus back to life. It was also God's act of overcoming the world of sin and its alienation and of establishing God's Lordship.

The eschaton, therefore, is the consummation of God's history with the world, for in it God's Lordship will be unquestionably established and God's identification and union with the created world will be brought to completion. It is the moment when the world's alienation is finally brought to an end, even if some individuals remain outside the world of the new creation. When, in the eschatological day, the world knows God and its union with God, the final vestige of the world's alienation will be overcome. In that day God will be all in all.

▶ THE ETHICAL DIMENSION OF FAITH

Belief in the doctrine of the end is more than believing that there will be an end. Many people in today's world believe that the world will come to an end. But such belief is not authentic Christian faith. Faith demands that we practice the Christian life in light of the end. Truly to believe in eschatology is to live with hope, patience, and the other virtues appropriate to eschatological existence. It is to stake the entirety of life on the movement of God into the world and to live for the consummation of that movement.

SUMMARY STATEMENTS

1. The eschaton is the realization of the new world that God is creating. The Christian life is accordingly oriented toward the future.

2. The return of Jesus Christ is the consummation of his revelation in the world.

3. The eschaton is the completion of God's judgment on the world. Judgment results in reward, which is the perfection of life in God, and punishment, which is life without God.

4. Resurrection is the perfection of our life in Christ and our transformation in the image of Christ.

5. The new creation culminates with the redemption and transformation of the world.

6. The Bible's prophetic texts are messages of warning and encouragement.

7. It is important to focus on the ethical and practical significance of eschatology and to avoid speculative issues.

8. God's union with the created world means that God takes the world's alienation into the divine being. The eschaton signifies the final overcoming of alienation.

QUESTIONS FOR REFLECTION

1. How does eschatology help us see the coherent, systematic character of the Christian faith?

2. In what ways does a correct understanding of eschatology shape the Christian life and Christian practice?

3. Why is it important to recognize the eschatological character of God's being?

THAT GOD MAY BE ALL IN ALL

FOURTEEN

THE TRINITARIAN LIFE OF GOD

OBJECTIVES

Your study of this chapter should help you to understand:

1. The relation of the divine and the human in Jesus Christ.
2. The divinity of the Holy Spirit.
3. The relation of Jesus Christ and the Holy Spirit to God the Father.

KEY WORDS TO UNDERSTAND

Christology	Monotheism
Exaltation	Nicene Creed
Homoousian	Perichoresis
Humiliation	Person
Incarnation	Pneumatology
Kenosis	Subordinationism
Logos Christology	Substance

QUESTIONS TO CONSIDER AS YOU READ

1. In what sense is Jesus Christ divine? In what sense is he human?
2. What does the doctrine of the Trinity affirm and what does it deny?
3. How does the New Testament's teaching about Jesus Christ and the Holy Spirit relate to the postbiblical development of these doctrines?

Come, Father, Son, and Holy Ghost,
    Whom one all-perfect God we own,
Restorer of thine image lost,
    Thy various offices make known;
Display, our fallen souls to raise,
Thy whole economy of grace.

Jehovah in Three Persons, come,
    And draw, and sprinkle us, and seal
Poor guilty, dying worms, in whom
    Thy [sic] dost eternal life reveal;
The knowledge of thyself bestow,
And all thy glorious goodness show.

Soon as our pardoned hearts believe
    That thou are pure, essential love,
The proof we in ourselves receive
    Of the Three Witnesses above;
Sure as the saints around thy throne
That Father, Word, and Spirit are one.

O that we now, in love renewed,
    Might blameless in thy sight appear;
Wake we in thy similitude,
    Stamped with the Triune character;
Flesh, spirit, soul, to thee resign,
And live and die entirely thine!

This hymn to the Trinity by the Wesleys expresses several vital Christian beliefs. It asserts that the Father, Son, and Spirit are together the "one all-perfect God" who is "pure, essential love" and that it is through their joint work that we are restored in the image of God. It then sets forth the saving effects of that joint work: raising our fallen souls, drawing us, revealing to us eternal life, showing us the divine goodness. Finally, it ends with a prayer that we, renewed in love, might come to reflect the character of the Trinity and thus, in every aspect of our lives, participate in the divine life.

▶ INTRODUCTION

In the preceding chapters, we have explored the theme of God's coming into the world. This is the fundamental truth of the Christian faith. Accordingly, the doctrine of the Trinity, which is the doctrinal exposition of God's coming into the world, is Christianity's most profound doctrine. Previous descriptions of God, such as the Creator or the lawgiver, were preliminary to this fundamental truth. They contained elements of the truth but only in the doctrine of the Trinity do we arrive at the fullest and most concrete theological account of God.

The doctrine of the Trinity asserts that God is the Father, the Son, and the Holy Spirit; that each of these is fully the divine being; and that they are, in their inseparable unity, the one God. The biblical basis of this doctrine is those passages in which the being and acts of God are presented in the togetherness of the Father, the Son, and the Spirit:

- "For through [Christ we] have access in one Spirit to the Father" (Eph. 2:18).
- "There is one body and one Spirit . . . one Lord . . . one God and Father of all, who is over all and through all and in all" (Eph. 4:4-6).
- "There are varieties of gifts, but the same Spirit; and there are varieties of services, but the same Lord; and there are varieties of activities, but the same God who activates all of them in everyone" (1 Cor. 12:4-6).
- "The grace of the Lord Jesus Christ, the love of God, and the communion of the Holy Spirit be with all of you" (2 Cor. 13:13).
- "Who have been chosen and destined by God the Father and sanctified by the Spirit, to be obedient to Jesus Christ" (1 Pet. 1:2).
- "Pray in the Holy Spirit; keep yourselves in the love of God; look forward to the mercy of our Lord Jesus Christ" (Jude 20-21).
- "I appeal to you, brothers and sisters, by our Lord Jesus Christ and by the love of the Spirit, to join me in earnest prayer to God" (Rom. 15:30).

These passages show us a tendency, within the New Testament, to think of the Father, Son, and Spirit together in the movement of God into the world. When New Testament writers thought about the Christian life and God's relation to the Christian life, they tended to think in terms of the Father, Son, and Spirit.

The doctrine of the Trinity is supported by other doctrines, which affirm that Jesus Christ is fully divine and fully human and that the Holy Spirit is fully divine. These form the background for understanding God's Trinitarian life.

▶ THE NEW TESTAMENT'S TESTIMONY TO JESUS' DIVINITY

The New Testament teaches that Jesus Christ is an object of worship and dwells in inseparable unity with the Father.

The New Testament affirms the divinity of Jesus Christ in various passages. One notable passage is Revelation's vision of heaven, where "The four living creatures and the twenty-four elders fell before the Lamb" (5:8), saying, "to the one seated on the throne and to the Lamb be blessing and honor and glory and might" (5:13-14). Here John portrays Jesus Christ as the object of worship and, implicitly, as a divine being, who is to be worshiped along with God the Father.

We find the fullest biblical development of the idea of Jesus' divinity in the Johannine tradition, which portrays Christ as the divine Word, dwelling with God in the beginning (John 1:1-2), and as "the true God" (1 John 5:20).

These affirmations raise the question of Jesus' relation to God, the Father. The Johannine tradition addresses this relation in considerable detail. It asserts the absolute unity of Jesus and the Father: "The Father and I are one" (10:30) and then goes on to help us understand the nature of this unity. It is not a unity of sameness, for Jesus is not the Father. Jesus and Father are not simply names for the same being. Instead their unity is found in a relation of mutual abiding: "The Father is in me and I am in the Father" (v. 38). Jesus and the Father, accordingly, are neither completely separate entities nor one and the same entity. Instead, they dwell in and through each other, distinct yet supremely and inseparably one.

Consequently, the relation between Jesus and the Father is of the most intimate sort: "The Father loves the Son and has placed all things in his hands" (3:35); "the Father loves the Son and shows him all that he himself is doing" (5:20); "the one who sent me is with me; he has not left me alone, for I always do what is pleasing to him" (8:29). So, when Jesus acts, it is the Father acting: "My teaching is not mine but his who sent me" (7:16); "I seek not to do my own will but the will of him who sent me" (5:30).

Because of the unity between the Father and Jesus and because their actions are done in unison, Jesus is the presence of God in the world and the agent of divine action:

> Just as the Father raises the dead and gives them life, so also the Son gives life to whomever he wishes. The Father judges no one but has given all judgment to the Son, so that all may honor the Son just as they honor the Father. Anyone who does not honor the Son does not honor the Father who sent him *(5:21-23)*.

This passage shows us the central Johannine conviction that Jesus performs the action of God and that, consequently, Jesus is to be worshiped along with God the Father.

▶ THE NEW TESTAMENT'S TESTIMONY TO JESUS' HUMANITY

The New Testament teaches that Jesus Christ is fully human.

The New Testament presents Jesus as a fully human being. Mention of Jesus' humanity is often made casually in the New Testament, as when Luke's Gospel notes that "Jesus increased in wisdom and in years, and in divine and human favor" (2:52) and when Acts states that "Jesus of Nazareth [was] a man [*aner*, a male human being] attested to you by God" (2.22). These sorts of passages assume without further comment that Jesus was human in every sense of the word.

However, we find in the Letter to the Hebrews a sustained effort to reflect on Jesus' humanity and to draw out its theological implications. Jesus, this letter notes, "had to become like his brothers and sisters [i.e., fellow human beings] in every respect, so that he might be a merciful and faithful high priest" (2:17). This passage indicates clearly that Jesus was fully human and that his full humanity was an essential prerequisite of his being the Savior. There was no aspect of human nature in its created goodness that Jesus lacked.

Hebrews goes beyond affirming Jesus' humanity. It asserts also that Jesus underwent the same sort of learning and disciplinary processes that we all experience: "It was fitting that God . . . should make the pioneer of their salvation perfect through sufferings" (2:10). Jesus' suffering points us to the fact that he was like us. But it was also the means by which he became fitted ("perfect") for his calling. Jesus, in other words, underwent a significant process of development that enabled him to be the Savior.

This point is emphasized when Hebrews states,

> In the days of his flesh, Jesus offered up prayers and supplications, with loud cries and tears, to the one who was able to save him from death, and he was heard because of his reverent submission. Although he was a Son, he learned obedience through what he suffered, and having been made perfect, he became the source of eternal salvation *(5:7-9).*

This important passage throws the humanity of Jesus into clear relief. By portraying Jesus as praying with loud cries and tears, we are reminded that Jesus at times experienced great anguish, as when his friend Lazarus died (John 11) and when, with the typically Jewish combination of despair and hope, he experienced alienation from God while dying on the cross: "My God, my God, why have you forsaken me?" (Mark 15:34). By observing that God heard Jesus' prayers because of Jesus' "reverent submission" we see that Jesus was a model of both piety and obedience. Jesus willingly adopted an attitude of humble obedience to God's will. By stating that he learned obedience through what he suffered, we are shown that, like the rest of us, Jesus' obedience to God was not purely spontaneous but was instead something that Jesus had to learn through the same difficult way that all humans must learn obedience. This helps us understand the significance of Jesus' temptations. If Jesus were simply divine and not human, he could not have been tempted. The fact that he experienced temptation tells us that he was authentically and fully human.

The New Testament, then, presents Jesus Christ as human in every sense of the word, even to the point of affirming that he had to learn to obey God. At the same time, it is just as insistent that Jesus' obedience was of such purity that we can characterize his life as sinless even amid temptation (Heb. 4:15; 2 Cor. 5:21).

▶ THE UNITY OF THE DIVINE AND THE HUMAN

The doctrine of the incarnation teaches that in Jesus Christ God has assumed human nature in its concrete, historical reality.

The unity of the divine and the human is expressed in the idea of *incarnation.* This term, which means enfleshment, is based on John 1:14 ("The Word became flesh and lived among us"). It states, in a word, the conviction that the Son, the Word of God, became human. But in its narrative context it says also that the Son became not just human but a particular human being at a particular moment in Israel's history. It tells us as well that the Son became this particular human being without ceasing to be the eternal, divine Son. Jesus Christ, then, was the divine Son existing as a human being.

The incarnation is one of the central paradoxes of the Christian faith, for it tells us that two realities (divinity and humanity) are unexpectedly found together. Ordinary experience furnishes us with no concepts with which to understand this paradox; it is impossible to imagine the reality that the idea of the incarnation signifies. Nonetheless, we can note some theological affirmations that result from it.

If Jesus Christ is truly the incarnation of the Son, then we may conclude that in Jesus God identifies with human beings. In Jesus the divine life passes over into one of its creations, human being. God becomes what God is not. Yet, in this becoming, God does not cease to be God. The incarnation is accordingly not a transformation from one thing into another. On the contrary, in the incarnation the divine life takes human being into itself and unites with it. In this assumption, the integrity of the divine and the human is preserved. Jesus was not less human because human nature had been assumed by the divine; the divine nature was not diminished because it embraced humanity.

Even though God remains God in coming into the world, God does not remain unaffected. In the Son's incarnation and death, God undergoes suffering. Paul expresses this truth when he wrote of Christ that "though he was rich, yet for [our] sakes he became poor, so that by his poverty you might become rich" (2 Cor. 8:9). The Son, in coming into the world, exchanged the glory of his preworldly existence for a lowly state. In the incarnation the divine life passes over into a state of lowliness. "Though he was in the form of God, [he] did not regard equality with God as something to be exploited, but emptied himself, taking the form of a slave, being born in human likeness" (Phil. 2:6-7). God's coming into the world, in other words, was accomplished without reserve. God did not hold back any part of the divine being but instead made a full and complete identification with humankind in its concreteness. As a result, God assumed the effects of sin even to the point of death and identified with us to the extent of being "humbled . . . and [becoming] obedient to the point of death—even death on a cross" (v. 8).

STATES IN THE LIFE OF GOD'S SON

Theologians have developed some terms to describe the states of or stages in the life of God's Son. The state of *exaltation* denotes the preworldly existence of the Son and the glorified, resurrected state of Jesus Christ. Taking a cue from Paul's words in Phil. 2, theologians designate the earthly life of the Son as the state of **humiliation.** The Greek word *kenosis* ("emptying") is often used in this context to portray the act by which the Son "emptied himself, taking the form of a slave" (Phil. 2:7).

▶ POSTBIBLICAL DEVELOPMENTS IN CHRISTOLOGY

Christian thinking about Jesus developed further after the writing of the New Testament and culminated in creedal statements.

One of the issues left unresolved by the New Testament writings pertained to Jesus' divinity and humanity: In what sense was Jesus divine? In what sense was he human? How was the Church to think about the relation of the divine to the human? These are questions of *Christology,* the doctrine about Jesus Christ.

There was an early (second to third century A.D.) tendency, often referred to as "adoptionist Christology," to think of Jesus as a human being upon whom the Word or Spirit descended, thus making him the Son. But by the fourth century the Church had largely decided that this was an inadequate understanding of Jesus. It really didn't do justice to the Johannine picture of Jesus as the incarnation of the Word and as divine.

An alternative to adoptionist Christology drew on the affirmation that Jesus was the incarnation of the divine Word (*logos*). According to this conception, the divine Word was joined to human "flesh." Scholars refer to this as the "Word-flesh" Christology. The main emphasis here was that Jesus Christ is God and that encountering Jesus Christ means encountering God, not (as in adoptionist Christologies) a man who had become the Son of God by receiving the Spirit or the Word. The proponents of the Word-flesh Christology wanted to affirm without equivocation or qualification that Jesus Christ is God.

However, this sort of Christology was a bit vague on the nature of the flesh that was united with the divine Word. Some of the proponents pictured the flesh of Jesus as his human body and soul; however, they expressly denied that Jesus had a human mind. This meant that the Word was united to a fragment of human nature (soul and body) and not to complete human nature (soul, body, and mind). If that were true, critics argued, human salvation would be incomplete, for if there were some aspect of human nature not united to the Word, that aspect could not be saved.

As a result of this critique, the Church steered away from the Word-flesh Christology and instead insisted that we think of Jesus Christ as fully divine and fully human. A letter written in A.D. 382 reporting the results of a council of bishops affirmed that Jesus' "flesh was not soulless nor mindless nor imperfect" and that "he became fully man for the sake of our salvation."

However, thinking of Jesus as fully divine and fully human proved difficult. In particular, the question arose of how we are to think of the unity of the divine and the human. Some suggested that the divine and human were joined together in such a way that he had two minds and two wills—a human mind and will joined to a divine mind and will. The Early Church rejected this notion but continued to seek a workable understanding of the unity of the two natures.

Two alternatives to the Word-flesh Christology were developed in the fourth and fifth centuries. One (customarily associated with the Church in Alexandria) placed great emphasis on the union of the divine and human in Jesus. The other (customarily associated with the Church in Antioch) thought it important to preserve some distinction between the divine and the human. They provided differing answers to the questions. When Scripture ascribes suffering, growth, and death to Jesus Christ, are we to think of the Word as suffering, learning, and dying? Or instead are we to think of Christ's human nature (but not his divine nature) suffering, learning, and dying? The first position (the Alexandrian), emphasizing the union of the natures, thought of the Word as suffering, growing, and dying in the human nature to which it was united. The second position (the Antiochene), emphasizing the distinction of the natures, denied that the Word could suffer, grow, and die in any respect and ascribed these properties strictly to the human nature.

Readers today often find the difference between these two views overly refined and subtle. But in the fourth and fifth centuries these two positions were highly polarized because supporters of each saw in the other view grave dangers to the Church's faith. Supporters of the Alexandrian position felt that the Antiochene view would drive a wedge between the divine and the human. They feared that we would think of Jesus possessing two minds, one human and one divine, and likewise two wills. The supporters of the Antiochene view felt that the Alexandrian view discounted Jesus' humanity. They did not see how, in it, Jesus could be regarded as a real human being who voluntarily obeyed God's commands and who was thus a role model for us.

In an attempt to resolve the difference between these views, a series of councils met, notably the council of Chalcedon (A.D. 451) This council agreed upon several points: It rejected extreme interpretations of both sides; it affirmed that the divine nature of Christ could not in any way suffer or die; it maintained the distinction between the divine and human natures of Christ; it rejected the Word-flesh Christology by affirming that Christ was truly human, possessing a complete human nature; and it rejected the view that Christ had only a single nature. On the contrary, it portrayed Jesus as possessing two natures, divine and human, which were perfectly united without either nature being changed from its essential properties. The council thus portrayed Jesus as a single person and being.

Not every ancient church affirmed the decision of the council of Chalcedon. Some churches felt that it leaned too far in the direction of affirming the two natures of Christ. They preferred to place much more emphasis on the unity of Christ and to speak of a single nature. For that reason, they are called the Monophysite (Greek for "one nature") churches. Other ancient churches felt that the council leaned too far in the direction of unity and preferred to place more emphasis on the two natures. They are called Nestorian churches, after Nestorius, a fifth-century bishop who helped formulate this view. The Monophysite and Nestorian churches still exist; however, in recent decades there have been significant efforts to overcome the barriers between these churches and those that accept the council of Chalcedon, which are called "Orthodox" because they adhere to the council.

On this issue of Christ's divinity and humanity, the creeds in our tradition have followed the council of Chalcedon. They affirm that the Word "took man's nature . . . so that two whole and perfect natures, that is to say, the Godhead and manhood, were joined together in one person, never to be divided, whereof is one Christ, very God, and very man."

▶ THE NEW TESTAMENT'S TESTIMONY TO THE SPIRIT'S DIVINITY

The New Testament affirms the divinity of the Holy Spirit by associating the Spirit with God's movement into the world.

The New Testament's affirmation of the Spirit's divinity is much more indirect than its affirmation of Jesus' divinity. This is because the apostolic preaching was focused on the good news of Jesus Christ. Nonetheless, the New Testament indicates that the Holy Spirit is an integral part of God's movement into the world just as Jesus was. We see this in what the New Testament says about God's love, revelation, new creation, and holiness.

Paul drew the closest of connections between the Holy Spirit and God's love by affirming that "God's love has been poured into our hearts through the Holy Spirit" (Rom. 5:5) and that love is the fruit of the Spirit (Gal. 5:22). In the Spirit, God's love becomes our love. In the Spirit, the God who is love draws us into the new creation and transforms us so that we come to have God's loving character. The Holy Spirit, accordingly, is God's movement into the world creating a people who love with God's love.

The Spirit is also closely connected to the revelation of God. Take, for example, the Book of Revelation. At the beginning of the book, John is in the Spirit when he hears the voice of Jesus (1:10-11). Later, in the Spirit, he receives a vision of heaven (4:2) and of the heavenly Jerusalem (21:10). These passages show us that John was able to receive the revelation only because he was in the Spirit. This point is made more prosaically in Ephesians:

> I pray that . . . [God] may grant that you may be strengthened in your inner being with power through his Spirit. . . . [And] that you may have the power to comprehend . . . what is the breadth and length and height and depth, and to know the love of Christ that surpasses knowledge, so that you may be filled with all the fullness of God *(3:16, 18-19)*.

Knowing God is here expressly grounded in the Spirit. Those who dwell in the world of sin are "without God in the world" (2:12) because they live outside the Spirit. But those who are in the Spirit have been enlightened by God's wisdom and revelation and thus authentically know God.

The Spirit is the power of the new creation. As Paul wrote, "The law of the Spirit of life in Christ Jesus has set you free from the law of sin and death. . . . To set the mind on the Spirit is life and peace. . . . If by the Spirit you put to death the deeds of the body, you will live. For all who are led by the Spirit of God are children of God" (Rom. 8:2, 8, 13-14). All of these things—freedom from the law of sin and death, life and peace, being a child of God—are ways of describing the new creation in Christ, and we receive all of them only in the power of the Spirit. The Johannine metaphor of rebirth makes the same point (John 3:5). To enter into God's new creation requires that we be born anew from the Spirit.

Finally, the Spirit is closely related to God's holiness. As the holy God comes into the world, the divine life creates a holy people. The Holy Spirit is the movement of God that makes us holy, as we see from the texts that expressly attribute sanctification to the Spirit (2 Thess. 2:13; 1 Peter 1:2). The Spirit not only is holy (Latin, *sanctus*) but also makes holy (Latin, *sancti-fication*). That is why godly fruit such as love are the fruit of the Spirit. They are the effects of the Spirit's making us holy. It is also why "those who worship [God] must worship in spirit [or Spirit] and truth" (John 4:24). Authentic worship takes place in the presence of the holy God; but for this we must be transformed by the Spirit and made holy so that we can stand before God. As we live in the Spirit, we participate in God's holiness and are drawn into the presence of God.

The New Testament, then, asserts that the Holy Spirit is the movement of God into the world by which we share in God's love, receive God's revelation, participate in the new creation, and become holy. Just as Jesus is the movement of God that is God's love and revelation and the new creation and God's holiness, so the Spirit is the movement of God that effects these realities in us and thus draws us into God's Trinitarian life.

▶ Postbiblical Developments in Pneumatology

Christian reflection on the Holy Spirit developed in the postbiblical period, culminating in creedal affirmations of the Spirit's divinity.

The doctrine about the Holy Spirit (**Pneumatology**) did not develop as rapidly and as fully as did Christian thinking about Jesus Christ. There were two reasons for this. First, the New Testament's teaching about the Spirit is far less extensive than its teaching about Jesus. Second, the difficulties associated with Christology seemed far more pressing than the difficulties associated with Pneumatology.

However, once the Church established the doctrine about Christ, attention turned to the doctrine of the Holy Spirit. The principal issue in the development of this doctrine was whether the Spirit is fully divine. It was customary, in the early Christian centuries, to think of the Spirit as simply the power of God extended into the world. In other words, the Spirit was generally not regarded as distinct from God the Father in the way in which the Son is distinct. By the fourth century, however, theologians had come to the conclusion that, if the Spirit were truly the presence of God in the world and the agent of our sanctification, then the Spirit must be fully divine in the sense in which the Son is fully divine. This conviction was enshrined in the Trinitarian creeds, which affirmed that the Spirit is the Lord and giver of life and is to be worshiped along with the Father and the Son.

The creeds in our tradition follow these creeds. They confess that "The Holy Ghost is of one substance, majesty, and glory with the Father and the Son, very and eternal God" and that the Spirit "is of the same essential nature . . . as the Father and the Son."

▶ GOD THE FATHER

The Father is the beginning and end of God's movement into the world.

So far, our discourse about God has focused on Jesus and the Holy Spirit. It is now time to consider God the Father. Consider these passages:

- "To the only wise God, through Jesus Christ, to whom be the glory forever" (Rom. 16:27).
- "There is one God, the Father, from whom are all things and for whom we exist, and one Lord, Jesus Christ, through whom are all things and through whom we exist" (1 Cor. 8:6).
- "Thanks be to God, who gives us the victory through our Lord Jesus Christ" (1 Cor. 15:57).
- Give "thanks to God the Father at all times and for everything in the name of our Lord Jesus Christ" (Eph. 5:20).
- "To the only God our Savior, through Jesus Christ our Lord, be glory" (Jude 25).
- "Do everything in the name of the Lord Jesus, giving thanks to God the Father through him" (Col. 3:17).

We observe in these passages a persistent pattern: All things come from the Father; praise and prayer and thanksgiving are consistently directed to the Father through Jesus Christ. Combined with the doctrine of the Spirit, this pattern tells us that God's acts in the world proceed from the Father, are enacted through the Son, are realized in the Spirit, and return to the Father as the Spirit evokes our praise and obedience.

The doctrine of the Trinity is the affirmation that what is true of God's coming into the world is true of God's eternal being. This being is a movement that proceeds from the Father, continues through the Son, and concludes as the Spirit embraces the fellowship between the Father and the Son. God's history with the world is thus a reflection of God's eternal, Trinitarian life.

The doctrine of the Trinity thus presents the Father as the beginning of all things, both in history and eternity. From the Father proceeds the eternal Son and the Spirit. From the Father through the Son comes the creation of the world.

At the same time, the Father is also the end of all things, a belief that finds its most extraordinary expression in Paul's words in 1 Corinthians:

> Then comes the end, when [Christ] hands over the kingdom to God the Father, after he has destroyed every ruler and every authority and power. . . . When all things are subjected to him, then the Son himself will also be subjected to the one who put all things in subjection under him, so that God may be all in all *(15:24, 28)*.

These verses picture Jesus at the right hand of God the Father, subduing the world of sin and its demonic powers. This is a symbol of the coexistence of the new creation and the world of sin. When that world has been finally overcome, when alienation has been conquered, then the Son will deliver the restored, transformed world to the Father. The great struggle of God for redemption will finally be over. Then, with the world of sin destroyed and chaos finally and decisively overthrown, God the Father will be all in all. Then a state of unity will exist such as existed in the beginning. That is why praise is so important—it is the Church's anticipation of the return of all things to God the Father. In praise the Church symbolically offers the world to the Father, through the Son, in the power of the Spirit. It thus looks forward to the end when the world will be reunited with God. The idea of the Father is, therefore, a thoroughly eschatalogical idea. To meditate on the Father is to contemplate both the beginning and the end of all things.

▶ POSTBIBLICAL DEVELOPMENTS IN THE DOCTRINE OF THE TRINITY

THE RELATION OF THE SON TO THE FATHER

In its creeds the Church affirmed the eternity of the Son and that the Son and the Father have one and the same essence.

The council of Chalcedon was an attempt to address one issue in Christology, namely the relation in Christ between the human and the divine. However, another important question was raised, the question about the relation between Jesus Christ the Son, and God the Father. The answer to this question determined the shape of the doctrine of the Trinity.

The leading way in which Christian writers in the second and third centuries thought about the Son was by means of the idea of the Word (*logos*). Hence this sort of thought is called **Logos Christology**. This idea, combining John's Gospel with elements of Jewish theology and Stoic philosophy, portrayed the Son as God's eternal thought, which, at a certain point in cosmic history, emerged from the depths of God's being as a distinct divine being.

The strengths of Logos Christologies were that they had close connections to the New Testament, especially John's Gospel; that they clearly presented the distinction between the Father and the Son (analogous to the distinction between a speaker and the speaker's words); and that they affirmed the unity of the Father and the Son (since the Son, as the Word, was the reflection of the Father, just as a spoken word reflects the mind and thoughts of the speaker). However, later writers were critical of the view that the Word emerged from the Father shortly before the act of creation. Such a view did not sufficiently preserve a sense of the Son's eternal being.

A different approach was taken by the great third-century theologian Origen (d. 253), who portrayed the Son (and also the Holy Spirit) as eternal. In Origen's view, the Son is eternal and utterly without beginning. Although, he argued, the Son is begotten from the Father, the act of begetting is not an event in time. If it were, then there would be a time before which the Son did not exist, a view that the Logos Christologies seemed to affirm. The Church eventually endorsed Origen's view of this issue.

There was another aspect of Origen's understanding of the Son that generated considerable controversy long after he was dead. This was his belief that, because the Father is the source of all, even the Son (since the Father begets the Son), the Father is intrinsically greater than the Son. This view came later to be known as **subordinationism**, because in it the Son is regarded as subordinated to the Father.

The development of Christology was furthered by a controversy in the early fourth century. The issue at stake was whether we should think of the Son as fully divine or as somehow less than fully divine. Proponents of the latter position (usually called Arians, after Arius [d. 336], an early proponent of this view) were convinced that in order to interpret the New Testament correctly, it was necessary to think of Jesus as the incarnation of a being who was divine but not as divine as the Father. Otherwise, they argued, how could we explain the temptation of Christ and his suffering? If Christ were simply divine, he could not have been tempted and have suffered. If he were simply divine, he could not function as a role model for us. Since, according to the Arians' theology, the Son is not fully divine, he is not eternal. In fact, they regarded the Son as a created being—the first and highest of all created beings but a part of the created world.

Controversy quickly ensued, with a group of theologians contending against the Arians. One of the leaders of this group was the bishop of Alexandria, Athanasius (d. 373). Athanasius embraced Origen's teaching about the Son's eternity. He argued, with Origen, that the Son must be eternal, for otherwise God would not always have had the Word, that is, the *logos*. If the Arian theology were correct, then God, prior to the creation of the Word, would have lacked *logos*—reason, thought, and speech. Like Origen, Athanasius regarded this as absurd. God could never have been without *logos*. Consequently, the Son must be eternal as the Father is eternal and not only eternal but infinite, omnipotent, and so on. Everything true of the Father must also be true of the preincarnate Son. In this way, Athanasius argued against Origen's teaching about the Son's subordination to the Father.

This issue proved to be quite contentious. Most leaders of the Church regarded the Arian theology as seriously flawed. Yet there were obstacles to embracing Athanasius's theology, for, if the Son were fully divine, it was difficult to see how he could suffer and die. Moreover, it was difficult to see how, according to Athanasius's view, the Son differed from the Father. If both were fully divine and possessed every divine attribute, in what sense did they differ? The majority of Church leaders felt most comfortable with a Christology along the lines of Origen. They affirmed the Son's eternity (and thus denied Arian theology) but they believed that the Son is in some sense subordinated to the Father.

A Christology that was agreeable to the majority of Church leaders was fashioned by two councils, meeting in A.D. 325 (Nicaea) and A.D.

381 (Constantinople). They produced statements that together are collectively referred to as the *Nicene Creed*. The Christological portion of this statement affirms belief "in one Lord Jesus Christ, the Son of God, begotten of the Father as only begotten, that is, from the essence [reality] of the Father . . . God from God, Light from Light, true God from true God, begotten not created . . . of the same essence [reality] as the Father."[2]

This creed has come to be almost universally endorsed by Christian churches. It begins with biblical language about Jesus (Lord, Son of God, only-begotten) but quickly moves to resolve points of controversy. It asserts that the Son is distinct from and depends on the Father; that the Son is divine as the Father is divine (since the Son's being is grounded in the Father's being); that the Son is eternal (since he was begotten and not created); and that the Son is of the same substance or essence ("consubstantial," in Greek *Homoousian*) as the Father.

With this creed the Church rejected the Arian view that the Son is of a different sort of divinity from the Father. On the contrary, it affirmed that because the being of the Son derives from the being of the Father, they share the same essence. As a result, whatever we say about the Father we are to say also about the Son, except that the Father begets the Son and the Son is begotten by the Father.

The creeds in our tradition follow the Nicene Creed very closely. They express faith in "Jesus Christ," who is "the Son," "the Second Person of the Triune Godhead," "the Word of the Father." They affirm that the Son is "eternally one with the Father," "very [i.e., truly] and eternal God," and "of one substance with the Father."

THE DOCTRINE OF THE TRINITY

The doctrine of the Trinity states that God exists as the Father, Son, and Holy Spirit, who dwell in an inseparable unity. Each of these is fully God and yet they are not three gods.

The classic formulation of the doctrine of the Trinity is the creed of Constantinople (A.D. 381):

We believe in one God, the Father all-governing . . . Creator . . . of heaven and earth, of all things visible and invisible; And in one

Lord Jesus Christ, the only-begotten Son of God, begotten from the Father before all time . . . Light from Light, true God from true God, begotten not created . . . of the same essence [reality] as the Father . . . through Whom all things came into being. . . . And in the Holy Spirit, the Lord and life-giver, Who proceeds from the Father, Who is worshiped and glorified together with the Father and Son, Who spoke through the prophets. . . . Amen.[3]

The principal points of this creed are that there is one God and that this God exists as Father, Son, and Holy Spirit. The first point is grounded in the Old Testament's uncompromising *monotheism*. It forbids us from worshiping any reality as divine except the God revealed to us as Creator and Redeemer.

The second point states that God is not a reality or being alongside the Father, Son, and Spirit. On the contrary, the one divine being exists completely in the three, whether we think of the three individually or collectively. It is not that each of the three constitutes one-third of the divine being, for the Father is God, the Son is God, and the Holy Spirit is God. Each is the fullness of the divine being. Yet we must not think of the three as though they were separate beings. In that case they would be three gods. Instead, we must think of the three in their unity.

The doctrine of the Trinity therefore denies several things. It denies that there is more than one God. It denies that the Son and Spirit are not fully divine. It denies that the Father, Son, and Spirit are only various names for the one God and that they are merely different appearances of God. It asserts that there is only one God. It asserts that the Son and Spirit are fully divine as is the Father. It asserts that the Father, Son, and Spirit are truly distinct from one another.

To express the distinction of Father from Son from Spirit, the creeds use the term *person*. This term designates the members of the Trinity considered with respect to what is distinct about each. The Father is a distinct person from the Son because the Father begets; the Son does not beget. To express the three persons in their unity, the creeds use terms such as *essence* and *substance*. The doctrine of the Trinity is thus the affirmation that the divine substance subsists in three persons.

TRINITARIAN TERMINOLOGY

In using Trinitarian terms, it is important to remember that the Church purposely chose neutral terms to avoid giving the impression that by their use we comprehend God. In particular, it is important that we not think of the Trinitarian persons as personalities in the modern sense. Doing so would leave us with the belief in three divine beings. Instead, *person* is used to signify the members of the Trinity in their distinctness.

Regarding the doctrine of the Trinity, the creeds in our tradition assert that "In [the] unity of this Godhead [i.e., divine nature] there are three persons, of one substance, power, and eternity—the Father, the Son, and the Holy Ghost" and that "these three are one in eternity, deity, and purpose; everlasting, of infinite power, wisdom, and goodness." We note in these words the creedal terms person and substance.

▶ THE MEANING OF THE DOCTRINE OF THE TRINITY

The doctrine of the Trinity is the affirmation that God's eternal life is a life of movement and of love. It is the affirmation that God enters the world, unites with the world, and thereby restores the world to the divine life.

The creeds are authoritative guides to us in thinking about God. They tell us that we should think of Jesus, in his humanity, as the coming of God into the world. They tell us that the life, death, and resurrection of this human being are in fact the life of God coming into our world of sin in order to create fellowship. They tell us that this life of God so identified with humanity in the person of Jesus Christ that it encountered death. Yet in this encounter and in this identification, God did not cease to be God. Even in death God remains God. Even in Jesus' humble submission, which is God's humble submission, God remains.

These affirmations signify that submission and death are not alien to God and that in fact nothing is alien to God. God is able to enter into and identify with the world of sin while remaining God. God can pass over into death and remain God, the source of life. So, when we say that in Jesus Christ two natures, divine and human, are united in one person, we are saying that God's identification with us is complete. We are saying that God has come into the world not casually or peripherally but in the entirety of God's being. We are saying that God has become one of us while remaining God. God is the Lord precisely because God can pass over into that which is not God and identify with it fully without ceasing to be God. The good news of the gospel is that in Jesus Christ God did exactly that.

The creeds tell us also that we should not think of God as the "supreme being." The term *being* does not help us very much in our thinking about God. This is because for us *being* means an individual and we are apt to think of individual in static terms. But if we are to think rightly of God, we must think of God's life as a life of eternal movement. That is why it is so important to see God's love, grace, and revelation as God's coming into the world for the purpose of creating fellowship with us. In the divine movement that proceeds from the Father through Jesus Christ and culminates in the Spirit, the life of God enters the world. If we think of God as a being, even the supreme being, we will puzzle over the doctrines of the Incarnation and the Trinity. It will strike us as odd that God is somehow three yet one and that the divine and the human are inseparably united. But if we keep in mind that God's life is essentially a life of movement, a movement that includes God's coming to us in Jesus Christ, then the puzzle over numbers such as one and three ceases. The doctrine of the Trinity, in other words, is not the solution to a puzzle about numbers. It is the Church's affirmation that God comes to us and identifies entirely with us in Jesus Christ and that this act of God is an instance of the eternal, moving life of God.

Thinking of the Trinity as a life of movement helps us understand God's love for the world. It is because of God's love that the Father sends the Son into the world. It is because the Father and the Son love the disciples that they will dwell in them through the Holy Spirit.

But the divine love is more than simply God's coming into the world through the sending of the Son and Spirit. This divine love is self-sacrificial. In the words of 1 John, God "loved us and sent his Son to be the atoning sacrifice for our sins" (4:10). More concretely, "He laid down his life for us" (3:16). The divine love did not merely come into the world. It identified with the world to such an extent that God entered into the nothingness of death. As Philippians puts it, the eternal Son "emptied himself" (2:7). God's love, accordingly, is not only the appearance of God in the world but also God's union with the world, even to the point of a shameful death. To speak of God's love, then, is to speak of God's coming into the world and becoming human and suffering.

God loves the world. What is more important is that God is love. God is the movement of love undertaken to redeem the world. God is eternally what God is in this movement. God is eternally the one who will come into the world and die—the lamb who was slain from the foundation of the world (Rev. 13:8). This movement, with its result in death and the overcoming of death, is the eternal life of God.

The doctrine of the Trinity, then, is the concrete way of describing the God who is love. Without the doctrine of the Trinity, our talk about God's love can be overly sentimental as we attribute human emotions to God. But in the context of the doctrine of the Trinity, God's love can mean only one thing—that the Father sent the Son to die as an atoning sacrifice and that the Holy Spirit has come to continue the ministry of Jesus and to bring about our response to God in the form of obedience and praise. To speak of God's love, to say that God is love, is to say that God is the movement of divine life from the Father, through the Son, and in the Holy Spirit.

Consequently, we should not think of God's love as an attribute. To do so is to treat the divine love too casually. It leaves open the possibility of thinking of this love as one attribute among many others. It risks allowing love to be thought of in overly sentimental terms, as though the principal thing were God's feelings for us. Instead, we must think of God's being as love and we must think of love as the movement of God into the world.

At the same time, the God who is love is the God who is holy. This means that even in coming into the world, even in uniting with the world, even in dying, God remains the Lord and the transcendent God.

Even in entering history in order to effect salvation, God does not cease to be God. In uniting with the world God does not cease to be transcendent. While dwelling in the world of sin, God's holiness is undiminished. Death is not the end of the divine life.

Affirmation of God's holiness reminds us that salvation—the work of the Father, Son, and Spirit—is only an extension of the eternal life of God into the world. In creation and new creation, this eternal life goes outward and creates and then saves the world by restoring that world to the eternal life of God. But the divine life is not limited to the creation and redemption of the world. On the contrary, creation and redemption are a brief episode in the infinite divine life of love.

Thinking about the Trinity in terms of the movement from the Father, through the Son, and in the Spirit helps us avoid a perennial pitfall, which is to overly distinguish the Trinitarian persons from each other. It is easy to think of the three Trinitarian persons as three personalities, each with intellect and will. To help us avoid this error, the creeds insist that the persons share one and the same divine substance. The Father, Son, and Spirit are the one God. They do not act or think as individuals. On the contrary, they are, in their inseparable togetherness, the way in which the divine life exists. The divine life, which is a life of movement, embraces and is the three persons.

That means that we should always think of the persons together. A term that theologians have used to help on this point is *perichoresis*. This Greek word (which suggests the picture of people dancing in unison around each other) is used to assert that the divine persons are not individually existent beings and that instead they live in and through each other. The Father would not be the Father without the Son. The Son would not be the Son without the Father. They exist in an inseparable unity that infinitely transcends the unity of individuals. Similarly, the Father and Son exist together in and with the Holy Spirit; the Holy Spirit would not be the Holy Spirit without the Father and the Son. Each Trinitarian person exists by virtue of its relation to the others. We think soundly when we hold the three persons together in our thinking and do not regard the persons as independently existing beings. The idea of *perichoresis* is a way of portraying the divine life as a life of movement.

▶ THE ETHICAL DIMENSION OF FAITH

Although Christology, pneumatology, and the doctrine of the Trinity are about Jesus Christ, the Holy Spirit, and the Father, they are also about the Christian life. This is because they are not theories about objects that we are studying but are an account of God's coming into the world to create fellowship. They are, accordingly, as much matters of practice as teachings to be believed.

For instance, Phil. 2 speaks of the Son not grasping after equality with God but instead becoming empty and humble. Although this is first of all an affirmation about Jesus Christ, it is also an affirmation about the character of the Christian life. Paul prefaced this passage with an admonition to his readers: "Do nothing from selfish ambition or conceit, but in humility regard others as better than yourselves. . . . Let the same mind be in you that was in Christ Jesus" (2:3, 5). For Paul, each of us is to reproduce in ourselves the Son's act of emptying and humiliation. The same is true of Christ's resurrection. Although it means new life for Jesus Christ, it means new life for us as well: "Just as Christ was raised from the dead . . . so we too might walk in newness of life" (Rom. 6:4). Belief in the resurrection of Christ necessarily includes our participation in that resurrection, the anticipation of which is a morally and spiritually transformed life.

Or, take the relation of the Father to the Son. If we approach this doctrine as though it were an incomprehensible mystery, then we miss its truth. Its truth is that God comes to us in Jesus Christ. But this movement of God is not merely toward us. It is a movement that embraces us and draws us into God's life. In other words, the movement of God toward us draws us into the fellowship of the Father and the Son and allows us to participate in that fellowship. The concrete form of this participation is our worship. Of special importance in this regard is that, for New Testament writers, our worship is directed *toward* the Father *through* the Son, as in Colossians: "Do everything in the name of the Lord Jesus, giving thanks to God the Father through him" (3:17). Our worship, accordingly, is not simply something that we do. It is something that we do as we are drawn into the fellowship between the Father and the Son. The doctrine of the Trinity, therefore, has an intensely practical dimension. It is not only about God. To believe in the Trinity is to faithfully practice the Christian life and thus be drawn into God's life.

▶ CONCLUSION

The eschatological destiny of the world is that God will be all in all (1 Cor. 15:28). This happens when, in the eschatological day, the world's participation in the Trinitarian life of God is complete, when all things share, through the power of the Spirit, in the fellowship between the Father and the Son. In the meantime, the eschaton remains an object of hope, the final act in the cosmic drama enacted by "the God of hope" (Rom. 15:13).

The Bible's eschatological message of warning and encouragement is clear: "What sort of persons ought you to be in leading lives of holiness and godliness, waiting for and hastening the coming day of God" (2 Pet. 3:11-12). Our calling is to "run with perseverance the race that is set before us" (Heb. 12:1), resolutely clinging to hope, offering to God our sacrifice of praise, confident that the world's future is union with God. This is the Bible's counsel to us. If we heed it, we will, in God's time, participate in the union of all things in and with God and thus arrive at our created destiny.

SUMMARY STATEMENTS

1. The New Testament teaches that Jesus Christ is an object of worship and dwells in inseparable unity with the Father.
2. The New Testament teaches that Jesus Christ is fully human.
3. The doctrine of the incarnation teaches that in Jesus Christ God has assumed human nature in its concrete, historical reality.
4. Christian thinking about Jesus developed further after the writing of the New Testament and culminated in creedal statements.
5. The New Testament affirms the divinity of the Holy Spirit by associating the Spirit with God's movement into the world.
6. Christian reflection on the Holy Spirit developed in the post-biblical period, culminating in creedal affirmations of the Spirit's divinity.

7. The Father is the beginning and end of God's movement into the world.

8. In its creeds the Church affirmed the eternity of the Son and that the Son and the Father have one and the same essence.

9. The doctrine of the Trinity states that God exists as the Father, Son, and Holy Spirit, who dwell in an inseparable unity. Each of these is fully God and yet they are not three gods.

10. The doctrine of the Trinity is the affirmation that God's eternal life is a life of movement and of love. It is the affirmation that God enters the world, unites with the world and thereby restores the world to the divine life.

QUESTIONS FOR REFLECTION

1. Why does the Bible say so much more about Jesus Christ than about the Holy Spirit?

2. What is at stake in the affirmation that Jesus Christ is divine—why does the Christian faith stand or fall with this affirmation?

3. Why is it important to affirm the full humanity of Jesus Christ?

NOTES

1. John H. Leith, ed. *Creeds of the Churches: A Reader in Christian Doctrine from the Bible to the Present,* 3d ed. (Atlanta: John Knox Press, 1982), 33.
2. Ibid., 30-31.
3. Ibid., 33.

INDEX

death
  goodness of creation,
    and, 50–51
  removed from God's
    presence, 72, 73,
    138, 258
  to the world of sin,
    209, 245–247,
    254, 277, 322
  and love, 254, 259
  spiritual, 137, 144,
    204
  to the law, 209
  existence after, 213,
    246, 302
  victory over, 207, 297
deification, 257, 297
demons, 130
dependence (human on
    God), 40, 47–48,
    63, 72, 80, 85, 112
depravity, 134, 137, 139
despair, 49, 50, 78
discernment, 236
discipleship, 185
discipline, 151, 252, 255,
    256, 280
divinity of Jesus Christ.
    See Jesus Christ,
    divinity of
divinity of the Holy
    Spirit. See Holy
    Spirit, divinity of
doctrine
  Christian, 12, 60–61,
    303
  disagreements on, 274
  For specific doctrines
    see: creation,
    election, God, new
    heavens and new
    earth, grace,
    redemption,
    resurrection,
    salvation, the end,
    Trinity
dogma, 272

dominion, 62, 64, 71,
    248
dualism (of soul and
    body), 68

E
ecological responsibility,
    53, 62
ego-centrism, 129
election
  and covenant,
    102–103
  and holiness, 100
  corporate vs.
    individual, 100,
    205
  doctrine of, 98–103,
    106
  of Israel, 98, 100, 106,
    157–158, 169,
    176, 266, 305
  of the Church,
    266–267, 288
end
  doctrine of the, 13,
    24, 306
  See also eschatological
    consummation (of
    all things)
enlightenment, 211, 227
entire sanctification. See
    sanctification,
    entire
eschatological
  consummation (of all
    things), 24, 48,
    213, 247, 267,
    285–288, 299, 335
destiny (of the world),
    25, 48, 63, 299
destiny (of human
    beings) 25, 69–71,
    82,165, 168, 298
existence of believers,
    234–237,
    247–249, 260,
    267, 293–294, 306
  See also Kingdom of

God, eschatological
    dimension of;
    Salvation,
    eschatological
    dimension of
eschatology
  and the doctrine of
    God, 24, 303–306
  ethical issues in, 62,
    302–303
  themes of, 25, 293
  definition of, 13, 25,
    293
  disputed topics in,
    274, 299
  hermeneutical issues
    in, 300
  eschaton, the, 138,
    293–296, 301,
    304, 306
eternal life, 101,
    137–138, 208,
    212–213, 237,
    239, 247
ethical
  dimension of faith. See
    faith, ethical
    dimension of
  order, 31, 43
  participation in the
    world, 62, 142,
    237–238
  transcendence over the
    world, 238
ethics
  systems of, 101–102,
    115, 142
  transformation of, 239
Eucharist, 278
eucharistia, 278
evil
  in personal form, 130
  natural, 51
exaltation, state of, 318.
    See also Jesus
    Christ, exaltation
    of